SUCCESSFUL PHOTOGRAPHY

Successful Photography

ANDREAS FEININGER

PRENTICE-HALL, INC.   ENGLEWOOD CLIFFS, N. J.

Library of Congress Catalog Card Number 53-5731

Thirteenth printing . . . . . . December, 1968

Printed in the United States of America
86461—T

ACKNOWLEDGMENT

The Author and Publishers would like to acknowledge their great indebtedness to

Crown Publishers Inc., 419 Fourth Avenue, New York, N.Y., for generously permitting the use of the photographs reprinted on pp. 145 bottom, 146, 147 ext. bottom right, 148-154, 156-160, 193-196, 198-199, 202-203, 205-208, which are taken from the author's book FEININGER ON PHOTOGRAPHY, copyright, 1949; and to the

Eastman Kodak Company, Rochester, N.Y., for permission to reprint, on pp. 162-164, 166, 181-184, and 186-189, fifteen of their excellent formulas.

CONTENTS

Introduction

This book was written to teach you "photography." I tried to make it a thoroughly practical guide that starts with essentials and then goes on from there to tell you what to do and how to do it until you become a competent and confident photographer.

Teaching implies learning. Even if photography is merely your "hobby," if you want to make it successful and rewarding, a certain effort on your part is necessary. A few technical terms and rules must be memorized. However, do not worry; what at first may seem strange and difficult, because it is new, will soon become familiar to you.

As you leaf through the following pages, it may occur to you that this is a rather "complete" book. You may even think: "What use do I have for a blue filter or infrared film? All this is much too complicated for me!" . . . *Right now* you might not need these things—in which case you simply skip such items when first studying this book. However, as your knowledge increases and your ambitions grow, you will find that the use of some of these less commonly used devices accounts for the difference between a mediocre picture and a successful photograph. *Then* you will be glad to have the necessary information handy. This book is organized in such a way that skipping the things you do not need at the moment neither interrupts the continuity of the whole nor makes the rest less easy to understand.

Part 1 tells you what it is all about. A short "indoctrination course" familiarizes you with the different steps involved in the making of a photograph. Operations later discussed in detail are here shown in their proper relationship to one another. This over-all view of photo-technique with par-.ticular emphasis on "controls" forms the background for all our future discussions.

Part 2 introduces you to your tools and materials. Accurately, precisely, thoroughly, yet free from nonessential technicalities, it tells you all you have to know about your camera, lens, film, lights, and those small but very practical accessories that greatly facilitate picture-taking.

Part 3 shows you how to take a picture. Subdivided into six sections, it contains meticulously detailed information on how to produce photographs that are sharp, have depth, contain the right degree of contrast, stop or suggest motion, and are correctly exposed. It also tells you how to use artificial light—photofloods, flash, and speedlights.

Part 4 teaches you how to develop your films and print and enlarge your negatives. You learn how to improvise an inexpensive darkroom—any time, any place. The "mysteries" of developing and printing are explained in such simple terms that, by the time you finish this chapter, you will agree with the author that modern film processing is "as easy as boiling a couple of eggs."

However, if, for the present, you want to let a commercial photo-finisher do your darkroom work, simply skip this chapter and save it for the day when you feel ready to attend to this fascinating phase of picture-making yourself.

Part 5 helps you to develop your critical faculties. Fifty-eight unusual pictures of different mistakes show you most of the things that can go wrong—complete with information for diagnosis, correction, and advice on how to avoid such faults.

Part 6 teaches you how to work with chemicals. Mixing your own solutions from basic components makes it possible to reduce the cost of your hobby or work. It furthermore enables you to use special solutions which, because of their instability, are not commercially available in prepared form—a bonus for the more advanced worker.

Part 7 shows you how to expand the scope of your work. Having acquired a sound foundation of basic photo-technique, you are now ready to explore, through tests and experiments, those subtle variations of technique and approach that will enable you to do "original" work of your own. You learn how to critically evaluate different types of cameras and lenses, and how to select those best suited to *your* needs. Furthermore, you learn, with the aid of eighty-five photographs and diagrams, how basic operations can be varied to an almost limitless degree in accordance with the demands of the subject of your picture.

Part 8 tells you how to use your "technique" to best advantage. Photography is picture language, and photo-technique is nothing but a means to an end: the picture with purpose and meaning. How to produce such pictures is the theme of this section which, in many ways, is the most important section in the book—and also the most interesting. It is hoped that the ideas discussed here will prove to be the turning point in your career or hobby, the spark that liberates your latent creative faculties.

You will notice that certain features are discussed several times, in different connections. Such apparent repetitions are necessary to better clarify the subject. In the making of a photograph, almost every step is the combined result of a number of operations so intimately connected that a change in one invariably demands corresponding changes in the others if the final result is to be satisfactory. Realization of this interdependency of the various factors that determine the outcome of a picture is one of the "secrets" that lead to consistently successful photographs. "Wasting" a few lines on repetitions seemed to the author the best guarantee of making sure that this is fully understood by his reader.

This book is not a novel. Rarely, if at all, will anyone read through it in a single session. But again and again it will be referred to for advice on specific questions. To be sure that you find accurate and complete answers to your photographic problems is my foremost consideration.

ANDREAS FEININGER

PART ONE

GENERAL PRINCIPLES

Advice to beginners, followed by a presentation of the principles of photo-technique
with emphasis on the interdependence of
the various operations and their controls

Imaginary and Real Difficulties

Here, at the very beginning, I shall give my reader a pleasant surprise by exploding an old myth which has been carefully kept in existence by technical writers and photo-magazine editors who seem to believe that their livelihood depends upon its preservation: the idea that "photo-technique is difficult."

This is definitely not true. Years ago, in the days of wet plates, large-size cameras, slow lenses and slower emulsions, photography was a craft that demanded the highest technical skill and years of experience before one could expect to master it. But today, in our streamlined era of "foolproof" cameras, super-fast lenses and films, standardized developing processes, and mechanized controls for every operation, photo-technique has become so simple that anyone who can spare the time to read instructions can also produce "technically perfect photographs."

I know this sounds like heresy, but it is not. In order to produce a "technically perfect photograph" a "technically perfect negative" is necessary. A technically perfect negative is sharp and has the right kind of contrast and the right degree of density. In other words, it is a negative that is neither fuzzy (because of faulty focusing) nor blurred (because of subject or camera motion), *neither* too contrasty *nor* too contrastless, and *neither* too black (dense) *nor* too transparent (thin). Sharpness or fuzziness results from proper or improper FOCUSING, and from holding or not holding the camera still while making an exposure. Contrast range and density degree are controlled through EXPOSURE and DEVELOPMENT. Today, a technically perfect negative can be made by anyone who knows how to use the following four control instruments: RANGE FINDER (or GROUND-GLASS) for focusing, EXPOSURE METER for exposing, and THERMOMETER and TIMER for developing. That, basically, is all there is to it.

A Short Cut to "Technical Perfection"

Most people who want to learn a trade or master a craft realize that before they can successfully execute their ideas in any medium they must learn the basic elements of "technique." They also realize that there is no better aid to success than practical experience. And that experience is the result of experimentation and hard work.

For example, the first thing an apprentice cabinetmaker learns is how to use a saw and plane—not by studying the finished work of advanced cabinetmakers, but by taking these tools into his own hands and finding out from his own experience how they work. To begin with, he learns how

3

to make a straight cut with a saw or how to smooth a rough board with a plane. He does *not* immediately try to construct an entire cabinet or a mahogany table; instead, he starts at the beginning. He learns through trial and error, practices to gain experience and not with the intent of producing salable goods at once. He methodically experiments, searches, and learns as he works. Later he will be taught the different types of saws, the different types of planes, and which is best suited to each specific type of work. But not until he has acquired a considerable degree of skill will he be allowed to attempt a "real" job—to make a simple salable piece of furniture.

This is the time-honored, sound, and practical method by which any apprentice learns his trade. Yet the amateur photographer, who may be likened to an apprentice, insists on producing "finished pictures" right from the start. Having spent a lot of money on his equipment, he apparently expects to get the skill to handle his tools as part of the deal. And, strangely enough, to a certain degree he is right. Modern photo equipment has been perfected to such a degree that, figuratively speaking, quite a lot of "skill" is built into a camera, exposure meter, etc., and if a photographer follows the manufacturer's instructions implicitly he can never go far wrong. On the other hand, his work will be little better than average. *Only if he explores the possibilities and limitations of his tools through laborious practice and experiment will he be able to make the fullest use of the inherent potentialities of the photographic medium, and only then will his pictures differ from those produced by the faithful instruction-follower.*

CONCLUSIONS

If a short cut to success in photography exists, it is through experiment. I know that the experiments recommended in Part VII will involve extra work at first. Actually, however, it will save time and much work later. By trying to make "finished pictures" right from the start, a photographer literally spends years in planless grubbing and in time-consuming trial-and-error attempts. He also wastes material which because of lack of specific knowledge is converted into mediocre pictures instead of interesting photographs. In comparison to this constant frustration, the time, money, and effort spent on essential experiments is wholly inconsequential, while the practical gain is enormous. By doing these experiments instead of merely reading about them, a photographer accumulates more useful knowledge in a few weeks than he otherwise could through years of planless fumbling. Besides, nothing creates more confidence in one's ability and the potentialities of the medium in which one works than a solid background of experience based upon personally performed experiments and tests.

4

Useful and Useless Knowledge

An ambitious photographer is constantly concerned with improving his work. To facilitate this he relies mainly upon reading books and magazine articles on photo-technique, being guided by more advanced photographers and writers on photographic subjects. This is basically a sound approach. However, it has its pitfalls, for unless the student's goal has been established, he may be led inadvertently into a morass of completely useless "knowledge."

An enormous number of books, booklets, and magazine articles have been written for amateur consumption on subjects that in no practical way help the amateur to improve the quality of his pictures. There are books upon books dealing with optics, chemistry, sensitometry, the history of photography—yes, even entire books devoted to such apparently simple matters as how to expose a negative! Complete with higher mathematics and logarithms, too! Believe it or not—before the average amateur could read, much less understand, some of these books he actually would first have to take a course in mathematics. And after he had finally waded through this complicated material he still would not know anything of practical value which his exposure meter would not have made apparent at a single glance.

CONCLUSIONS

Superficially, photography may appear to become more intricate each year, but actually the opposite is true. All the complicated gadgets—photo-electric exposure meters, lens-coupled range finders, synchronized shutters, flash and speedlights, cameras with built-in this and built-in that, etc.—actually are designed to make work much simpler for the photographer by (1) eliminating guesswork and (2) providing, in meter settings and dial readings, facts which previously he could learn only through practical experience. And just as one can operate a radio or television set without knowledge of electronics, or drive a car without knowing the theory of the internal-combustion engine, so anyone can use a modern camera, exposure meter, ready-mixed developer, etc., without studying optics, electronics, or chemistry.

THIS IS WHAT HAPPENS
WHEN YOU MAKE A PHOTOGRAPH

1. **Light** emitted by a natural or artificial source of illumination strikes the subject, is reflected by it, and thus makes it visible to the lens of the camera as well as to the eye.

2. **The lens** of the camera refracts the rays of light reflected into it by the subject, forms an image of this subject and, if properly focused, projects this image onto the sensitized emulsion of the film.

3. **The film** responds (within certain limits) to the light that strikes it in direct proportion to the amount of exposure. A "latent," i.e., invisible, image is formed by chemical interaction of the light quanta with the crystals of the light-sensitized emulsion.

4. **Development** transforms the latent image into a visible one, the parts that received more light being correspondingly darker than those that received less light. The result is a "negative" image of the subject. The values of light and dark are reversed. To make such a negative impervious to further exposure to light, it must be "fixed" in a chemical solution ("hypo"). To make it permanent, it must be cleansed of all extraneous chemicals by washing before it is ready to be dried and printed.

5. **Printing** again reverses the tone values of the image, resulting in the final "positive" picture on paper. Printing, whether "directly" by contact, or "indirectly" via an enlarger, is basically nothing but a repetition of the processes of exposing and developing a negative. Now the image contained in the negative is projected onto the light-sensitized emulsion of the paper, where interaction between light and emulsion once more produces a latent image which, after being developed, fixed, and washed, becomes our final photograph.

The "Technically Perfect Negative"

The starting point for any technically perfect photograph is a technically perfect negative. Such a negative combines sharpness of rendition with the right degree of density (neither too dense nor too thin) and the proper contrast or "gradation" (neither too contrasty or "hard," nor too contrastless or "soft"). And, of course, any technically perfect negative is absolutely clean, free from spots, streaks, smears, dust, and—fingermarks.

Negatives that are not sharp produce fuzzy, unclear pictures.

Negatives that are too dense are difficult to print and often excessively "grainy."

Negatives that are too thin produce prints that are lacking in shadow detail.

Negatives that are too contrasty produce prints that are deficient in intermediate shades of gray.

Negatives that are too contrastless produce prints that are deficient in strong blacks and whites.

Negatives that are not clean produce dirty prints.

THREE VITAL FUNCTIONS

The three operations which determine whether or not a negative will be "technically perfect" are FOCUSING, EXPOSING, and DEVELOPING. Of these vital functions, FOCUSING controls the *sharpness of rendition;* EXPOSING (which is a function of the combined effects of DIAPHRAGM STOP * and SHUTTER SPEED), in conjunction with DEVELOPING, determine *density and contrast* of the negative. How these functions and the results they produce are interconnected is shown in the following diagram:

* A device to reduce the effective diameter of a lens (see p. 28).

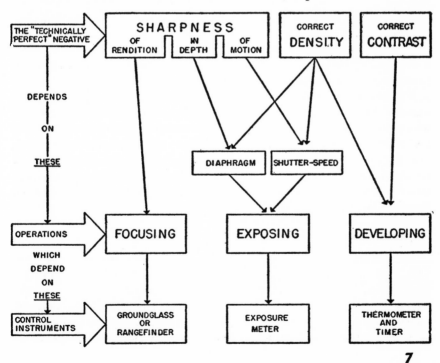

Footnote on "Sharpness"

The attentive reader has doubtless noticed that three different kinds of sharpness are listed in the diagram above. Basically, "sharpness" is controlled by focusing, but additional factors exist which under certain circumstances can also produce the effect of "unsharpness."

1. **Unsharpness Due to Faulty Focusing.**—This is the most common type of unsharpness. Unless the lens is properly focused on the subject the picture will be more or less unsharp; the degree of its unsharpness will depend on the extent to which the image was "out of focus."

2. **Unsharpness Due to Faulty Diaphragm Adjustment.**—A lens can be focused only on a certain plane at a certain distance from the lens. If the camera is properly focused on a subject which has no "depth," such as a painting, or a wall, a sharp picture will result. However, when confronted with a subject of greater extension in depth, such as a whole room, or a landscape, the photographer can still focus only on a certain plane at a certain distance from the lens. As a result, *theoretically*, everything in front of and behind this plane of focus appears increasingly unsharp the farther it is from the plane of focus. *Practically*, this kind of unsharpness is easily overcome with the aid of the diaphragm. The more the diaphragm opening is reduced (an operation known as "stopping down the lens"), the greater the depth of the sharply rendered zone. (For detailed instructions see p. 69.)

3. **Unsharpness Due to Faulty Shutter-speed Adjustment.**—If stationary subjects are photographed the shutter speed theoretically has no influence whatsoever on the sharpness of the picture. When photographing subjects in motion, however, the image of the subject moves across the surface of the exposing film, with the result that it will be rendered more or less blurred unless one uses a shutter speed fast enough to "freeze" the image on the film. See p. 84.

4. **Unsharpness Due to Motion of the Camera.**—Practically, it does not matter whether the subject moves while the camera is stationary, or whether the camera moves while the subject is stationary—both result in a blurred negative. To avoid this very common fault, a photographer should learn to *hold his camera perfectly still while making an exposure*. He should brace himself, hold his breath, and gently "squeeze" the shutter-release button as carefully as a sharpshooter "squeezes" the trigger in order not to spoil his aim. Furthermore, he should remember that, as a rule, *only* shutter speeds shorter than 1/25 of a second can be "hand-held" without danger of moving the camera during the exposure. If possible, exposures longer than 1/25 sec. should be made with the camera firmly supported, by either a sturdy tripod or other suitable means. Unsharpness due to motion of the camera is one of the most common mistakes made by a beginner—and one that can be most easily avoided.

CONTROLS FOR FOCUSING, EXPOSING, AND DEVELOPING

The tremendous advance in photography during the last decade or two has made it possible to mechanize fully the technical side of producing a photograph. Instead of relying on his eyes, his sense of time, and previous experience, the modern photographer relies on mechanical devices, instruments, dial settings, and meter readings—and produces photographs that are "technically" superior to any produced before. To "estimate" the subject-to-camera distance, to "guess" the time of exposure, or to develop "by inspection" under the red glow of a darkroom lamp, is now as obsolete as riding around in a horse and buggy.

Focusing Controls

"Focusing" means adjusting the lens-to-film distance in accordance with the lens-to-subject distance to produce a sharp image. The device for accomplishing this is either a *groundglass* * or a *lens-coupled range finder*.

Groundglass. The main advantage of *groundglass focusing* is that a groundglass produces an image that is the same size as the negative. Furthermore, it clearly indicates the degree to which sharpness extends in depth.† And, finally, it facilitates composition. Its disadvantage lies in the fact that, as the diaphragm is stopped down to increase sharpness in depth, the image darkens. However, this disadvantage can be overcome in two ways: (1) by means of an "automatic diaphragm" which permits focusing with the diaphragm wide open but closes down automatically to a pre-set stop when the shutter is released; and (2) by having the groundglass image produced by a separate finder lens (Rolleiflex type of camera, the "twin-lens reflex cameras"). However, as previously mentioned, the latter solution precludes direct observation of the extent to which sharpness in depth is produced. Some cameras are so constructed that the groundglass image is visible until the moment of exposure (all single-lens reflex cameras such as the Graflex, Kine-Exakta, Pentacon), or even continuously—before, during, and after the exposure (twin-lens reflex cameras such as the Rolleiflex, Rolleicord, Kodak Reflex, Ansco Reflex).

Lens-coupled Range Finder. The outstanding features of the lens-coupled range finder are compactness, speed of operation, and the fact that complete focusing control exists at all times—before, during, and after

* A negative-size piece of frosted glass onto which the image can be projected.
† Exception: all twin-lens reflex cameras, in which the groundglass image is not produced by the lens that takes the picture but by a separate finder lens.

9

the exposure. In other words, the image is always brightly visible and neither darkens nor disappears at the moment of exposure. Disadvantages of the range finder are the relative smallness of its image (photographers who wear glasses sometimes have difficulty in working with a range finder), the fact that it is not very accurate at short ranges, that it can never be used at extremely short subject-to-lens distances, and that it does not show the degree to which sharpness extends in depth.

Exposure Controls

The right amount of light must be admitted to the film in order to produce a "correctly exposed negative."

Overexposed negatives are too dense (too black). Highlights (the darkest parts of the negative) are frequently surrounded by "halos." These spill over into adjacent parts of the image, causing a certain degree of unsharpness through diffusion of light within the emulsion. Negative grain * is more pronounced than in correctly exposed negatives made on the same type of film. Over-all contrast is usually too low.

Underexposed negatives are too thin (too transparent). The darkest parts of the subject (the thinnest parts of the negative) are often as clear as glass and devoid of any detail. Over-all contrast is usually too high.

A WORD OF ADVICE

The exposure should always be determined with the aid of an exposure meter. (See p. 47.) Many beginners may feel that they don't need or can't afford an exposure meter, that it is too "professional" an instrument, expensive and complex. I disagree. In my opinion an exposure meter is almost as important as a camera to any photographer who wants to get the maximum from his work or hobby. To begin with, nothing is more disappointing than discovering that an important shot turned out poorly because of bad exposure. And furthermore, we all know that photography is a rather expensive hobby; but with the aid of an exposure meter each exposure can be correct, and waste due to poor exposure can be eliminated. A good exposure meter easily lasts ten years. I leave it to my reader to figure out how soon an exposure meter will pay for itself even if it should save only one bad exposure out of every three shots—which is a conservative estimate.

The two controls by means of which we regulate the exposure are the DIAPHRAGM STOP and SHUTTER-SPEED SETTING, each of which, incidentally, has a double function:

---

* Any photographic emulsion contains minute particles of metallic silver called "grains" (see p. 43).

10

the diaphragm regulates
$\begin{cases} \text{the amount of light admitted to} \\ \quad \text{the film} \\ \text{the extension of sharpness in} \\ \quad \text{depth} \end{cases}$

the shutter speed regulates
$\begin{cases} \text{the amount of light admitted to} \\ \quad \text{the film} \\ \text{the degree of sharpness with} \\ \quad \text{which subjects in motion are} \\ \quad \text{rendered} \end{cases}$

Diaphragm and Shutter Speed. By selecting a larger or smaller diaphragm opening we admit a wider or narrower beam of light, while by selecting a slower or faster shutter speed we permit this beam of light to strike the film for a longer or shorter time. This means that we can produce a correct exposure in many different ways: the effect of a "larger diaphragm opening plus faster shutter speed" is, in negative exposure, the same as a "smaller diaphragm opening plus slower shutter speed."

To use an analogy: let us assume that we have to fill a vessel with a predetermined amount of water—for example, one gallon. If we draw the water from a pipe with a large diameter (corresponding to a large diaphragm opening) we keep the faucet open for a shorter time (corresponding to a short shutter speed) than if we draw the same amount of water from a pipe with a small diameter (corresponding to a small diaphragm opening). In order to compensate for the slower flow, we keep the faucet open for a correspondingly longer time (corresponding to a slower shutter speed). In either case, by correlating the diameter of the pipe (or diaphragm opening) and the duration of the flow (the time the faucet or the shutter, respectively, is open), we achieve the identical result: to draw exactly one gallon of water (or to admit identical amounts of light to the film).

VERY IMPORTANT

The whole secret of correct exposure is the selection of the most suitable combination of diaphragm opening and shutter speed. The basis for any such selection, i.e., for setting the DIAPHRAGM and SHUTTER, is determined by an exposure meter. (See p. 88 on how to use your exposure meter correctly.) Its correctly adjusted dials show the photographer simultaneously all the possible combinations of diaphragm opening and shutter speed which will produce a correctly exposed negative. Which of these combinations is finally selected depends on the following factors:

1. Extension in Depth of Subject.—If depth is considerable and must be rendered sharply, a relatively small diaphragm stop is needed (how small

11

the diaphragm stop should be will be discussed later, on p. 68). And, as previously stated, a relatively small diaphragm opening must be "compensated" for by a relatively slow shutter speed to avoid underexposure.

2. Motion and Speed of Subject.—If the subject is not stationary but in motion, a relatively fast shutter speed must be used to "stop" the motion and to make a picture sharp. The higher the speed of the subject, or the more rapid the change in action, the faster the shutter speed must be (how fast the shutter speed should be will be discussed later, on p. 83). And, as previously stated, a relatively fast shutter speed must be "compensated" for by a relatively large diaphragm opening to avoid underexposure.

3. Hand-held or Tripod Exposure.—To avoid unsharpness due to movement of the camera, only exposures faster than 1/25 sec. should normally be "hand-held." Longer exposures should be made with the camera firmly supported by a tripod or other suitable means. Consequently, if the exposure has to be made "hand-held," a shutter speed not slower than 1/25 sec.—and preferably somewhat faster—should be selected when computing the exposure. The corresponding diaphragm opening can easily be found by consulting the exposure meter.

This may sound rather complicated, but it is in reality extremely simple. A practical example may make it clearer: let us assume that the emulsion speed of your film (see p. 41) is 125 ASA (22° DIN), and that your correspondingly pre-set Weston exposure meter indicates a light-intensity reading of 25. Under these conditions you would have a choice of the combinations of diaphragm opening and shutter speed listed in the following diagram. This diagram also shows the effects of these different combinations as far as accuracy of focusing, extension of sharpness in depth, and ability to "stop" motion are concerned.

Diaphragm stop numbers	1.5	2	3.5	4.5	5.6	6.3	9	11	16	22	32
Corresponding shutter speeds	1/1200	1/800	1/250	1/150	1/100	1/80	1/40	1/25	1/12	1/6	1/3
Focusing	Decreasing sharpness in depth demands increasingly accurate focusing.			Increasing sharpness in depth compensates for less accurate focusing.							
Extension of sharpness in depth	very limited - limited - medium - increasingly extensive										
Rendition of objects in motion	very sharp - sharp - slightly blurred - increasingly blurred										
Conclusions	The faster the action or the motion of the subject, the faster shutter speeds are necessary to produce sharp pictures.			The greater the depth of the subject, the smaller diaphragm stops must be used to produce sufficient sharpness in depth.							
	Exposure times short enough to be handheld. Tripod should be used.										

VERY IMPORTANT

It is of the highest importance for the beginner to realize how closely the functions of the three controls—FOCUSING, DIAPHRAGM setting, and SHUTTER speed—are related. Change of one almost invariably necessitates readjustment of one or both of the others if the result is to be a technically perfect negative. In practice, ideal solutions of this problem are rare. In most cases the best one can do is find *the most advantageous compromise* between the conflicting effects resulting from the double functions of the diaphragm and shutter.

In order to achieve the best possible results the following contrary demands must be considered and, what is more, fulfilled as far as practically feasible:

If the lens is focused accurately everything is all right, and the selection of diaphragm stop and shutter speed can be made exactly as outlined above.

If the lens, however, is focused more or less at random either because the camera is not equipped with range finder or groundglass, or because a "snapshot" must be taken quickly, leaving no time for accurate focusing,* then the danger of producing an out-of-focus negative must be counteracted as far as possible. This is done by using a relatively small diaphragm opening, which automatically produces a relatively large "safety zone" of sharpness extending in depth. However, as previously stated, a relatively small diaphragm opening must be "compensated" for by a relatively slow shutter speed to avoid the danger of underexposure.

Diaphragm opening should be as small as possible to produce the greatest extension of sharpness in depth; but not so small as to cause underexposure.

Diaphragm opening should be as large as possible to permit the use of the highest possible shutter speed to prevent unsharpness due to movement of subject or camera.

Shutter speed should be as short as possible to "stop" motion of the subject and to prevent unsharpness due to motion of the "hand-held" camera; but not so short as to cause underexposure.

Shutter speed should be as long as possible to permit use of the smallest possible diaphragm stop in order to produce the greatest extension of sharpness in depth.

---

* See p. 70 for a valuable "system" for such occasions.

Summing up the good and the less desirable effects of different settings of focusing, diaphragm, and shutter speed, we arrive at the following conclusions:

	Advantage	*Disadvantage*
Accurate focusing	Guarantees the highest degree of sharpness of rendition.	The time taken for focusing accurately may cause the photographer to miss a shot or the peak of action.
Random focusing	Takes practically no time, is often the only way of making "snapshots" when one has to act fast.	Danger of out-of-focus pictures necessitates use of smaller diaphragm opening to increase zone of sharpness in depth as a "safety-measure"; this calls for slower shutter speeds to avoid danger of under-exposure and can become the cause for unsharpness due to motion of subject or camera.
Small diaphragm	Increases extension of zone of sharpness in depth; reduces the danger of over-exposure in very bright light.	The relatively small amount of light admitted to film creates danger of under-exposure; to prevent under-exposure, slower shutter speeds must be used, increasing danger of unsharpness due to motion of subject or camera.
Large diaphragm	Admits plenty of light, making under-exposure less likely; permits use of fast shutter speeds that aid in avoiding unsharpness due to motion.	Extension of sharpness in depth is limited; focusing has to be done especially carefully; danger of over-exposure exists.
Fast shutter speed	Prevents danger of unsharpness due to motion of subject or camera; reduces danger of over-exposure in very bright light.	Necessitates use of larger diaphragm opening to counteract danger of under-exposure due to the fact that the faster the shutter speed, the less light admitted to the film.
Slow shutter speed	Allows use of smaller diaphragm opening resulting in greater extension of zone of sharpness in depth; reduces danger of under-exposure.	Increases danger of unsharpness due to motion of subject or camera; increases danger of over-exposure in very bright light.

14

Realization of *the interdependence of the three controls—focusing, diaphragm setting, and shutter speed—*and of their effects upon the negative! —should make it clear that they must never be considered separately; instead, they must be treated as a unit. The following survey demonstrates in graphic form all the factors which determine the outcome of an exposure.

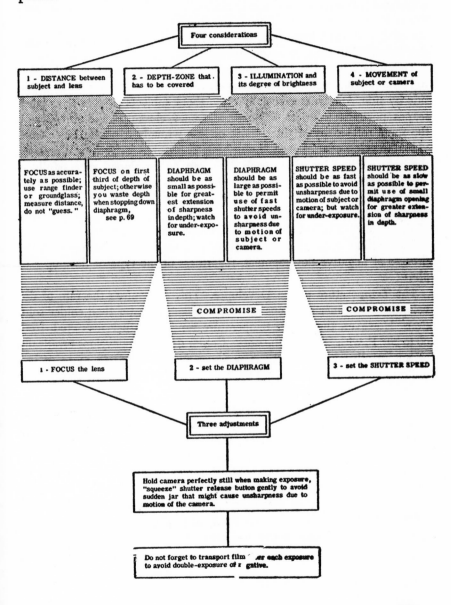

Four considerations

1 - DISTANCE between subject and lens	2 - DEPTH-ZONE that has to be covered	3 - ILLUMINATION and its degree of brightness	4 - MOVEMENT of subject or camera

| FOCUS as accurately as possible; use range finder or groundglass; measure distance, do not "guess." | FOCUS on first third of depth of subject; otherwise you waste depth when stopping down diaphragm, see p. 69 | DIAPHRAGM should be as small as possible for greatest extension of sharpness in depth; watch for under-exposure. | DIAPHRAGM should be as large as possible to permit use of fast shutter speeds to avoid unsharpness due to motion of subject or camera. | SHUTTER SPEED should be as fast as possible to avoid unsharpness due to motion of subject or camera; but watch for under-exposure. | SHUTTER SPEED should be as slow as possible to permit use of small diaphragm opening for greater extension of sharpness in depth. |

COMPROMISE   COMPROMISE

1 - FOCUS the lens	2 - set the DIAPHRAGM	3 - set the SHUTTER SPEED

Three adjustments

Hold camera perfectly still when making exposure, "squeeze" shutter release button gently to avoid sudden jar that might cause unsharpness due to motion of the camera.

Do not forget to transport film after each exposure to avoid double-exposure of r gative.

15

Developing Controls

In the days of large-size glass plates and individual sheets of cut film, developing each negative individually and, if necessary, in a specially prepared developer, made sense. Then, best results could be most consistently produced by adapting the process of development to the particular requirement of each exposure in accordance with the type of illumination, the contrast range of the subject, the inherent qualities of the negative material, and, most important, the desired qualities of the finished negative in regard to contrast range and density.

Today, however, the most commonly used type of negative material is roll film. On roll film, subjects extremely different in character are recorded side by side. Amateurs especially often shoot subjects as diverse as landscapes, portraits, interiors, backlighted scenes, close-ups, and still lifes on the same roll—many of them more or less wrongly exposed. Since individual development of each "frame" * is impossible for technical reasons, the only method by which such films can be developed successfully is standardization of the whole process in accordance with the requirements of what might be called "the average negative," and by performing the necessary operations in a strictly mechanical manner. This modern way of developing is called the TIME-AND-TEMPERATURE METHOD.

This method is based upon the two following factors which govern the process of negative development, regardless of the type of developer or film:

The Temperature of the Developer.—This determines the rate of development—warmer solutions develop a negative faster than colder solutions. However, the usable temperature range is rather restricted—from 60 to 80° F. with 68° F. as the norm. Colder developer develops erratically or not at all; warmer solutions produce over-all "fog" (a more or less uniform veil of gray overlaying the image) and can cause the emulsion to melt and to run off its base.

The Time of Development.—This determines density and contrast range of the negative. The longer the development, the denser (blacker) the negatives become, and the higher their contrast (the greater the difference between light and dark); and vice versa. This fact is of great practical value for controlling the contrast range of negatives and will be discussed later in more detail (see p. 80).

The "normal" time of development (at the "normal" temperature of 68° F.) varies considerably with the type of developer and the type of film. For specific cases consult the instruction sheet that always accompanies the film.

---

* The individual negative on a film strip.

16

The beauty of the time-and-temperature method is that it simplifies development to such a degree that even a rank beginner can produce consistently good results from the start. All he has to do is to use the developer that is recommended by the film manufacturer, consult the instruction sheet that comes with his film to find the recommended time of development, and be sure that the temperature of his developer is exactly 68° F. The only control instruments he needs are a THERMOME- TER and a TIMER. With their aid (and the manufacturer's instruction sheet), negative development today is no more difficult than boiling a couple of eggs.

Pointers for Beginners

The three control instruments—EXPOSURE METER, THERMOMETER, and TIMER—are just as important for ultimate success as your camera and film. Train yourself to consult them constantly. There is no excuse for guess- work.

The secret of the "technically perfect negative" is revealed in the dia- gram on p. 15; memorize the four considerations—DISTANCE, DEPTH, ILLU- MINATION, MOTION; and the three adjustments—FOCUS, DIAPHRAGM, SHUTTER SPEED.

Always expose for shadows; highlights will then take care of themselves. When in doubt, overexposure is better than underexposure.

To avoid blurred negatives, train yourself to hold the camera perfectly still when making an exposure; "squeeze" the shutter release button gently. Remember to wind or change the film after each exposure.

Study the instructions that accompany your camera, film, and developer; they contain, in essence, what you need to know to use them to best advantage.

Learn to evaluate your subjects in terms of black and white and shades of gray, and to disregard color; unless, of course, your camera is loaded with color film.

Pay attention to background; branches appearing to grow out of people's heads are amusing but not particularly beautiful . . . and fuzzy bright spots of no particular shape in the background of a picture are most distracting. A neutral background is never wrong . . . and the open sky is the best background for portraits and pictures of people.

Close-ups invariably make more interesting pictures than shots that are taken from afar; distant views, beautiful as they appear to the eye, notoriously produce some of the most disappointing photographs.

17

PART TWO

TOOLS AND MATERIALS

Descriptions and evaluation of the tools and materials a photographer needs for the production of "technically perfect photographs"

Photography is as simple or as complex as you wish to make it. "Prize-winning" pictures have been taken with box cameras loaded with a "nameless" brand of film. On the other hand, possession of hundreds of dollars worth of equipment is still no guarantee for the production of outstanding work. All of which only helps to prove the generally accepted but commonly ignored fact that it is the photographer who "makes" the picture, and not his camera, lens, or film.

On the other hand, without adequate information on equipment and material, no one can make an intelligent selection and acquire the things he needs for doing a certain type of work. The following chapter contains this information. It is accurate and complete—perhaps too complete for your present needs. In that case, read what is of interest to you now and skip the rest. You can always return to it later, if and when you need it. You will probably find that some devices which now seem highly specialized to you may eventually become essential in order to achieve particular effects.

THE COMPONENTS OF THE CAMERA
AND THEIR FUNCTIONS

Any camera,

from the cheapest to the most expensive, is basically nothing but a light-tight box or sleeve connecting two vital parts:

the LENS that produces the image, and

the FILM that retains it.

All other parts are auxiliary devices whose purpose is to facilitate the three operations by which the negative is produced:

AIMING,

FOCUSING,

EXPOSING.

Controls for Aiming

Aiming a camera is as important as aiming a gun. To aim the photographer needs a finder. He has the choice of two basically different types: *eye-level finders* through which he looks with the camera held against his eye; and *waist-level finders* into which he looks from above with the camera held near waist level. Pictures taken with cameras equipped with eye-level finders show more or less the same type of perspective as that which we see, which is never really wrong but often somewhat dull. Pictures taken with waist-level finders usually have a more or less "worm's-eye view" perspective which tends to make them less usual and consequently more interesting. Cameras equipped with eye-level finders are "quicker on the draw"—the reason why this type of finder is used on most 35-mm. and all press-type cameras. However, its image is often very small, does not always correspond exactly with the extent of the picture, and, except in prism-reflex cameras, indicates neither the zone of sharpest focus nor the extension of sharpness in depth. Waist-level finders are of two types:

The brilliant finder, found only on simple and inexpensive cameras. The image it produces is always sharp, regardless of whether or not the camera has been focused properly, and it does not indicate extension of sharpness in depth.

The reflex-type groundglass finder. It shows the image produced by the lens that takes the picture (or by its twin), in the full size of the negative, clearly indicating whether or not it is in focus, and how far sharpness extends in depth. Cameras equipped with this most versatile type of finder are, among others, the Hasselblad and Bronica in the 2¼ x 2¼-inch size; the Leicaflex, Nikon F, Pentax in the 35-mm. size; and all twin-lens reflex cameras of the Rolleiflex type. (However, for technical reasons and to gain other advantages, the reflex finders of the last type do not show the degree to which sharpness extends in depth. See p. 215.)

Controls for Focusing

Focusing means adjusting the lens-to-film distance in accordance with the lens-to-subject distance to produce *an image that is sharp.* To do this two devices are needed: (1) *an optical control (the range finder or the groundglass)* by means of which we see whether or not the image is in focus; (2) *a mechanical control (the helical lens mount or the rack-and-pinion drive* operated by a focusing knob) by which we can adjust the distance between lens and film until the optical control device shows that the image on the negative will be "in focus"

22

Controls for Exposing

Exposing means admitting the right amount of light to the film to produce a negative of desired density and contrast. We accomplish this with the aid of two controls:

1. *The diaphragm,* which regulates the "effective" diameter of the lens, admitting more or less light to the film.

2. *The shutter,* which regulates the length of time that light is admitted to the film. There are two basically different types of shutters: *between-the-lens shutters,* which are built into the lens, and *focal-plane shutters,* which are built into the camera. The first type, at its best, is more accurate, and easier to synchronize for flash and speedlight; the second type permits faster shutter speeds, but is often less accurate and more difficult to synchronize for flash and strobe. Single-lens reflex cameras and 35-mm. cameras are usually equipped with focal-plane shutters, and twin-lens reflex and view-type cameras with between-the-lens shutters. Some press-type cameras are equipped with both types of shutters, each of which can be used separately.

The following diagram shows in graphic form the relationship between the different camera controls and their effects:

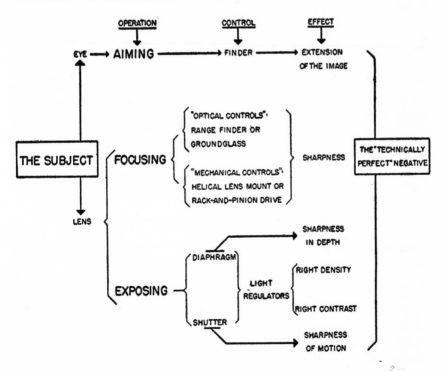

The Lens

There are almost as many different types and sizes of lenses as there are breeds of dogs. However, all lenses, whether simple or complicated, have certain fundamental properties in common, and are subject to the same optical laws. As stated previously: you do *not* have to know *how* a lens produces an image; you do *not* have to know the laws of optics; you do *not* have to know what refraction is, or astigmatism, or spherical aberration, or curvature of field, or coma, or nodal points—in order to be able to select *your* lens intelligently and use it to best advantage. All you have to learn is the meaning of the terms FOCAL LENGTH, RELATIVE APERTURE, and COVERING POWER which are explained below:

THE FOCAL LENGTH OF A LENS

The focal length of a lens determines the scale of the image on the negative: the longer the focal length, the larger the image. Focal length and image size are directly proportional: a lens with twice the focal length of another lens produces an image twice as large as that produced by the "shorter" lens. Consequently, if a photographer wants to increase the scale of a rendering he must use a lens with a longer focal length, and vice versa.

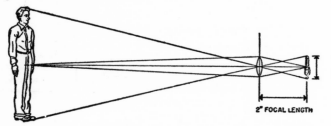

2" FOCAL LENGTH

SHORT FOCAL LENGTH--SMALL IMAGE

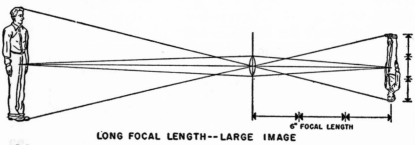

6" FOCAL LENGTH

LONG FOCAL LENGTH--LARGE IMAGE

24

The focal length of a lens is the distance from (approximately) lens center to film at which the lens produces a sharp image of an object that is "infinitely" far away—for example the sun. To roughly estimate the focal length of a lens, hold it toward the sun and measure the distance at which the smallest, sharpest, and hottest image is produced. However, if you project the image onto the palm of your hand, be careful not to get burned. A photographic lens is basically nothing but a burning glass, and on a sunny day you can light a cigarette with it.

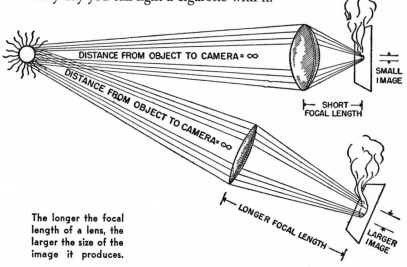

The longer the focal length of a lens, the larger the size of the image it produces.

The focal length of a lens is measured either in inches, centimeters, or millimeters, and is normally engraved on the lens mount. The focal length is the shortest distance between lens center * and film at which the lens will still produce a sharp image. In this position, the lens is said to be focused "on infinity." In order to produce sharp images of closer subjects, the distance from lens center to film must be increased in accordance with the lens-to-subject distance—the lens must be "focused." To produce an image that is the same size as the subject (rendition "in natural size"), the distance from lens center to film must be roughly twice the focal length of the lens; and in order to produce an image in twice natural size (of an extremely close, very small subject—for example, an insect or a small flower), distance from lens center to film must be three times the focal length of the lens; and so on. The shortest subject-to-lens distance at which a lens can still produce a sharp image is equal to the focal length of the lens; in such a strictly hypothetical case, however, distance between lens center and film would have to be infinitely great.

* More accurately: the "node of emission," which in telephoto and "retrofocus" wide-angle lenses may lie outside the lens.

According to their focal lengths, lenses are frequently referred to as "standard," "short-focus," and "long-focus" lenses. Such a differentiation, however, is not absolute. The same lens that has a relatively short focal length when used to cover a large negative has a relatively long focal length when used to cover a negative of small size. For example: a wide-angle lens for an 8- by 10-inch negative has a focal length of 6 inches; this same lens, however, if used on a 4- by 5-inch camera, would act as a "standard lens," since the "normal" focal length for a 4- by 5-inch negative size is 6 inches; and if used on a 2¼- by 2¼-inch single-lens reflex camera, this lens which originally was a wide-angle would now act as a "telephoto" lens, since the "standard" focal length for a 2¼- by 2¼-inch negative size is 3 inches.

The "normal" or "standard" focal length for any negative size is roughly equal to the length of the diagonal of the negative. Any lens with a focal length greater than the diagonal of the negative it covers is a "long-focus lens"; if its focal length is shorter than the diagonal of the negative, it must be considered a "short-focus lens."

THE RELATIVE APERTURE OF A LENS

The relative aperture is a measure of the light transmission of a lens. The larger the diameter of a lens in proportion to its focal length, the larger its "relative aperture," the more light it admits to the film, and the higher is its "speed."

THE RELATIVE APERTURE OF THIS LENS IS f/3

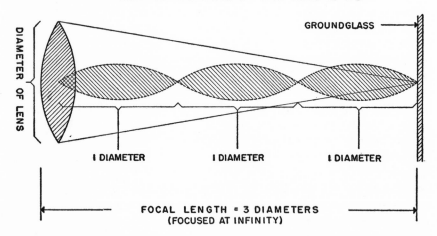

The relative aperture of a lens cannot be measured directly as can the focal length, since it is a function of two factors: lens diameter and focal length. It is expressed in the form of a ratio: relative aperture equals

26

focal length divided by the diameter of the front surface of the lens.* It is expressed in f-numbers. If, for example, the diameter of a lens is 23½ mm. and its focal length is 150 mm., all you have to do to determine roughly its relative aperture is to divide 150 by 23½, and you get as a result an f-number of 6.3. This f-number can be written in several ways—either as "f.6.3" or as "f/6.3" or as "1 : 6.3."

To better understand the importance of the relationship between lens diameter and focal length, let us consider an analogy:

Imagine a circular window with a three-foot diameter. This window illuminates a small room, and the distance between window and opposite wall is nine feet. Image a second room, illuminated by a circular window with a three-foot diameter; but this room is twice as deep, and the distance between window and wall is eighteen feet. Obviously, despite the fact that both windows are of equal size, the second wall receives less light than the wall in the first room, since it is farther away from the window. Actually, since the wall in the second room is twice as far away from the window as the wall in the first room, and since light intensity is inversely proportional to the square of the distance between object and source of illumination, the wall in the eighteen-foot room receives only one quarter of the illumination of that of the nine-foot room, even though it is only twice as far from the window.

This example should make it clear why the formula for the "speed" of a lens must include *two* factors: diameter and focal length. By itself, the diameter indicates nothing about the speed of a lens. Only if we know the distance between the lens ("the window") and the film ("the wall") can we compute the amount of light that will reach the negative and determine the exposure. The simplest way to express the values of *both* lens diameter and focal length in *one* formula is in the form of a ratio: "focal length divided by lens diameter." According to this formula, the f-number of the three-foot window in the nine-foot room is 9:3, or f/3; while the f-number of the three-foot window in the eighteen-foot room is considerably lower—to be exact: 18:3, or f/6.

A fact that seems to cause the beginner considerable trouble is that *the higher* the speed of a lens the *lower* its f-number. An f/1.5 lens is considerably faster than an f/3.5 lens, which in turn is much faster than an f/6.3 lens, and so on. Why this is so was shown in the above analogy —lens speeds are expressed in the form of a ratio: focal length divided by lens diameter.

---

* Strictly speaking, this is not quite correct. Actually, the "effective diameter" of a lens must be used to determine the relative aperture—usually it is a fraction larger than the diameter of the front surface of the lens.

The relative aperture is equivalent to the largest diaphragm opening of a lens. This diaphragm opening indicates its highest possible "speed." However, shooting pictures with the lens "wide open" is not always desirable for two reasons:

1. The larger the diaphragm opening, the smaller the extension of the zone of sharpness in depth (see p. 68).

2. The larger the diaphragm opening, the greater the danger of over-exposure. When light is extremely bright (at the beach, in snow scenes in sunshine, on glaciers), the shutters of most cameras do not provide speeds fast enough to avoid overexposure if a picture is taken with the lens wide open.

The means for reducing the relative aperture—for "slowing down the lens"—is the diaphragm, which is built into the lens. It is calibrated in f-numbers which are computed by dividing the focal length by the diameter of the respective diaphragm opening. Diaphragm openings, or "stops" as they are commonly called, are calibrated in such a way that each consecutive f-number requires twice the exposure of the preceding larger diaphragm opening—i.e., smaller f-number. In other words, *as the diaphragm opening is reduced from one f-number to the next, the exposure must be doubled.* The following table shows the relationship between f-numbers, comparative exposure factors, sharpness in depth, and brightness of the groundglass image:

The American f-number system:	1	1.4	2	2.8	4	5.6	8	11	16	22
Comparative exposure factors:	1	2	4	8	16	32	64	128	256	512
The German f-number system	1.3	1.6	2.2	3.2	4.5	6.3	9	12.5	18	25

Diaphragm openings get larger	Diaphragm openings get smaller
Stop numbers get smaller	Stop numbers get larger
Sharpness in depth decreases	Sharpness in depth increases
Exposure times decrease	Exposure times increase
Groundglass image brightens	Groundglass image darkens

The ratio between exposures at different f-numbers is equivalent to the ratio of the f-numbers multiplied by themselves.

For example: the ratio of f/3.5 to f/8 is equal to $(3.5 \times 3.5):(8 \times 8)$, which is equivalent to 12.25 : 64, or 1 : 5.22. If we had to expose 1/100 sec. at f/3.5 but wanted to stop down to f/8, we should have to expose $1/100 \times 5.22$ or roughly 1/20 sec. in order to get a negative with the same density.

F-numbers are indicators of the brightness of the image (on the ground-glass or on the film). For example, an f-number of 4.5 always indicates the same degree of brightness of the image—and necessitates the same exposure—regardless of whether it represents the relative aperture (i.e., highest possible speed) of an f/4.5 lens, or the diaphragm stop of an f/1.5 lens which was stopped down to f/4.5. It is of no consequence whether the lens is a giant telephoto lens of a 5- by 7-inch "Big Bertha," or a tiny wide-angle lens of a 35-mm. camera—as long as each has a relative aperture of f/4.5, or is stopped down to f/4.5, there is no difference between the two as far as image brightness and exposure duration are concerned.

Light Loss in Lenses

NOTE: Lenses are made of glass, and, however transparent it may appear, all glass absorbs a certain amount of the light that passes through it, and even more is lost through reflection from the surfaces of the individual lens elements. In most ordinary lenses this loss of light is negligible as far as computation of the exposure is concerned; moreover, in exposure meters certain allowances are made for such light losses. However, superfast lenses contain up to seven individual elements with up to ten different glass-air surfaces. In such lenses light losses can reach 50 per cent of the total illumination. Consequently, when working with one of these superfast lenses, the photographer should increase the meter reading by 30 to 50 per cent in order to avoid underexposure.

Recently a new and much more accurate method of calibrating lenses and diaphragms has been introduced; it is based upon T-stops ("T" stands for "transmission"). This method carefully measures and takes into account all light losses due to absorption and reflection. As a result, T-stops of identical numbers always indicate identical image brightness, whether the lens consists of two thin or ten thick individual elements.

There are several independent laboratories which recalibrate f-stops to T-stops. This is a service of special interest to a color photographer, for accuracy of exposure is much more important in color than in black-and-white photography, in which exposure latitude of the film compensates for minor inaccuracies. It is to be hoped that in the near future all new lenses will be factory-calibrated in T-stops.

The speed of a lens is not absolute, but depends on the lens-to-subject distance. Remember that the "speed" of a lens is a function of both focal length and lens diameter. "Focal length," however, is merely a shorter term for "distance between lens and film when the lens is focused on infinity." When the lens is not focused on infinity but on a closer subject, distance between lens and film increases—and the closer the subject is, the greater the distance between lens and film. And since "distance from lens to film" is part of the formula of the "speed" of a lens, any change in this distance naturally must affect this formula.

Minor increases in lens-to-film distance above "standard" (i.e., focal length) can be safely disregarded. The resultant loss in lens speed is so slight that the ability of the film to absorb a certain amount of under-exposure will compensate for it. However, *focusing on a very near subject* increases distance between lens and film to such an extent that the resulting loss of lens speed causes serious underexposure unless compensated for by a proportional increase in exposure. To refer to the analogy of the window and the two rooms: if the nine-foot distance from window to wall corresponds to the "focal length of the window," we arrive, by the computation shown above, at a "speed" of f/3. But if the same window-lens were used to make a close-up with the image in natural size, the window-to-wall distance would have to be increased to twice the "focal length of the window-lens" for the subject to be in focus (see p. 25). This would necessitate a window-to-wall distance of eighteen feet—the same as the window-to-wall distance of the second room. However, as demonstrated above, the "effective" speed of the window-lens would then be f/6, or only one quarter of what it was when focused at infinity!

Such a serious loss of lens speed naturally affects the exposure. Since the intensity of an illumination is inversely proportional to the square of the distance between light source (the lens) and illuminated object (the film), focusing a lens on a close subject for rendition in natural size (necessitating a lens-to-film distance equal to twice the focal length of the lens) increases the exposure by 2^2 times (as indicated by the exposure meter) and 2^2 equals 4! In other words, *close-ups in natural size must be exposed four times as long as shots focused at infinity.*

The necessary increase in exposure for any lens-to-film distance greater than the focal length of the lens can be computed according to the following formula:

$$\frac{\text{lens-to-film distance} \times \text{lens-to-film distance}}{\text{focal length of lens} \times \text{focal length of lens}}$$

For example: we want to take a close-up of a flower, using a lens with a focal length of six inches. The distance between lens and film (bellows extension) after focusing measures ten inches.

To find the exposure factor for this particular setup we use the following equation:

$$\frac{10 \times 10}{6 \times 6} = \frac{100}{36} = \text{approximately } 3$$

This means that the exposure for the flower must be three times as long as the exposure meter indicated. For example, if the meter indicated an exposure of 2 seconds at f/32, we now have to expose 2×3 (or 6) seconds at f/32 in order to get a correctly exposed negative.

The following table shows the ratio between close-up and corresponding increase of exposure:

	Subject-to-lens distance in multiples of focal lengths:						Lens-to-film distance in multiples of focal lengths:						
	∞	100	20	10	5	3	2	2-1/2	3	4	5	6	7
Image magnification	0	01	05	.11	.25	.50	1 Nat'l size	1-1/2	2	3	4	5	6
Exposure factor	1	1.02	1.1 1	1.23	1.56	2.25	4	6	9	16	25	36	49

For practical purposes, increases in exposure are necessary only if the subject-to-lens distance is shorter than five times the focal length of the lens (see arrow in diagram above). From that point on, however, the shorter the subject-to-lens distance (or the greater the increase in the distance from lens to film), the higher the exposure factor. *For such close-ups, exposure times as indicated by the exposure meter must be multiplied by the corresponding factor if the result is to be a "technically perfect negative."*

THE EFFECTIVE APERTURE KODAGUIDE made by the Eastman Kodak Company is an ingenious little device for immediate determination of the exposure factor for close-ups. It consists of a card with an attached dial which, after proper setting, shows both the exposure factor and the degree of magnification.

THE COVERING POWER OF A LENS

The covering power determines whether or not a lens can be used in conjunction with a certain negative size. The greater the covering power of a lens, the relatively larger the negative size it will "cover" ("relative" in comparison to the focal length of the lens).

Covering power has nothing to do with focal length. A lens with a great focal length may have very little covering power, or vice versa. The 3-inch "telephoto lens" of a movie camera, for instance, has just enough covering power to cover the tiny rectangle of the cine-film; the 3-inch "standard lens" of a Rolleiflex covers the much larger negative size of 2¼ by 2¼ inches; and the 3-inch Zeiss Dagor f/9 "wide-angle lens" has such an enormous covering power that it covers the comparatively huge negative size of 4 by 5 inches.

Any lens produces a circular image. However, the quality of this image is not uniform. It is always sharpest near the center, gradually becoming less sharp toward the rim of the circle. For photographic purposes only the inner, sharply rendered part of the image is of use. The outer zones are valueless. For this reason, the negative size must always "fit" within this inner "useful" circle, the diameter of which consequently must never be smaller than the diagonal of the negative.

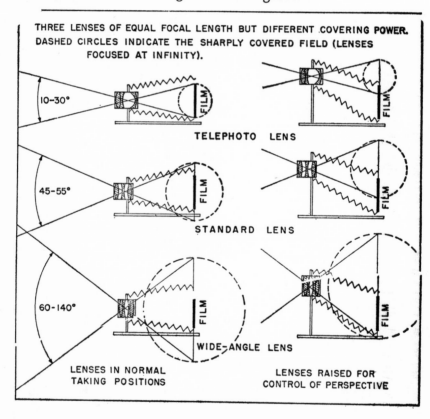

THREE LENSES OF EQUAL FOCAL LENGTH BUT DIFFERENT COVERING POWER. DASHED CIRCLES INDICATE THE SHARPLY COVERED FIELD (LENSES FOCUSED AT INFINITY).

10-30°   FILM   FILM

TELEPHOTO LENS

45-55°   FILM   FILM

STANDARD LENS

60-140°   FILM   FILM

WIDE-ANGLE LENS

LENSES IN NORMAL
TAKING POSITIONS

LENSES RAISED FOR
CONTROL OF PERSPECTIVE

We can imagine this inner "useful" circle to be the base of a cone with the apex at the center of the lens. (The lens should be focused on infinity to make the height of the cone equal to the focal length of the lens.) The angle formed by the sides of this cone is the measure of the covering power of a lens. "Standard lenses" cover an angle of 45° to 55°, "telephoto lenses" cover a narrower angle, while "wide-angle lenses" cover an angle of 60° to 140°. A few super wide-angle lenses have been produced to cover angles up to 210°—which literally means that such lenses can "shoot backwards."

The covering power of most standard lenses is just about sufficient to sharply cover the negative size for which they are intended. This is satisfactory as long as such lenses are used in cameras without "swings" * or facilities for raising and lowering the lens. *Lenses intended for use on cameras with "swings" must have greater than "standard" covering power.* Otherwise, use of the "swings," or raising or lowering the lens, would cause part of the picture to be outside the sharply covered circle, with the result that only part of the image would be sharp. For this reason, it is often advisable to use the "wide-angle lens" of a 5- by 7-inch camera as a "standard lens" on a 4- by 5-inch swing-equipped view camera. Its focal length would be identical to a "standard lens"—6 inches—but the covering power of the wide-angle lens would be considerably greater than that of the standard lens. With this additional covering power, perspective can be controlled and sharpness still maintained even though full use of "swings" is made.

The covering power of most lenses increases as the diaphragm is stopped down. In some instances, this increase is so considerable that the stopped-down lens will cover a negative one size larger than the size it covers "wide open" (for example, the Goerz Dagor lenses). Whenever it is desirable that the entire negative be perfectly sharp (especially in copy work), the lens should be stopped down to the optimum f-stop to utilize its full inherent covering power.

The covering power of every lens increases as lens-to-subject distance decreases. This phenomenon is especially useful for the making of close-up photographs in natural or more than natural size. Whenever the bellows or extension tubes of a camera are not long enough to allow the necessary lens-to-film distances required for such close-ups, the problem may be solved by substituting a lens of much shorter focal length for the "standard lens." Lenses of 1 to 3 inches in focal length are especially suitable for close-up photography with 4- by 5-inch cameras. For example, a lens with a focal length of 1 inch, originally designed to cover nothing larger than a 16-mm. moving-picture frame, will cover a 4- by 5-inch negative perfectly at a distance of 10 inches from the film, and produce an image of 9-times magnification.

---

* A provision for independent adjustment of camera front and back.

The Film

Modern negative material is available in a great variety of different types, each especially well suited to certain specific purposes. To ask a photo store clerk for "a roll of film" without further specification would be as foolish as to ask him for "a camera" without specifying the type. A certain amount of theoretical knowledge is required to select and use the proper film as it is required to select a camera or lens. But just as in the case of a camera or a lens, all the different types of negative material can be classified as variations of *a few basic qualities*. Once a photographer becomes familiar with the fundamental properties of negative material he will be able to evaluate any type of film and determine which film each type of work requires.

Modern negative material varies with regard to the following five major qualities:

1. *Type:* roll film, filmpack, sheet film, glass plates, in various sizes.
2. *Color sensitivity:* blue-sensitive (process film), orthochromatic (red-insensitive), panchromatic (sensitized to all colors), infrared-sensitized.
3. *Speed:* slow, medium, fast, super-fast.
4. *Graininess:* fine grain, medium grain, coarse grain.
5. *Gradation:* contrasty, normal, soft.

Aside from these differences, and the resulting differences in exposure time and method of development, all negative material must be treated according to the same rules as far as handling and storing are concerned.

10 DOs AND DON'Ts

1. Don't touch the negative emulsion with your fingers—indelible spots caused by the always present acid moisture of the skin may result.

2. When handling negatives, hold them by the edges only, for the reason stated above.

3. Negative material should be stored in a cool dry place. Dampness and heat slowly destroy unexposed film, and slowly but inevitably deteriorate finished negatives. In summer, for instance, the glove compartment of a car is much too hot a place for keeping film.

34

4. Always load your camera in the shade. No "daylight-loading" film is so light-tight that it can stand direct exposure to the sun without fogging along the edges. If there is no shade, turn from the light and use the shadow cast by your body.

5. When buying film, you should look at the expiration date stamped on the cover—it is your guarantee of freshness. Old film may have lost some of its speed, may be less contrasty and partially or wholly fogged.

6. Be sure that roll film is always wound tight. Don't let it loosen when loading the camera, or your negatives may become light-struck. Thread the endpaper carefully into the slot of the empty spool. Fold it over sharply so that it does not make a bulge, or the film may become light-struck.

7. Filmpacks are very delicate. Hold them by the edges only. Don't squeeze them by pressing on their flat sides, or light might penetrate and fog the film.

8. Pull filmpack tabs s-l-o-w-l-y. If you don't, friction may generate static electricity which causes "discharge marks" (see p. 147). Be sure to pull tabs straight and all the way out (until a straight line shows), or all the following exposures will be partly "cut off" by the end of the incompletely pulled film.

9. When loading sheet film holders, be sure that the emulsion side faces the slide. All sheet film have identification notches that differ for each make and emulsion type. (See instruction sheet packed with film.) The emulsion side *faces you* if the film is held vertically and the notches are in the upper right-hand corner.

10. When shooting pictures in bright light, don't leave the camera uncovered longer than necessary. If you use filmpack or sheet film, cover the holder with the slide or the focusing cloth as long as the slide is pulled.

THE TYPES
OF NEGATIVE MATERIAL

There are four types of negative material which have the following characteristics:

1. **Roll Film.**—Long strips of film wound on a spool containing material for 6 to 50 consecutive exposures, depending on the size of the individual "frame." It is available in a great number of different emulsions and sizes, from "sub-miniature" (8-mm. movie film) to film 10 inches wide by 100 feet long for large aerial cameras.

35

Roll film is the most compact form of negative material. It is easily loaded in daylight, and easier to use and process than any other type. Its disadvantages in comparison to other types: individual shots cannot be processed individually; impossibility of changing from one emulsion type to another without sacrificing the remaining unexposed portion on the roll (only the 35-mm. Contarex and the 2¼ x 2¼-inch Hasselblad and Bronica single-lens reflex cameras provide interchangeable film backs which permit changing from one roll film to another without losing a single frame). Roll film adapters are available for some press-type and view cameras.

2. **Filmpack.**—16 individual sheets of film packed flat in a container called a cassette. It is available in a rather limited number of different emulsions and sizes. Most common sizes: 3¼ by 4¼ and 4 by 5 inches; for German cameras: 9 by 12 cm. Filmpack combines the ease of handling of roll film with the advantage that individual shots may be processed individually and exposed sheets taken from the pack without sacrificing the remainder. It can be loaded and unloaded in daylight, and, since each filmpack is in a separate adapter, change to another emulsion type, or to sheet film, is possible without sacrificing unexposed film. Disadvantages: Filmpack is the most expensive form of negative material. Damp atmospheric conditions may cause the film to buckle out of the plane of focus, resulting in unsharp negatives.

3. **Sheet Film.**—Individual sheets of film with a base heavier than filmpack. This film must be loaded individually into separate holders. It is available in a great variety of emulsions and in sizes from 2¼ by 3¼ to 8 by 10 inches and larger. Individual shots can be processed individually without waste of film.

Advantages: It is cheaper than filmpack and usually stays flatter in the holder than filmpack sheets. This makes it preferable for use in conjunction with lenses of great focal length or high speed in which deviation of the film from the plane of focus immediately causes unsharpness. Disadvantages: Loading must be done in the darkroom. Each holder takes only two sheets of film—one on each side. Weight and bulkiness: material for only half a dozen shots takes almost as much space as the camera itself.

4. **Glass Plates.**—Are now used only for making positive transparencies, color-separation negatives, photo-engravings, and for certain scientific purposes, particularly in astronomy.

Different Sizes of Negative Material

Various sizes of negative material offer different advantages and disadvantages. For those photographers who haven't quite decided whether

36

to buy a large, medium, or small camera, the following evaluations may be of aid in making a choice.

Large negatives (3¼″ x 4¼″ and up) have the following advantages over small sizes:

1. *Sharper pictures:* large negatives need proportionally less magnification during enlarging than small negatives. Texture rendition is better, as are detail and definition in "long shots."

2. *Better tone values and richer gradation:* degree of enlargement is lower and consequently tone values are not "torn apart" until the film grain becomes apparent and breaks up the smoothness of the gray shades.

3. *Less danger of "grain"* (see p. 43): lower degree of negative magnification permits use of standard developers, which are faster, cheaper, and simpler to use than special fine-grain developers (see p. 114).

4. *Higher "effective" film speed:* elimination of the danger of "grain" permits use of standard developers. As opposed to special fine-grain developers, these developers do not demand increases in exposure (see p. 114).

5. *Compositional advantages:* since excessive magnification is not necessary, small sections of the negative can be enlarged to become effective pictures—a simple substitute for a telephoto lens. Cutting off superfluous detail strengthens the composition and increases the impact of a picture.

6. *Film processing is easier:* specks of dust and lint, minute scratches and almost unavoidable blemishes do not show half as much as in enlargements made from smaller negatives where magnification is much higher.

Against these advantages, the following disadvantages must be weighed:

1. *Considerably higher cost* per exposure.

2. *Bulk and weight* of the negative material. For example, two sheets of 4 by 5 film in a holder take almost as much space, and weigh as much, as material for 100 shots on 35-mm. film.

3. *Larger, heavier, and more conspicuous cameras* are of course needed for handling larger-sized negatives. This means slower operation, which restricts the photographer in his choice of subjects. Less extension of sharpness in depth exists at any given stop because lenses with longer focal lengths are required. If depth is necessary, small diaphragm stops, and consequently slower exposures, must be used.

Small negatives (35 mm.) have the following advantages over larger sizes:

1. *Considerably less cost* per exposure.

2. *More pictures can be taken of each subject* since cost of film is relatively low. This insures more complete coverage and reduces the danger

37

of missing the dramatic climax, the peak of action, or the most expressive gesture. . . .

3. *Equipment is compact and light,* and therefore permits rapid and inconspicuous shooting. It has the advantage of film magazines containing material enough for whole picture-series, and of rapid-winding mechanisms which permit shooting pictures at a pace of several per second.

4. *Lenses of much higher speed* are available for small-size cameras. In longer focal lengths necessary to cover larger negative sizes, such lenses would be prohibitively heavy and expensive.

5. *Superior sharpness in depth* exists at any given stop due to shorter focal lengths of the lenses, permitting the use of generally higher shutter speeds.

6. *Negative material for dozens of exposures* takes less space than a package of cigarettes.

Against these advantages, the following disadvantages must be weighed:

1. *Inferior sharpness* of the picture, especially noticeable in big enlargements.

2. *Danger of film grain* is always present. To avoid film grain, slower fine-grain films (see p. 43) and speed-reducing fine-grain developers (see p. 114) must be used.

3. *Inferior gradation* because of need for higher negative magnification which tends to "tear apart" the tone values.

4. *Loss of "effective" film speed* (see explanation above under 2).

5. *More difficult processing* because higher magnification brings out minute specks of dust and lint, scratches, and similar almost unavoidable blemishes. And ultimately, in spite of all precaution and care, the photographer still ends up with prints that are technically inferior to those made from larger-size negatives, mainly because of reasons stated in 1 and 3.

Large film sizes are recommended for the slow and deliberate worker, the man with a calm temperament, the perfectionist who demands technical quality, the photographer who specializes in inanimate subjects, one who likes texture, sharpness, and fine definition.

Small film sizes are recommended for the fast and impulsive worker, the man with a quick temperament and an "itchy trigger finger," the reporter who looks for "life" rather than "texture," the traveler who must travel light.

Medium film sizes (2¼" x 2¼" and 2¼" x 3¼") are recommended for the average amateur.

38

In black-and-white photography, subject colors are translated into shades of gray. In order to obtain as natural-looking pictures as possible, the brightness values of these must correspond as nearly as possible to the brightness values of the colors they represent. For example, yellow—a "light" color—should be translated into a lighter shade of gray than blue, which to the eye appears darker. To accomplish such translation of color into corresponding shades of gray, film is "color-sensitized." However, because of technical obstacles, no single type of film as yet exists which permits the translation of *all* colors *equally well* into corresponding shades of gray.

According to their different degrees of color sensitivity, we distinguish between the following types of negative emulsions:

1. **Blue-sensitive emulsions** are sensitive only to ultraviolet, violet, and blue radiation, and "blind" to all other colors. As a result, they render blue as "white"; red, orange, yellow, and green are rendered as "black." Today, such emulsions are used only for certain special purposes (astronomy, photo-engraving, etc.) where this lack of general color sensitivity is a virtue, not a fault. For ordinary photographic purposes these emulsions are, of course, completely unsuitable.

2. **Orthochromatic emulsions** are more or less sensitive to all colors except red, which they render as "black." They are, however, overly sensitive to blue, which they render too light, almost as "white." Wherever necessary, this oversensitivity to blue can be corrected by using a yellow filter (see p. 49).

Orthochromatic emulsions are used when it is desirable to render reddish and pink tones darker than their actual brightness value; in portraiture, for example, this insensitivity of ortho-film to red often improves the rendition of flesh tones. Aside from such special purposes, orthochromatic emulsions are used mostly by amateurs because they can be developed by red light (one can see what one is doing); or simply because they are less expensive than the all-color-sensitized panchromatic emulsions, compared to which they are inferior in color rendition and smoothness of gray tones.

3. **Panchromatic emulsions** are more or less sensitive to all colors of the spectrum. They are, however, overly sensitive to blue and red, which they render somewhat lighter than they appear, and somewhat insensitive to green, which they render too dark. These shortcomings can be corrected by means of special "correction filters" (see p. 50).

Because of their sensitivity to all colors, panchromatic films must be developed in total darkness by the "time and temperature method" mentioned on p. 16. Particularly for the development of roll films, however, this is absolutely the best method to follow for consistently good results, since individual treatment of single frames is impossible for technical reasons. Consequently, since development in total darkness is no "disadvantage," and since sensitivity to all colors is definitely a most desirable quality, panchromatic films must be considered the best general-purpose negative material available today.

4. Infrared films have panchromatic emulsions whose sensitivity to red has been extended beyond the visible spectrum into the "invisible" infrared. Infrared radiation is "heat radiation," and consequently it is possible, for example, to photograph a hot iron in total darkness on infrared film. Since infrared radiation has extraordinary haze-penetration power, infrared-sensitized films are ideally suited to tele- and aerial photography when atmospheric haze and mist are too dense to permit the use of "ordinary" negative material. Even though a faraway "view" may be completely invisible, it may still register with perfect clarity on infrared film. For everyday purposes, infrared material is not recommended because of the "un-natural" way in which color values are rendered. Water and blue sky, for example, are rendered black in infrared pictures, while foliage and meadows appear white. This strange rendition, however, is not dependent upon the actual color of the subject. It is entirely dependent upon whether an object can reflect or absorb infrared radiation, and since such radiation is "invisible," there is no way to predict how light or how dark a certain color will appear when photographed on infrared. Water and blue sky appear black on infrared—*not* because they are "blue," but because they absorb infrared; and foliage and meadows appear white —*not* because they are "green," but because plant chlorophyll permits infrared radiation to be reflected.

Since infrared emulsions are also sensitive to visible light, it is necessary to use special filters in order to get the typical "infrared effect." For most purposes the Kodak Wratten Filters No. 25, 29, or 70 are perfectly satisfactory even though these filters transmit some visible red. If a photograph must be taken primarily by infrared radiation, a special "black" filter, such as the Kodak Wratten Filter No. 87 or 89B, must be used. For best results, follow the recommendations on the instruction sheet that accompanies the film.

A relatively new branch of photography is the taking of pictures in total darkness on infrared film with the aid of special "infrared flashbulbs." Such flashbulbs are coated with a black lacquer which practically absorbs all visible light but transmits infrared radiation. No special filter is needed, since no visible light is present to "spoil the effect."

40

5. Ultraviolet. All photographic emulsions are highly sensitive to invisible ultraviolet radiation. Generally, this is of no consequence, since under ordinary conditions the ultraviolet content of visible light is negligible. At high altitudes (aerial and mountain photography), however, ultraviolet radiation can become so strong as to amount to a "photographic nuisance." Ordinary lenses are not corrected for ultraviolet radiation, which they focus in a plane different from that of visible light. As a result, an unsharp UV-image is superimposed upon the sharp image made by visible light. As long as the UV-image is weak, it remains "invisible." But if the UV-radiation becomes too strong, the out-of-focus image created by its action becomes the cause of "unexplainable" unsharpness of the visible image. To avoid this, a special ultraviolet-absorbing filter (Kodak Wratten Filter No. 2-B) which prevents the ultraviolet from reaching the film must be used.

THE SPEED
OF NEGATIVE MATERIAL

To make accurate calculation of exposure data possible, negative emulsions have been assigned "speed ratings" which provide the basis for setting the dial of the exposure meter. Unfortunately, at present, several different systems for measuring film speeds are in use, but only two are important: the ASA (American Standard Association) system which today is in general use in the USA, and the German DIN (Deutsche Industrie Normen) system. Speed ratings of films are subject to occasional changes by the manufacturer, and to list them is unnecessary, for they can be found in the instructions that accompany the film.

The higher the speed rating of an emulsion, the "faster" the film—the shorter the exposure, and the smaller a diaphragm stop can be used for greater extension of sharpness in depth. Fast films produce well-exposed negatives under conditions where slower emulsions must fail—when light is poor, when fastest shutter speeds must be used, or when smallest diaphragm stops are needed to create a maximum of sharpness in depth. For these reasons it may seem that fast films are "better" than slower emulsions. But actually the contrary is true. Fast films have two undesirable qualities which become more pronounced as film speed increases: coarser "grain" (see p. 43), and softer "gradation" (see p. 44). For this reason, *the "best" film is always the slowest film that is still fast enough to do a perfect job.*

The "Effective" Film Speed

The "effective" speed of a negative emulsion is not a constant factor but depends to a large degree upon the color of the illumination. For this reason, until recently, all films had two different speed numbers, one for daylight and one for tungsten light illumination. However, experience has shown that the response of photo-electric exposure meters to these two types of light is, as a rule, so similar to the response of panchromatic films that the same speed number can be used for both types of light. With orthochromatic films it is, of course, still necessary to use lower speed ratings for tungsten illumination than for daylight because these films are mainly sensitive to blue, and tungsten light contains less blue than daylight.

"Effective" film speed furthermore depends to a large degree on the type of developer and the method of development used. In this respect, the following factors must be considered:

1. *Type of developer:* fine-grain developers usually demand certain increases in exposure—the exact factor depends on the type of developer. However, such developer-caused "losses in effective film speed" may range as high as 65 per cent of the total film speed (see p. 114).

2. *Duration of development:* longer-than-standard duration of development increases the rated speed of an emulsion, sometimes as much as 100 per cent. Such "overdeveloped" negatives are always much more contrasty and "grainy" than correctly developed negatives. However, under difficult circumstances, overdevelopment may be the only way of "getting the picture"—and a contrasty and grainy negative is still better than no picture at all. Besides, such a negative can always be printed on paper of soft gradation (see p. 116).

Conversely, shorter-than-standard development reduces the rated speed of an emulsion—the exact speed loss depends on the amount by which the "standard time" of development is shortened. Since decreased development produces negatives with lower-than-standard contrasts, this method may be the only way of producing satisfactory pictures of extremely contrasty subjects (see p. 75). In such cases, exposure should be increased by 50 to 100 per cent to compensate for the loss in negative density due to the shortening of development.

For practical purposes, films can be classified in four speed groups. in practice, a film having a speed number twice as high as another is also twice as fast and, under otherwise identical conditions, can be exposed at twice the shutter speed of the slower film.

1. **Slow emulsions,** with ASA speeds of 32-40, are characterized by very fine grain and comparatively "contrasty" gradation. These films are

ideal for a photographer who uses a 35-mm. camera—provided their speed is not too slow for his particular type of work.

2. **Medium-fast emulsions,** with ASA speeds around 125, are characterized by fine grain and "normal" gradation. These are the typical "all-round films" which in most instances produce the best results.

3. **Fast emulsions,** with ASA speeds around 400, are characterized by somewhat coarser grain and relatively "soft" gradation. They are best to use when light is poor, for taking photographs indoors by artificial light, for candid night and stage photography, sports, and action pictures.

4. **High-speed emulsions,** with ASA speeds as high as 1250, are characterized by coarse grain and relatively soft gradation. Films of this type can produce usable results when exposed as if rated from 1500 to 2500 ASA, provided, of course, that the subject contrast is low and the negatives are given longer than normal development. Films belonging to this group should only be used under marginal light conditions when their enormous speed is really needed to get any picture at all.

THE GRAIN
OF NEGATIVE MATERIAL

The light-sensitive component of photographic emulsions consists of innumerable tiny particles of silver salts. Development transforms the exposed silver salts into tiny grains of metallic silver which form the negative: the denser the layer of silver grains, the darker the part of the image. The size of the individual grains is so small that they can be seen only under a microscope. However, under certain conditions, they clump together and accumulate to such a degree that they become visible to the eye. When this happens, the picture appears "grainy." Graininess is always most prominent in the medium-gray shades, which lose their "smoothness" and appear as a sandpaper-like texture. Graininess, furthermore, destroys sharpness by making contours "ragged."

Graininess is principally an inherent quality of an emulsion. As a rule, the faster the film, the coarser the grain. However, in addition, the degree of graininess is subject to the following factors:

1. **Exposure:** overexposed negatives are always more "grainy" than correctly exposed films of the same type.

2. **Developer:** "fine-grain developers" produce negatives with a finer grain than standard developers. However, this advantage is always connected with a certain loss of film speed; i.e., films that must be fine-grain-developed must be exposed longer than films of the same type which are developed in standard developers.

43

3. Development: the size of the negative grain increases with prolonged development. On the other hand, shorter-than-normal development produces negatives with finer-than-normal grain, a useful phenomenon which will be discussed later on p. 114.

4. Enlargement: the higher the degree of enlargement, the more apparent the grain. This fact explains the comparatively high degree of "graininess" of most enlargements made from 35-mm. negatives.

5. Paper: the more contrasty the gradation * of the printing paper, the more pronounced the film grain, and vice versa. Consequently, gains achieved through shorter-than-normal development are valueless if they result in negatives so lacking in contrast that they must be printed on paper of hard gradation.

---

* "Gradation" is the quality of a light-sensitive emulsion that determines the manner in which it reproduces contrast.

THE GRADATION
OF NEGATIVE MATERIAL

The gradation of an emulsion is the measure of its ability for contrast rendition. In this respect we must distinguish between the following three types:

1. Films with hard gradation produce negatives in which contrast between light and dark appears † higher than it appeared in the subject.

2. Films with medium (normal, standard) gradation produce negatives in which contrast between light and dark appears more or less as it appeared in the subject.

3. Films with soft gradation produce negatives in which contrast between light and dark is lower than it appeared in the subject.

As a rule, the higher the speed of an emulsion, the softer its gradation, and vice versa. However, gradation is not an unalterable factor. Regardless of the gradation group to which a film belongs, the gradation of the negative always partly depends on the following factors:

1. Subject Contrast: contrasty subjects always produce more contrasty negatives than subjects in which contrast is low.

2. Illumination: contrasty illumination, with brilliant highlights and deep black shadows, always produces negatives of higher contrast than soft and diffused illumination. Controlling the contrast range of the illumination is one of the most efficient means for controlling the contrast range of the negative.

---

† Note: The term "appears" is used deliberately. Almost without exception, subject contrast in nature is higher than the image contrast of the negative.

3. Exposure: overexposure as well as underexposure tends to produce negatives of lower contrast than correctly exposed negatives.

4. Developer: rapid developers increase, and fine-grain developers decrease, negative contrast in comparison to negatives developed in standard developers at equal developing times.

5. Development: prolonged development increases, and shortened development reduces, negative contrast in comparison to standard development.

For the average needs of the amateur, a film with a "medium" gradation is most suitable. Such films combine sufficient speed with sufficiently fine grain. For special purposes, however, a softer or harder gradation may be preferable. If a very contrasty subject must be photographed—such as dark-skinned Indians in front of white adobe houses, and brilliant sunlight creates deep black shadows—a film with a softer gradation will give better results, for it permits the photographer to reduce natural contrasts to a degree where they do not exceed the contrast range of the photographic paper. On the other hand, if a subject which is very low in contrast must be photographed—such as the sky line of a big city seen from afar, which appears weak and pale because of intervening haze and smoke, so that the buildings seem scarcely darker than the sky—a film with a harder gradation will give better results, for it permits the photographer to strengthen the weak contrasts of the subject and to render the sky line in a pictorially more effective form.

The following table represents an attempt to classify some of the more popular films in accordance with their gradation, graininess, and speed.

GRADATION:	RELATIVELY HARD	MEDIUM	RELATIVELY SOFT
Slow films with ASA speeds 16-64	Kodak Copy Films Kodak Contrast Process Films	Adox KB-14, R-14 Agfa Isopan FF, F Ilford Pan F Kodak Panatomic-X	
Medium-slow films, ASA speeds 80-160		Adox KB-21, R-21 Agfa Isopan SS Ansco Allweather Pan Ansco Versapan Ilford FP3 Kodak Plus-X Kodak Verichrome Pan	Ansco Vivipan
Fast films with ASA speeds 200-400		Agfa Isopan U Agfa Isopan Rekord Ansco Triple S Pan Ilford HP3 Kodak Tri-X Pan	Kodak Royal Pan sheet film
High-speed films with ASA speeds 500-1250		Polaroid's 3200 and 10,000 speed films	Ilford HPS Kodak Royal-X Pan

Type of negative material: roll film is the most compact negative material. It is easily loaded in daylight, easier to use and process than any other type.

Color sensitivity: panchromatic films are the only films that are sensitive to all the colors of the spectrum. Why limit yourself voluntarily by using ortho-films, which are "blind" to one of the most important colors: red?

Speed: the "best" film is always the slowest film that is still fast enough to do a perfect job.

Film grain: the slower the film, the finer the grain. However, many other factors influence the size of the grain. Wrongly treated, even fine-grain films will produce astonishingly "grainy" prints. On the other hand, properly processed, practically "grainless" prints can be made from the fastest films.

Gradation: for average purposes, films with a "medium" gradation offer the best "compromise solution," combining sufficient speed (typical of softer emulsions) with sufficiently fine grain (typical of harder emulsions). However, many other factors influence the gradation of a negative, and properly treated, any type of film can be made "harder" or "softer" (i.e., more or less contrasty) in accordance with the demands of the subject (see p. 80).

The best film: today, all films made by reputable manufacturers are of equally high quality, though their characteristics may differ. In the hands of an expert, any one of these films will give equally satisfactory results. "Experts" are people who know. Conclusion: try different films to find out which one you like best, *then stick to it!* Experiment, and familiarize yourself with its qualities, because *it is your knowledge of its behavior under different conditions which makes this film better than any other film on the market— for you!*

The number of gadgets and accessories available today is truly over-whelming. The Leitz catalogue alone lists over 200 different items—*designed for use with one single camera, the Leica!*—from which the interested photographer can choose. And in photo magazines almost twice as many pages are devoted to advertisements of gadgets and accessories as to editorial matter. No wonder that so many amateurs collect gadgets the way philatelists collect stamps—they are not satisfied until they own the whole line.

The serious amateur, however—the working photographer whose interest is in pictures and not in hardware—needs no more accessories than he can count on the fingers of one hand. Everything else may increase his fun in photography, but it certainly is not necessary for increasing the quality of his pictures. Apart from lighting and darkroom equipment, which will be discussed later, this is what he should have:

> Exposure meter
>
> Color filters
>
> Lens shade
>
> Cable release
>
> Tripod

EXPOSURE METERS

The starting point of every "technically perfect negative" is correct exposure. To trust the outcome of the exposure to "guesswork" or "experience" is *not* the sign of a seasoned photographer, but just plain foolishness. The human eye is a very poor instrument when it comes to measuring light intensities. It adapts itself so quickly to changes of brightness that they usually pass unnoticed. Most professional photographers are aware of this fact, and in spite of all their experience do not trust their eyes—they trust their exposure meters. Being professionals, they cannot afford to "miss" on an exposure. Amateurs can do no better than follow their example, and one of the soundest investments an amateur can make is a good exposure meter.

Exposure tables, guides, or charts don't measure light intensities. They interpret light conditions in terms of everyday experience. They are simple and reliable only within the limits of their applicability. Because of their

47

simplicity, they often prove more useful to the beginner than genuine exposure meters, which are much more accurate but also more difficult to use. They cost no more than ten or twenty-five cents.

Extinction-type exposure meters can be used to measure any kind of illumination, but their accuracy depends to a rather high degree on the skill and experience of the user. With the meter aimed at the subject, the photographer looks through an eyepiece, and, rotating a gray wedge, tries to determine the exact moment at which a number (or the scene as viewed through the aperture) becomes extinct. A calculator then indicates the correct data for diaphragm stop and shutter-speed settings. Such meters are relatively inexpensive.

Photo-electric exposure meters work completely automatically, giving the same results in the hands of an amateur or an experienced photographer. When the meter is pointed toward the subject (or toward the camera, if incident light is measured), reflected light (or direct illumination) strikes a photo-electric cell which generates an electric current in proportion to the intensity of the illumination. This current acts upon a measuring unit which indicates light values in the form of numbers. Transferred to a calculator, these numbers are automatically translated into terms of diaphragm openings and shutter speeds.

There are two types of photo-electric exposure meters:

1. Meters for measuring *reflected light;* they must be pointed toward the subject.

2. Meters for measuring *incident light;* they must be pointed toward the camera.

Meters of the first type are equally well suited to photographic work indoors and outdoors. Meters of the second type are excellent for indoor use, but, in the opinion of the author, are less suited to outdoor work, except at fairly close subject-to-camera distances. Most photo-electric exposure meters for reflected light can be transformed into meters for measuring incident light by means of an adapter. Prices range from ten to one hundred dollars—and more. (See page 88 on "How To Use an Exposure Meter Correctly.")

COLOR FILTERS

Color filters change the response of a photographic emulsion to light of a certain color. They are used to render this color either lighter or darker in the print than it would have been rendered without a filter. For example, a fashion shot of a girl in a green dress trimmed with red is required. The particular attraction of the dress is the sharp contrast between the green and the red. Photographed without a color filter, both green and red may appear as gray shades of approximately equal value, and the effect of the dress would be lost. Even though such a rendering might be "true" as far as translation of colors into shades of gray is concerned, it would be in effect an unsuccessful photograph—a "flop."

Contrast Filters

Such unsatisfactory color rendition can be improved through the use of "contrast filters." Photographed through a red filter, for instance, the red of the dress would be rendered lighter and the green darker. The color contrast would be translated into "graphic" contrast of light and dark, and the effect of the dress would be retained in terms of black and white.

Another more common example is the rendition of a blue sky with white clouds. In a photograph the cloud effect is usually more or less lost, owing to the oversensitivity of all films to blue, which they render almost as light as "white." However, with the aid of a yellow filter, most of the sky-blue can be prevented from reaching the emulsion, with the result that the sky is rendered a darker gray against which the white clouds stand out effectually.

These examples contain the whole "secret" of "filtering": in the first case *red* was rendered lighter through the use of a *red* filter—a filter of the same color as the color that had to be rendered lighter. In the second case, *blue* was rendered *darker* through the use of a *yellow* filter—a filter of a color which is "complementary" to the color that had to be rendered darker.

To render a color lighter—use a filter of the same color.

To render a color darker—use a filter of the complementary color.

Complementary color pairs are:

> red and blue-green
> orange and blue
> yellow and purple-blue
> green-yellow and purple
> green and red-purple

For selection of the correct type of "contrast filter" consult the following table, which lists the more commonly used Kodak Wratten Filters for color separation. Wherever several filters are mentioned in one box, the first will make the least, and the last will make the greatest, change in color rendition.

49

Color of subject	Wratten filter that will make color lighter	Wratten filter that will make color darker
Red	G, A, F	C5, B
Orange	G, A	C5
Yellow	K2, G, A	80, C5
Green	X1, X2, B	C5, A
Blue	C5	K2, G, A, F
Purple	C5	B

Correction Filters

While the "contrast filters" described above deliberately "distort" the color rendition of negative emulsions, another type, the "correction filters," are used for just the opposite purpose: to improve the accuracy of color rendition. As previously mentioned in the section on the color sensitivity of films (p. 39), no emulsion now exists which permits the simultaneous translation of all colors into their corresponding shades of gray. This deficiency can be overcome through the use of "color-correction filters" which partially absorb those colors to which the emulsion is oversensitive and thus restore the "color balance." Because of differences in color sensitivity, different types of film need different types of correction filters. In order to avoid the necessity for a special type of filter for each film, films of similar color response have been grouped together and assigned the same type of correction filter. The following table lists the Kodak Wratten Filters for use in color correction and the factors by which they prolong exposure, which must be used in connection with panchromatic Kodak films if a "true" ("monochromatic") color rendition is desired:

WRATTEN FILTERS AND FILTER FACTORS FOR MONOCHROMATIC COLOR RENDITION

Kodak 35 mm and 120 films	Daylight	Tungsten
Panatomic-X Plus-X Verichrome Pan Royal-X Pan	K2, 2x	X1, 4x
Tri-X Pan	K2, 2x	X1, 3x

Filter Factors

It is the purpose of a filter to absorb part of the light that otherwise would be available for the exposure. Naturally, to compensate for this filter-caused loss of light, and to prevent underexposure of the negative, a

50

corresponding increase in exposure becomes necessary when a filter is used. The amount of increase (the "filter factor" by which exposure must be multiplied) depends on three factors: the type of filter, the type of film, and the color of the illumination (daylight or tungsten illumination, i.e., predominantly bluish or reddish light). To simplify matters, films with similar color sensitivity have been grouped together and assigned a common filter factor for each type of filter; see the following tables:

ANSCO FILMS
(Classified according to color sensitivity)

Group I Non-Color Sensitized	Group II Orthochromatic	Group III Panchromatic
Process Commercial	Super Hy-Ortho Sheet Film	Versapan Vivipan Super Hypan Triple S Pan Superpan Press Superpan Portrait

WRATTEN FILTER FACTORS FOR ANSCO FILMS

Filter	Color Sensitivity Classification Group			
	Group II—Orthochromatic		Group III—Panchromatic	
	Daylight	Tungsten	Daylight	Tungsten
K1—Light Yellow	2	1.5	1.5	1.5
K2—Yellow	3	2	2	1.5
G—Deep Yellow	6	3	3	2
X1—Light Green	4	3	4	3
X2—Green	6	4	5	4
A—Red	—	—	8	5
B—Dark Green	8	4	7	6
C5—Deep Blue	4	4	6	10

KODAK FILMS
(Classified according to color sensitivity)

Non-color-sensitized	Orthochromatic	Panchromatic
Commercial Projector Slide Plates Fine Grain Positive	Royal Ortho Super Speed Ortho Portrait Contrast Process Ortho Kodalith Ortho Kodak Copy Films	Royal-X Pan Tri-X Pan Super Panchro Press Type B Plus-X Panatomic-X Verichrome Pan Contrast Process Pan

WRATTEN FILTER FACTORS FOR KODAK FILMS *

Filter	Non-color-sensitized		Orthochromatic		Panchromatic	
	Daylight	Tungsten	Daylight	Tungsten	Daylight	Tungsten
K1—Light Yellow	4	3	2	1.5	1.5	1.5
K2—Yellow	12	10	2.5	2	2	1.5
K3—Deep Yellow	20	16	2.5	2	2	1.5
X1—Yellow-Green	—	—	—	—	4	3
G—Dark Yellow	—	—	5	3	3	2
A—Red	—	—	—	—	8	6
F—Deep Red	—	—	—	—	25	12
47B—Blue	—	—	6	8	8	16

* The filter factor for a specific film may vary somewhat from this listing. See individual product instructions.

51

POLARIZERS AND GLARE CONTROL

Polarizers are special filters which filter not color but "glare." Most of my readers are familiar with Polaroid sunglasses and the way they reduce glare on a highway. Polarizers work in the same way. They are used in front of the lens like ordinary filters. Through their use, unwanted glare and reflections can be partially or completely eliminated from a photograph, the degree of reduction depending on the angle of the reflected light (the glare or reflection). At angles of approximately 30°, glare reduction is more or less complete; at 90°, glare is not affected at all; in between, glare is partially eliminated. However, only glare consisting of already polarized light is affected by polarizers. Most reflecting surfaces polarize light as they reflect it—water, window glass, paint, varnish, polished wood, glossy paper, to name only a few. Metallic surfaces, however, do not polarize light as they reflect it, and consequently, highlights and reflections from metallic surfaces are not affected by polarizers.

In color photography, the use of polarizing filters is the only practical method of darkening pale blue skies.

Since polarizers and color filters work on entirely different principles which do not interfere with each other, they can be used together. This makes it possible to control color rendition and reflections simultaneously, and very often one will aid the other. Thus elimination of glare will often bring out colors which were obscured by reflections, while the color filter will translate them into gray shades of desired brightness.

To produce the desired effect, polarizing filters must be used in definite positions. Hold the polarizer up to your eye, look through it at the subject, then slowly rotate the filter and watch the effect on highlights, glare, and reflections. When the desired degree of extinction is reached, place the filter in front of the lens *in exactly the same position as you held it*—i.e., don't accidentally rotate the filter while transferring it from eye to lens, or you will lose part of the effect.

It is neither necessary nor advisable always to use a polarizer in its position of maximum efficiency. Sometimes, reducing glare to a printable level is better than complete extinction, which often results in dull and lifeless effects.

The filter factor for a polarizer is usually 2.5. If a polarizer is used together with a color filter, the factor of one must be multiplied by the factor of the other to determine their combined factor. The combined factor must in turn be multiplied by the exposure time indicated by the exposure meter.

LENS SHADE

Only light reflected by the subject, or emitted by sources within the field of view of the camera, theoretically, should fall upon the lens. All other light is potentially dangerous as a source of lens-flares and halation (see p. 149); it should be kept from the lens by means of an effective lens shade.

Though inexpensive and insignificant in appearance, a lens shade is extremely important in the production of crisp, sharp, halation-free pictures. To be effective, it must be long enough to really shield the lens from unwanted light without cutting off part of the picture. To be practical, it must permit the simultaneous use of a color filter. Without an adequate lens shade, a lens is incomplete. Some lenses, especially the more expensive telephoto lenses, have built-in lens shades. But usually it is up to the photographer to equip his lens with this indispensable accessory which protects it not only from undesirable light but also from raindrops and snowflakes, besides saving it from many accidental fingerprints.

CABLE RELEASE

Movement of the camera during the exposure is one of the most frequent causes of unsharp pictures. To avoid movement, exposures longer than 1/25 sec. should be made with the camera firmly supported. However, even then unsharp pictures can result if the camera is accidentally jarred when the "button" is pressed.

Such accidental jarrings can be avoided if a cable release is used to trip the shutter; its flexibility absorbs any accidental motion and prevents it from moving the camera. A shutter is incomplete without a cable release. It is another of those "insignificant" accessories which lack the flashy appeal of more expensive gadgets, but whose importance in the production of "technically perfect negatives" can hardly be overemphasized.

TRIPOD

Possession of a tripod permits a photographer to practically double the scope of his work: time exposures at night; close-up work in which fractions of an inch make the difference between sharp and unsharp pictures; interior shots made with wide-angle lenses and small diaphragm stops;

53

architectural pictures in which perspective is controlled by "swings"; telephotography with long-focus lenses; pictures at home with photofloods; copying and reproductions; table-top photography—all these fascinating fields are open to the possessor of a tripod, and only to him.

The best tripod is the strongest tripod; it is also the heaviest, and the most expensive. It is always possible (and even advantageous!) to put a light camera on a heavy tripod, but it is *not* recommended to put a heavy camera on a light and flimsy support. Consequently, in choosing a tripod, be sure it is strong enough to support your camera safely, otherwise your money will have been wasted.

A tripod with a built-in "elevator" is especially useful. It has a center post that can be raised or lowered by turning a crank. It is particularly useful for close-up work in which fine adjustments in height are constantly necessary: they can be made by a simple turn of the handle, instead of the complicated readjustment of three legs. Such elevator tripods are made by several manufacturers in different models for lighter or heavier cameras. Considering the years of useful service they afford, and the constant annoyance that is eliminated, they are well worth their higher price.

Lighting Equipment

Knowledge of the different types of lights and their characteristics is one of the first requisites for arranging effective illumination. A man who knows his lights can do more interesting things with two lamps than one who does not with ten. As a matter of fact, more pictures are spoiled—artistically—by too much light and too many lights than by lack of light. "Overlighting" destroys form, roundness, and delicate shades of gray; multiple lights wrongly handled cast multiple crisscrossing shadows—one of the graver faults in "lighting."

Most subjects can be lighted adequately with two lights—a "main light" that sets the key for the illumination, and a "fill-in light" which slightly lightens the shadows cast by the main light—just enough so that the shadows will not print too black. If an additional light—an "accent light" for a highlight or two—is available, anyone with a "feeling" for light should be able to arrange a thoroughly "professional" illumination. (More about this on p. 97).

There are four basically different types of photographic lights:

1. **Photofloods** are incandescent bulbs of 250 and 500 watts, respectively, which give considerably more light than ordinary "household

54

bulbs" of the same wattage. But they last only three and six hours each. Photofloods should be used in correctly designed, large aluminum reflectors (see p. 57). They give a bright but soft and even light which makes them equally suitable as "main lights" or as "fill-in lights." If used with a "diffuser"—transparent drafting paper or spun glass—their light is practically shadowless; this is particularly desirable for fill-in purposes to avoid crisscrossing shadows.

2. **Spotlights** concentrate the light by means of an optical system consisting of a parabolic mirror behind, and a condenser lens in front of, the bulb. All the better spotlights can be "focused"—i.e., the diameter of the field of illumination can be made wider (and less intense) or narrower (and more intense) by adjusting the position of the bulb in relation to the reflecting mirror.

Compared to photofloods, spotlights give a much sharper, more intense illumination, and cast "blacker" and more sharply defined shadows. They are well suited for use as main lights or accent lights, but cannot be used as fill-in lights.

Spotlights come in all sizes, from tiny "baby spots" of 150 watts to the giant 5000-watt "sun spots" used in commercial studios.

3. **Flashbulbs** deliver a wallop of light within a fraction of a second—then burn out. This characteristic makes flash the most expensive type of light per exposure. On the other hand, it offers the tremendous advantage of using flash for instantaneous exposures of shortest "action-stopping" duration through "synchronizing" the firing of the bulb and the action of the shutter by means of a "flash gun."

There are two different types of flashbulb: bulbs to be used for synchronization with "between-the-lens shutters," which are characterized by

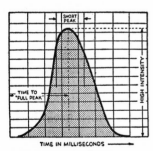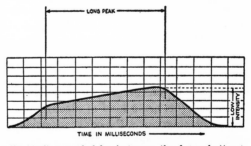

Left: Characteristic curve of a flashbulb intended for between-the-lens shutters. Notice the short peak and the high intensity of the flash. Right: Characteristics of a flashbulb intended for focal-plane synchronization. Notice the greater length of the peak, indicating a longer duration of the flash at more or less uniform intensity, which however, is much lower than that of the flashbulb at left. Instead of being concentrated in one quick punch of tremendous intensity, the light output of flashbulbs for focal-plane shutter synchronization is spread out over a relatively long time with corresponding decrease in intensity per time unit.

55

a "short peak"—i.e., high intensity of very short duration; and bulbs to be used for synchronization with "focal-plane shutters," which are characterized by a "long peak"—i.e., somewhat lower intensity and relatively longer duration to insure uniform exposure over the entire negative as the curtain passes across the film. *It is of vital importance for correct synchronization to use the type of flashbulb that is required by the type of shutter.*

Flashbulbs of both types are made in several sizes for higher or lower light-output. For the majority of purposes of the amateur, the smallest size, the so-called "peanut bulb," is entirely sufficient.

The means for synchronizing flash and shutter is the flash gun. It operates on battery current, using two, three, and sometimes four flashlight batteries, which should test no lower than 9 amperes. The flash gun fires the bulb and automatically compensates for the time lag between maximum light-output of the flashbulb (usually reached in 20 milliseconds) and maximum shutter opening (usually reached in 5 milliseconds). In most cases it also releases the shutter by an electromagnetic tripper.

The last word in flash guns is the "BC-synchronizer"—the "battery capacitor gun"—which stores electricity in a small condenser (capacitor) and releases only the amount of energy needed for firing the flash and tripping the shutter (the batteries of conventional synchronizers are drained as long as the button is pressed). According to their manufacturers, batteries in BC-synchronizers last for several years.

The most dependable method of flash synchronization is an internally synchronized shutter. Mechanical flash synchronizers (which use an adjustable cable to connect flash gun and shutter) and electromagnetic trippers occasionally get "out of sync" so that flash and exposure don't coincide, and the negative is either badly underexposed or completely unexposed. Synchro-shutters avoid this, since their built-in contacts cannot get out of adjustment. Furthermore, their construction altogether eliminates the need for an electromagnetic tripper—and trippers consume a relatively large amount of current. With tripper, batteries last for about a hundred flash exposures; with synchro-shutter, they will dependably fire from five to ten times as many bulbs.

4. **Speedlights** are a kind of electronic super-flash which have the following advantages over the conventional type of flashbulb: repeating-type flash tube which produces well over a thousand flashes before it must be replaced; extremely short flash duration of only 1/500 to 1/10,000 sec.; and a flash which because of its extremely short duration is almost invisible and, in portraiture, much easier on the eyes of the "sitter." Disadvantages: relatively low light-output (comparable to a "peanut flashbulb" for the smaller portable units); potentially dangerous (operating on high voltage of approximately 2000 volts); and quite expensive.

56

A speedlight unit consists of four basic parts: the gun with flash tube and reflector; the powerpack containing the condensers (and, in portable units, the battery); the cord between gun and shutter; and the trip cable with push button for remote-control firing. Maximum flash rate for most speedlights is from 4 to 6 flashes per minute since the condensers need time to recharge. For best results, internally synchronized shutters are recommended.

Two different types of speedlights are available: portable units which contain their own power supply in the form of batteries; and batteryless units which must be plugged into an AC-current wall outlet. Batteries usually last for 100 to 150 flashes before recharging becomes necessary. Special battery chargers that plug into 115-volt, 60-cycle AC outlets are available. In some units they are built directly into the powerpack.

Most speedlight units permit simultaneous use of two separate flash tubes, in which the total light-output of the unit is divided between the two tubes. For multiflash shots, any number of units can be hooked up together by interconnecting cables. The most modern method is synchronization by means of photo-electric cells, which eliminates cable connections and the danger of tripping over wires; in this case the distant "slave units" are set off by the flash of the "master unit."

"Balanced lighting equipment" is absolutely essential for the creation of balanced light effects. A spotlight that is too weak or too powerful in comparison to the photofloods with which it is used is practically valueless. An excellent light-combination consists of three units: two photofloods of 500 watts each, and one 250- or 500-watt spotlight. Spotlights of less than 250 watts are of little practical value, except for very small setups.

To "balance" the light of the two photofloods, place the "main light" relatively close to the subject and slightly to one side, place the "fill-in" light about twice as far away, in line with but higher than the camera. Finally, use the spotlight as an "accent and background light."

Reflectors and light-stands: To be able to choose, from the great variety of different shapes and sizes, the reflector that is most suitable to a specific purpose, a photographer must know the following:

The smaller a reflector, the harsher and more concentrated the light. The larger a reflector, the softer and more diffused the light.

Narrow reflectors produce somewhat of a "spotlight effect" with more sharply defined shadows, and are more suitable as main lights. Wide reflectors disperse the light more evenly, produce "paler" shadows with softer outlines, and are more suitable as fill-in lights.

Parabolic and hyperbolic reflectors produce a more concentrated beam of light than spherical reflectors, which produce a more evenly diffused illumination.

57

Reflectors with pressed-in ridges produce a softer, more diffused light than smooth reflectors.

All these considerations apply to photoflood as well as to flashbulb reflectors. In addition, some flash reflectors make it possible to "focus" the light beam at shorter or longer subject-distance merely by moving the reflector back and forth along its axis.

For the traveling photographer: reflectors that "stack" take considerably less space. "Clamp reflectors" can be attached to any projecting object, and often eliminate the necessity for a special light-stand. Reflector "floods" completely eliminate the need for reflectors.

Light-stands should be strong and light—aluminum is best.

A *"boom light"* that permits overhead illumination is an invaluable asset on most jobs. It gets the light into any desired place and keeps the light-stand out of the picture. Particularly to be recommended is the "Mini-boom"—a crossbar that fits on any light-stand. It is counterbalanced, light, swivels, tilts, turns, and gets a light into any possible (and seemingly impossible!) position. In addition, it is very reasonably priced.

POINTERS FOR PHOTO-FRESHMEN

Next to the camera, the most important piece of equipment is an exposure meter.

The surest way to improve the quality of most outdoor pictures is through use of a yellow filter. The difference is enormous, the cost negligible.

An efficient lens shade is the "secret weapon" of the consistently successful backlight photographer. Backlight is the most "dramatic" type of light.

A tip for backlight enthusiasts: use a coated lens (see p. 219).

A tripod is the "secret weapon" of the four-by-fiver who produces needle-sharp pictures, crisp texture rendition, and negatives that can be enlarged successfully to photo-mural size.

Practice with your camera; learn how to focus lightning-fast; be ready when your opportunity arrives.

Lenses with longer-than-standard focal lengths automatically produce more concentrated pictures, cut off superfluous elements that surround the subject, improve space rendition by minimizing distortion, strengthen the impact of any photograph; ideal for portraits, too.

Soft-focus effects are dangerous and tricky—not for the expert who knows what he is doing, but for the beginner who steps where angels fear to tread. Best for backlight and soft blond hair.

Too much light and too many lights spoil any indoor photograph.

PART THREE

HOW TO TAKE A PICTURE

Discussion of the functions of the camera in terms of sharpness, depth, contrast, motion-rendition, and exposure. Explanation of the principles of good illumination. Advice on the use of photofloods, flashbulbs, and speedlights

HOW TO TAKE A PHOTOGRAPH

Mastery of "technique" is the first requirement for taking good photographs. Without the means for expression, creative work in any field is not possible. No matter how talented or industrious, the painter who has not learned how to mix and apply his pigments, the sculptor who has not learned how to use a chisel and mallet, the writer who has not learned how to construct sentences and write dialogue, will never be able to produce a work of art—simply because he will not be able to present his ideas in a form which makes it possible to express them to others. This also applies to photographers. Without a period of apprenticeship—dedicated to searching, experimenting, and learning from mistakes—no one becomes a master. But while a master, a highly skilled craftsman, does not necessarily have to be an artist, every artist must be a master—a master of the techniques for expression in his chosen field.

A photographer may have the artistic genius of a Michelangelo—but unless he also has his manual dexterity, his talents will never take form. He may be highly sensitive to beauty, he may perceive a truth which others fail to see, he may suffer with the oppressed, or be privileged to witness great events—but his gifts and experiences will be of no avail unless he knows how to express them in concrete black and white on film and sensitized paper. In photography, the base and the sublime are inseparably connected, and the potentially most stirring picture may never evolve because of poor "technique."

Most amateurs make the mistake of expecting too much too soon. They don't want to "practice," they want "results" immediately. Perhaps they still remember a period in their profession which required hard work and entailed frustration. If photography is their hobby, they want nothing of that sort in it. A hobby, they think, should be fun and a relaxation. But it is neither amusing nor relaxing when things don't go the way they should and pictures turn out disappointingly because of poor "technique." And there is only one way to avoid this—to start with fundamentals, and to learn systematically the elements of the craft. These are presented in the following sections.

One of the basic requirements of a good negative is sharpness (unless of course, unsharpness is used deliberately to create a special effect). However, sharpness in photography is a rather vague concept. Most negatives are partly sharp and partly unsharp. Where actually does sharpness end and unsharpness begin?

DEFINITION OF SHARPNESS

Theoretically, sharpness exists when a point-source of light (for example a star) is rendered on the negative in the form of a point. Practically, of course, this is impossible because the image of even the faintest star is never rendered in the form of a point (which has a diameter of zero) but as a circle. Similarly, the image of any subject does not consist of an infinite number of points, but of an infinite number of tiny overlapping circles which are called "circles of confusion." The smaller these circles of confusion are, the sharper the image appears. Consequently, "sharpness" is always a matter of degree since "absolute sharpness" is an impossibility.

For practical purposes, the definition of "sharpness" has been related to the size of the negative for the simple reason that small negatives must be "sharper" than large negatives because they must stand higher magnification during enlargement. Generally, depth-of-field scales and tables (see p. 69) are computed on the basis that negatives 2¼ by 2¼ inches and larger are "sharp" if the diameter of the circle of confusion is not larger than 1/1000 of the focal length of the lens that is standard for each negative size. A 35-mm. negative is considered "sharp" if the diameter of the circle of confusion is no higher than 1/1500 of the standard lens, which corresponds to a diameter of 1/30 mm. (1/750 inch).

Whether or not this desirable degree of sharpness is actually achieved in practice depends mainly upon three factors: the sharpness of the lens; the sharpness of the film; and the accuracy of focusing.

The Sharpness of the Lens

It is a well-known fact that some lenses are sharper than others. As a rule, the sharpest lenses are relatively slow (f/6.3 to f/9), but not all slow lenses are sharp. Standard lenses are generally sharper than wide-angle and telephoto lenses. Sharpness can be improved by stopping down the diaphragm. The optimum is usually reached around two stops from maximum aperture. Use of smaller diaphragm stops increases extension of sharpness in depth ("depth of field"), but decreases the actual sharpness of rendition. When "effective apertures" of f/32 or smaller are reached, which happens in super close-ups where images of the subject are several times natural size (see pp. 25-27, 30), definition deteriorates rapidly and everything appears uniformly "soft" owing to the appearances of diffraction and interference phenomena.

The Sharpness of the Film

Strange as it may sound, all other factors being equal, some films produce sharper images than others Generally, the thinner the film emulsion, the finer the grain, and the better the anti-halo protection, the sharper the image; and vice versa.

The sharpness of a film is measured in terms of its acutance which is determined by exact measurement: a knife-edge is laid upon the film, the film is exposed to light, developed, and the silhouette of the knife edge is examined under a microscope. Because light is scattered within the film emulsion, the transition from light to dark is not abrupt but somewhat gradual. It is the zone between pure white and black which, micro-densitometrically evaluated, is the measure of the sharpness of the film: the narrower it is, the higher the acutance and the sharper the image which the film will produce.

The previously used measure of sharpness, the resolving power of a film in terms of lines per millimeter, is now considered obsolete.

IMAGE STRUCTURE CHARACTERISTICS OF SOME KODAK FILMS

Film	Grain structure	Sharpness (acutance)
Royal-X Pan	coarse	medium
Tri-X Pan, rolls, 35mm	fine	very high
Plus-X Pan	extra fine	very high
Panatomic-X	extra fine	very high
Verichrome Pan	extra fine	very high
Super Panchro Press Type B	medium	medium
Portrait Panchromatic Sheets	medium	medium-low
Super Speed Ortho Portrait	medium-coarse	low

The Accuracy of Focusing

Focusing means adjusting the lens-to-film distance in accordance with the lens-to-subject distance (see p. 22). No matter how good the lens and how sharp the film, the negative is bound to be unsharp unless the camera is properly focused. The most accurate and most direct way of focusing is by means of a groundglass (see p. 9). For critical work, use of a ten-power magnifier is recommended. Focusing via a lens-coupled range

63

finder (p. 9) is bound to be less accurate because it is not possible to mass-produce range finders which, in conjunction with a variety of lenses of different focal lengths, are accurate at all distances. Besides, range finders sometimes get out of adjustment; see p. 217 on how to check for accuracy of synchronization. Cameras without either groundglass or range finder (roll-film folding cameras of the old-fashioned "Kodak" type) have to be focused by the foot scale through measuring or guessing the subject-to-lens distance. Unavoidable inaccuracies can be compensated for by use of a relatively small diaphragm opening, which creates a "safety zone" of sharpness in depth. Fullest use of this principle is made in the "fixed-focus cameras" of the box type which don't have to be focused at all. Their lenses are set for a subject-distance of fifteen feet, and their apertures of approximately f/11 or f/15 produce sufficient sharpness in depth.

FOCUSING FOR DEPTH

Independent of the size of the diaphragm opening, considerable extension of sharpness in depth can be produced in oblique angle shots with the aid of the swing-back of a view-type camera.

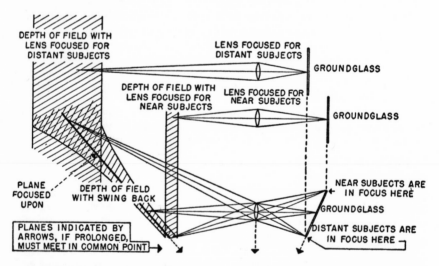

Tilt the camera-back backward (or swing it sideways, respectively) until imaginary lines drawn through the planes of subject, lens, and film meet in a common point (see sketch). Even though the diaphragm is wide open, everything within this oblique plane of focus will be rendered sharply. If the subject, as for example a map, is perfectly flat, subject-plane and plane of focus coincide, and no stopping down is needed. If parts of the subject protrude from this oblique plane of focus, the diaphragm must be stopped down sufficiently to bring these parts back into focus. However, instead of having to cover the entire depth of the subject, such stopping down requires covering only the relatively small distance between the oblique plane of focus and the protruding parts of the subject. Consequently, only a comparatively small amount of stopping down is necessary—a fact which in practice results in a substantial gain in exposure speed.

Such "extended focusing" is applicable regardless of whether the camera is pointed up or down, or is used for taking oblique side views of a subject. When oblique shots of subjects with great extension in depth must be taken, "focusing for depth" is often the only practical approach. This applies when use of the smallest available diaphragm stop fails to create a sufficiently extended zone of sharpness in depth; or if subject movement must be considered and a small diaphragm stop would result in exposures which would be too long to be practical.

CLOSE-UP FOCUSING

Photographers using cameras with front-focusing may encounter considerable difficulty when trying to focus on small subjects for close-ups in near-natural, natural, or more than natural size. Difficulty in photographing close-ups exists because moving the lens forward not only changes the lens-to-film distance, but also changes the lens-to-subject distance. Usually, lens-to-subject distances are so great that the minute decreases due to racking out the lens are, by comparison, completely inconsequential. But in close-ups, such decreases amount to a comparatively large percentage of the total lens-to-subject distance. As a result, front-focusing, by simultaneously changing both lens-to-film and lens-to-subject distances instead of adjusting one to the other, often makes it impossible to achieve the proper balance between the two, and therefore the image may never become really sharp.

The easiest way out of this difficulty is to focus the lens approximately on the close-up, and then either move the whole camera slowly back and forth until the image appears sharp on the groundglass or move the subject until it appears in focus.

Photographers who take close-ups frequently should use a view-type camera equipped with rear-focusing. In such cameras, the lens remains stationary and the back is racked back and forth to bring the image into focus. In this way the subject-to-lens distance remains constant, and the lens-to-film distance can be adjusted without difficulty.

Even with the sharpest lens and film and the greatest care in focusing, it is still possible to get unsharp pictures for the following reasons:

Dirt on the lens. Fingermarks on the glass or a film deposit of grease and dust act as diffusers and produce general softness of the image. Instructions for cleaning lenses correctly are given on p. 217.

Dirty filter. Filters should be treated as carefully as lenses. They should be carried in separate cases, and their glass surfaces should never be touched. Dirty filters act as diffusers and should be cleaned as carefully as a lens.

Camera movement. This is one of the most frequent causes for unsharp pictures (see p. 8). In larger-size reflex cameras, the upswinging heavy mirror sometimes jolts the whole camera at the critical moment of exposure and thus makes slow shutter speeds impractical. A lens board that does not fit tightly enough, or a camera front that has too much play, can also cause unsharp pictures.

Subject movement. If the shutter speed is too slow to "stop" the motion of the subject, rendition becomes blurred (see pp. 12 and 83). Often, however, a slight degree of blur suggests motion, and therefore should not always be considered as a fault.

Inferior filter quality. Cheaply made filters are often not flat enough for photographic purposes. Inexpensive filters made of solid glass are especially likely to produce unsharpness. On the other hand, the finest filters, the "optical flats," are also made of solid glass; they can be identified by their thickness and high price. The longer the focal length of a lens is, the better the optical quality of the filter must be since long-focus lenses magnify not only the image but also the defects in a filter. For this reason, filters that prove adequate for use with standard lenses may produce unsharp pictures when used on a telephoto lens.

Buckling film. Because of its flexibility, film does not always remain as flat as desirable in the camera. Especially under humid conditions, film, because of its affinity for dampness, tends to buckle and bulge from the plane of focus, and this tendency increases with increase in film size. For this reason it can occasionally become impossible to get sharp pictures on a large-size filmpack. To minimize the danger of total or partial unsharpness due to the buckling of the film, it is necessary to stop down the diaphragm in order to create a "safety zone" of extended sharpness in depth.

Heat haze. Objects seen or photographed through rising currents of hot air appear more or less blurred. This phenomenon can be seen by looking along the metal roof of a car standing in the sun—the hot air above it undulates. Hot air rising from chimneys is often the cause of "unexplainable" unsharpness. Other potential sources of difficulty in which hot air may act as an obstacle are: hot radiators (in buildings when shooting pictures from a window); steam locomotives and sun-heated railroad tracks; smokestacks and boilers of steamers. The only way to avoid unsharpness caused by heat haze is to be sure that one does not "shoot" across a current of hot air. If necessary, change the position of the camera.

Ultraviolet radiation. Normally too weak to be of any consequence, ultraviolet radiation can be the cause of unsharpness when photographing at high altitudes (aerial and mountain photography; see p. 41). Use of a filter, such as the Kodak Wratten 2B, which absorbs ultraviolet and requires no increase in exposure, prevents this type of unsharpness.

Difference between groundglass and film. While all modern filmholders and filmpack adapters fit any make of camera of a corresponding negative size, it may occasionally happen that they are either too thick or too thin, and consequently the film is not in exactly the same plane as that of the groundglass. When this happens, the negative will be more or less unsharp in spite of the fact that the greatest care may have been taken in focusing. Whenever pictures taken on sheet film or filmpack are unsharp for no apparent reason, it is advisable to use a depth gauge to check the planes of the groundglass and film to determine whether they coincide. In addition, be sure that filmholder or filmpack adapter makes complete contact with the camera; sometimes the ridge that forms the light trap at its short end does not quite fit into the corresponding groove in the camera, and the film, consequently, is set too far back.

Range finder out of synchronization. Range-finder-equipped cameras need a periodical checkup to make sure that the range finder is still "in sync" with the lens (see p. 217).

Camera front too weak. Heavy lenses may bend the camera front down, especially if they demand double- or triple-bellows extensions and thus exert a considerable lever effect. In such cases, the whole optical system is thrown out of alignment and unsharp negatives result. To prevent this, reinforce the camera with a flat aluminum rail ¼ by 2 inches in cross section, and attach it to the camera box with screws that fit into the tripod sockets.

Focus shift. Some otherwise excellent high-speed lenses shift the plane of focus in accordance with the diaphragm stop. If a photographer focuses such a lens with the diaphragm wide open, and then stops the diaphragm down without refocusing, he will get a more or less unsharp negative, the degree of unsharpness depending on the ratio between the two diaphragm stops. The only way to get sharp pictures with such lenses is to both focus and take the picture with the same diaphragm stop.

67

How to Get Sharpness in Depth

Most photographic subjects are three-dimensional; in addition to height and width, they have "depth." This fact immediately raises two questions: Which depth zone of my subject shall I focus on? and: How can I extend sharpness beyond the plane of focus in order to cover the entire depth of my subject?

AN EXPERIMENT

The simplest and most instructive way to learn how to create sharpness in depth is by way of experiment: take a groundglass-equipped camera, mount it on a tripod, focus it obliquely on a subject with great extension in depth, let's say, a picket fence, and observe the groundglass image.

The first step: With the diaphragm wide open, focus on a pale about three feet from the camera. Notice that the pale you focused on is perfectly sharp; that the pale in front of it and two or three behind it appear reasonably sharp; but that all the others are definitely out of focus and that they appear increasingly blurred the farther away they are from the plane of focus—i.e., the pale you focused on.

The second step: With the diaphragm wide open, focus on a pale about fifteen feet from the camera. Notice that now several pales in front of the one you focused on appear sharp, and that a greater number are also rendered sharply beyond the plane of focus.

The third step: With the diaphagm wide open, focus on a pale fifty feet or more away. Notice that this time ten or more pales in front of that on which you focused appear sharp, and that beyond the plane of focus everything is sharp.

The fourth step: Focus on a pale about fifteen feet from the camera, and *while gradually closing down the diaphragm* observe the image on the groundglass. Notice that more and more pales are covered sharply as the diaphragm opening is decreased.

CONCLUSIONS

In evaluating the results of such an experiment you should arrive at the following conclusions, which, incidentally, contain the whole "secret" of creating sharpness in depth:

1. A certain amount of "sharpness in depth" is inherent in any lens. Even though we always focus a lens on a definite "plane," objects in front of or behind this plane will still, within certain limits, be rendered sharply. The "slower" the lens, the shorter its focal length, and the

farther the plane of focus is from the camera, the deeper this "inherent" zone of sharpness in depth.

2. In most cases, the "inherent depth" of a lens is insufficient to cover the entire depth of the subject. It then becomes necessary to artificially increase the zone of sharpness in depth. The means for this is the diaphragm.

3. The more the diaphragm is stopped down, the more extensive the zone of sharpness in depth.

4. However, the more the diaphragm is stopped down, the darker the image becomes and the greater the necessary increase in exposure time, with all its attendant disadvantages.

5. As a result, practical considerations make it desirable to create a maximum amount of sharpness in depth with a minimum of stopping down.

6. Stopping down the diaphragm increases the zone of sharpness in depth in two directions from the plane of focus: toward and away from the camera. Consequently, it would be wasteful to focus on either the beginning or the end of the depth zone which must be rendered sharply. For example, focusing on infinity and stopping down the lens is always wasteful, since "depth beyond infinity" is useless.

---

7. Stopping down the diaphragm creates proportionally more sharpness in depth behind the plane of focus (away from the camera) than in front of the plane of focus (toward the camera). Consequently, the best way to cover a three-dimensional subject is to focus the lens on a plane situated approximately one third within the subject-depth, and to stop down the diaphragm until the whole depth is covered sharply.

HOW MUCH TO STOP DOWN

The simplest and most accurate way of determining the diaphragm stop necessary to cover a given zone in depth is to observe the image on the groundglass. Cameras without a groundglass (or twin-lens reflex cameras which do not show the extension of depth on the groundglass) are usually equipped with a depth-of-field scale which is engraved on either the lens mount or the focusing knob. To use this scale to fullest advantage, focus first on the closest, then on the most distant, part of the subject to determine their distances from the camera. Note each distance as registered on the foot-scale. Refocus the lens until identical diaphragm stop numbers appear on the depth-of-field scale opposite the foot-numbers which correspond to beginning and end of the zone that must be covered sharply.

69

Leave the lens as focused and stop down the diaphragm to the stop-value that appears opposite the foot-numbers that correspond to the distances at beginning and end of subject-depth. In this way, a maximum of depth is created with a minimum of stopping down.

Summing up our findings, we should arrive at the following results:

1. *Generally speaking*—the smaller the diaphragm opening, the greater the extent of the sharply covered zone in depth. The actual extent of this zone (the "depth of field"), however, is largely dependent on two additional factors:

2. *The subject-to-lens distance.* The farther away the plane of focus is from the camera, the greater the extension in depth covered by any given diaphragm stop; and vice versa. For this reason, close-ups generally require smaller diaphragm openings than long shots, since at short distances stopping down is "less efficient."

3. *The focal length of the lens.* The shorter the focal length, the greater the extension in depth sharply covered by any given diaphragm stop; and vice versa. For this reason, the best outfit for candid photo-reporting is a 35-mm. camera equipped with a lens of 35-mm. focal length (moderate wide-angle lens). If this lens is focused at a distance of approximately twelve feet and stopped down to f/11, it covers everything from approximately five feet to infinity.

Great extension of sharpness in depth results from:	*Limited extension of sharpness in depth results from:*
small diaphragm opening great subject-to-lens distance short focal length of the lens	large diaphragm opening short subject-to-lens distance long focal length of the lens

A Snapshot System

The three factors *subject-to-lens distance, focal length,* and *diaphragm opening* are so dependent upon each other that it is possible to speak of "optimum combinations" which produce maximum depth-coverage with minimum stopping down. By presetting controls, the photo-reporter can convert his camera into a "picture shotgun" with which he can score hits without having to "aim" too accurately. Thus prepared, he can forget the mechanics of the camera and pay undivided attention to his subject. At the right moment he then simply points his camera and "fires," confident of a "hit." The following table contains settings recommended for different camera sizes. Shutter speeds must be preset in accordance with exposure-meter readings.

70

Camera settings for MEDIUM CLOSE-UP SHOTS			Recommended snapshot settings	Camera settings for MEDIUM DISTANCE TO INFINITY		
f/stop	Focus at	Depth of field	FOCAL LENGTH	f/stop	Focus at	Depth of field
8	10'	7' - 15'	5 cm (2") and 7 1/2 cm (3")	8	30'	15'- ∞
11	15'	8' - 35'	35mm and 2 1/4 x 2 1/4" cameras	11	30'	12'- ∞
8	10'	8' - 12'	10 1/2 cm (4 1/8")	8	60'	30' - ∞
11	10'	7' - 14'	Type 2 1/4 x 3 1/4" camera	11	50'	25' - ∞
8	15'	12' - 18'	15 cm (6")	8	100'	50' - ∞
11	15'	11'6"-20'	Type 4 x 5" camera	11	75'	38' - ∞

These data are useful to you only when available at the moment of taking the picture. Copy the data that concern you into your camera case with India ink.

The Hyperfocal Distance

It frequently happens that a photograph must be sharp from a specific distance from the camera to infinity. To accomplish this with a minimum of stopping down, *the lens must be focused on a plane twice as far from the camera as the plane where sharpness should begin,* and the diaphragm must be stopped down accordingly. In such a case, the camera is said to be focused on "hyperfocal distance."

For example: A shot must be taken with a Contax equipped with an f/1.5 Sonnar lens with a focal length of 5 cm., and everything from 3 m. to infinity must be sharply rendered. To do this, the lens must be focused at 6 m., and, according to the depth-of-field scale on the lens mount, the diaphragm must be stopped down to a little more than f/8.

The hyperfocal distance can be defined as follows: when a lens is focused on infinity, sharpness extends from infinity to the "hyperfocal distance"; how far from the camera this is depends on the focal length of the lens and the diaphragm stop. If then the lens is refocused on "hyperfocal distance," and the diaphragm opening remains the same, everything from half the hyperfocal distance to infinity will be rendered sharply. Such a combination of focus and diaphragm produces the maximum depth of field for that particular lens and f-number.

The hyperfocal distance for any lens of any focal length in conjunction with any diaphragm stop can be determined by means of the following formula:

$$\text{Hyperfocal distance (in inches) equals } \frac{F^2}{f \times C} \text{ inches}$$

In this formula F is the focal length of the lens in inches

f is the diaphragm-stop number

C is the diameter of the circle of confusion in fractions of an inch

71

For example: A photographer wants to shoot pictures in which sharpness in depth extends from infinity to a plane as close to the camera as possible. He uses a 5-inch lens, and light conditions permit to stop down to f/8. Sharpness of his negatives should be governed by the requirements stated on p. 62, according to which the diameter of the circle of confusion must not exceed 1/1000 of the focal length of the lens. In this case, this would be equal to 5/1000 or 1/200 of an inch. In order to produce the maximum extent of sharpness in depth, he must focus the lens at hyperfocal distance. Then everything from half this distance to infinity will be rendered sharp. To find the hyperfocal distance he uses the formula given above and gets the following equation:

Hyperfocal distance equals

$$\frac{F^2}{f \times C} = \frac{5^2}{8 \times \frac{1}{200}} = \frac{25}{8} \times 200 = 625'' = 52 + \text{ feet}$$

Consequently, by focusing his lens at approximately fifty feet and stopping down to f/8, he creates a sharply covered depth-zone which begins at twenty-five feet (one half the hyperfocal distance) and extends to infinity.

Conversely, the f-number that will cover any depth-zone from infinity to any given distance from the camera can be determined by the following formula:

$$f \text{ (stop number) equals } \frac{F^2}{H \times C}$$

In this formula F is the focal length of the lens in inches
H is the hyperfocal distance in inches
C is the diameter of the circle of confusion in fractions of an inch

For example: A photographer wants to shoot pictures in which sharpness extends from infinity to twenty-five feet. He uses a 5-inch lens, and wants his negatives to be sharp in accordance with the specifications stated on p. 62, assuming a circle of confusion of 1/200 inch in diameter. He knows that, in order to get a maximum of depth, he must focus his lens at twice the distance of the nearest plane to be sharply rendered, or, in this case, at fifty feet. But how far must he stop down the diaphragm in order to create a zone of sharpness in depth sufficiently large to cover the distance from twenty-five feet to infinity? Here is the answer:

$$f = \frac{F^2}{H \times C} = \frac{25}{600 \times \frac{1}{200}} = \frac{25}{600} \times 200 = \frac{5000}{600} = 8.3$$

Consequently, by focusing his lens at a distance of fifty feet and stopping down to f/8.3, he can create a sharply covered depth-zone which

72

begins at twenty-five feet (half the hyperfocal distance) and extends to infinity.

With the aid of these two formulas, anyone who is interested and has half an hour to spare can easily compute a chart of hyperfocal distances at different diaphragm stops. Such a table will prove invaluable when light conditions are poor and a maximum of depth must be covered with a minimum of stopping down to conserve lens speed and reduce exposure times.

Why Stopping Down Improves Sharpness in Depth

Let us imagine two luminous points, A and B (see following sketch), at different distances from the camera. Each point sends out light in all directions either by radiation (the sun) or by reflection (any non-luminous object). But only a cone of light emitted by each point, with its apex at the source of light and its base at the surface of the lens, is utilized in producing the image. If the lens is focused on point A, light leaving the lens will be refracted to form a second cone of light inside the camera. The apex of this cone will just touch the plane of the film, and a "sharp" image of the luminous point will be formed at a. However, since a lens can never be focused simultaneously at two different distances, the image of the nearer point, B, would theoretically fall behind the film. Since this is impossible (because the film intercepts the light), the image of point B must in this case be rendered "unsharp" in the form of a circle with a diameter corresponding to the diameter of the cone of light at the plane of intersection with the film. This circle is the "circle of confusion."

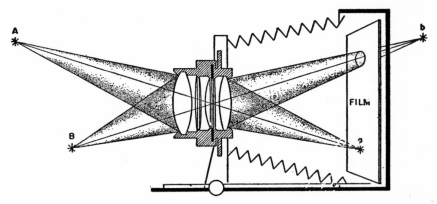

In order to render the image of point B sharp without refocusing the lens, the diameter of the circle of confusion must be reduced. As we already know, this is done by stopping down the diaphragm. Why this operation increases sharpness in depth is illustrated in the following sketch:

73

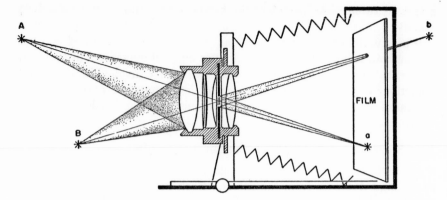

Decreasing the effective aperture of the lens by means of the diaphragm narrows the cone of light that leaves the lens. As a result, when this cone meets the plane of the film, it is already so narrow that the resulting circle of confusion becomes small enough to appear to the eye as a "point" —the image of point *B* appears "sharp."

How to Get Good Contrast

Many of the world's most colorful and exciting sights are notoriously disappointing when photographed. The reason for this is not so much the fact that color is absent in black-and-white photography as that photographers often do not know how to create "graphically effective" black-and-white contrasts, which alone substitute successfully for the absence of color. In itself, absence of color should not be considered a disadvantage. As a matter of fact, time and again good photographers transform commonplace subjects into striking photographs just because of this absence of color. Many subjects, if rendered on color film in the most "natural" form imaginable, are unenduringly boring and trite. These same subjects, however, if rendered imaginatively in black-and-white photographs, with brilliant whites and "graphic" blacks, become surprisingly new and exciting.

In a black-and-white photograph, the film automatically translates the colors of the subject into black and white and intermediate shades of gray. As far as many photographers are concerned, these automatically produced values are quite adequate. Beginners, especially, seldom suspect any necessity to change this simple method of color translation. However, as they progress and become more critical, they usually begin to realize that many of their pictures turn out unsatisfactorily because, somehow, they didn't succeed in capturing the essence of their subjects. Especially if vivid natural colors are vital to the subject, the reason for their failure usually is the inability to produce pictures in which "color" is translated into graphically effective contrast.

Contrast control becomes necessary for two different reasons: first, because black-and-white film does not translate color "literally" enough into shades of gray; and secondly, because it also translates color "too literally." Here is the explanation of this paradox:

Color translation not literal enough: As yet, no negative material exists which simultaneously translates the brightness aspect of all colors into corresponding shades of gray (see p. 39). Panchromatic film, for instance, in portraits made in tungsten light, renders lips too light. Ortho-film is overly sensitive to blue, and consequently renders blue sky too light, with the result that white clouds don't stand out effectively. In such cases—i.e., when a "literal" translation of color into shades of gray is desirable—the color translation must be improved. The means for doing this are the color-correction filters discussed on p. 50.

Color translation too literal: In reality, differentiation of form is mainly based upon differentiation of color. Red roses glow against a background of green leaves; in fall, golden and yellow trees stand out against a dark blue sky. . . . Color is everywhere, and most of this color is neither very light nor very dark. Translated into black-and-white photographs, however, these "medium" colors appear as "medium" grays. The previously exciting contrast of different colors is, therefore, lost in the monotony of almost identical grays. Contrast is lacking, objects blend into one another, and clarity of form and space is gone. Unless a photographer knows how to preserve the "effect" of color in the form of "exaggerated" contrast of light and dark, the result will be disappointing.

THE MEANS FOR CONTRAST CONTROL

In the majority of cases, contrast control is used to produce photographs in which contrast between light and dark *is greater* than it originally appeared in the subject. This is desirable for two different reasons: to "separate" colors that are different in hue (red, blue, green, etc.) but identical in brilliance (lightness or darkness); or to improve the appearance of subjects in which natural contrast is too low to be "graphically" effective (for example, long-distance shots in which atmospheric haze makes everything appear "blue-in-blue" or "gray-in-gray.") Occasionally, however, contrast control is necessary to reduce excessive subject-contrast to the range of the negative material (for example, pictures in which brilliant illumination alternates with pitch-black shadows). The following summary lists the different means used to control subject contrasts in accordance with the demands of graphically effective rendition:

75

1. *Negative material* (consider two qualities: color sensitivity and gradation).
2. *Color filters* (distinguish between two types: contrast filters and color-correction filters; see p. 48).
3. *Illumination* (distinguish between different types of light; see p. 54; and different ways of using a specific type of illumination: see pp. 79-80).
4. *Exposure* in conjunction with development (see p. 80).
5. *Paper gradation* (for over-all correction of unsatisfactory contrast of the negative).
6. *Dodging* (local contrast control in the print during enlarging).
7. *Combinations* of several or all of these means for contrast control.

1. Negative Material

Differences in color sensitivity are important in regard to the rendition of red and green. Orthochromatic films are insensitive to red, and render it as black. However, pure red is rare in nature. Most "reds" contain some yellow, blue, or green. As a result, most so-called "reds" are not rendered by ortho-film as "black" but merely appear darker than they appeared to the eye. In portraiture, for example, differentiation between the pink flesh tones and the red of lips is important. Orthochromatic film, because of its insensitivity to red, often produces better separation between "pink" and "red" than panchromatic film, which generally renders red too light. On the other hand, this insensitivity of ortho-film to red makes it inferior to panchromatic film in almost every instance except where green is the predominant color. Panchromatic film is low in green sensitivity, and generally renders green darker than it appeared to the eye. As a result, predominantly green subjects (landscapes, trees, foliage) often appear better when photographed on ortho-film, provided that its oversensitivity to blue is reduced through use of a yellow filter. However, unless specific reasons, such as those mentioned here, make the use of ortho-film desirable, panchromatic film is generally preferable because of its all-color sensitivity, which permits the use of "dramatizing" red filters; its high sensitivity to red, which makes it the ideal film for taking pictures by incandescent light, which is rich in red; and its generally higher speed, which is an especially valuable asset in night and/or indoor photography.

Differences in the ability of films to render contrast can be used advantageously for preserving, increasing, or reducing the brightness contrast of a subject. As a rule, the slower the speed of a negative emulsion, the more contrasty the image; and the faster the film, the softer the rendition. See pp. 44-46 for complete information.

Before selecting the most suitable type of film for a specific job, the photographer must first determine whether subject-contrast should be preserved, increased, or reduced to achieve the most desirable effect. Accordingly, he will narrow down his choice to a group of films with the required gradation—normal, hard, or soft. However, this is only the first step. Next he must consider the color scheme of his subject and decide which would produce better results: an orthochromatic or a panchromatic film. Accordingly, from the group of films chosen for gradation characteristics, he will now select a film with the most suitable color sensitivity.

2. Color Filters

We have the choice of correction filters and contrast filters.

Color-correction filters improve the representation of color in terms of gray so that the natural lightness or darkness of a color (as it appeared to the eye) is translated into a gray of corresponding lightness or darkness (so-called "monochromatic" color rendition). Consult the table on p. 50 for Kodak Wratten filters for use in color correction and their factors which, in conjunction with different types of Kodak films, will produce monochromatically correct color rendition in black and white.

Contrast filters alter the response of a negative emulsion with regard to specifically selected colors. Unlike color-correction filters, which often diminish contrast in the negative, contrast filters permit the photographer to reproduce colorful subjects in graphically effective black and white. Correction filters produce what might be called "scientifically correct" or "literally true" color rendition, though the pictorial effect is often dull. On the other hand, contrast filters permit the photographer to produce contrast in accordance with the characteristics of the subject and to create, therefore, what might be called "emotionally true" pictures. And since, by its very nature, any black-and-white photograph is an "abstraction"— "unnatural" in that color is "symbolized" by shades of gray—one might as well accept the logical consequence and, instead of trying for a "literally true" rendering, try one that is "emotionally true"—a presentation which alone can adequately express the subject.

Selection of a contrast filter is governed by two rules:

1. To make a color appear lighter in the picture than it appeared in nature, a filter of the same color must be used. Conversely, to make a color appear darker, a filter of the complementary color must be used. Such complementary color pairs are:

> red and blue-green
> orange and blue
> yellow and purple-blue
> green and red-purple
> purple and green-yellow

77

2. If two colors that are different in hue but similar in brightness must be separated in the black-and-white "translation," the warmer, more aggressive color should usually be rendered lighter, and the cooler, more passive and receding color should be rendered darker.

Warm and aggressive colors	Neutral colors	Cool and passive colors
Red	green-yellow	blue-green
Orange	green	blue
Yellow	red-purple	purple-blue

For complete information on filters and filter factors, see pp. 48-51. The following list of filters and their use is intended mainly as a guide for beginners.

FILTER	USED IN CONJUNC-TION WITH	EFFECT OF FILTER	COMMON USE	APPROXIMATE FILTER FACTOR (see p. 50)
Very light yellow (K1)	Ortho and pan film	darkens blue moderately	to improve cloud rendition	1.5
Dark yellow (K3)	Ortho and pan film	darkens blue considerably	to darken pale blue sky; more dramatic cloud rendition	2
Red (A)	Pan and infrared film	renders blue almost black; darkens green; renders red almost white	most dramatic cloud rendition; long-distance and telephotography; haze penetration	8
Orange (minus blue)	Pan film	practically the same as red	best all-round filter for aerial photography	6
Black (87C)	Infrared film	obliterates haze and dust; renders blue sky and water black, green foliage white	extreme telephotog-raphy; high-altitude aerial shots; fake night and moonlight effects shot in daylight	20-30
Yellow-green (X1)	Ortho and pan film	renders green foliage lighter and more detailed; darkens red	landscapes and foliage; monochromatic rendi-tion for tungsten light on Type B pan film (p. 51)	3-4
Green (B)	Ortho and pan film	darkens red; lightens green	a rarely used filter of little practical value	8
Blue (80)	Ortho and pan film	darkens red considerably; lightens blue	to darken red lips in portraits taken by incandescent light	3-4
Ultraviolet (2B)	Ortho and pan film	absorbs ultra-violet radiation	aerial and ground pho-tography above 5,000 feet	1.5

78

3. Illumination

The purpose of any illumination is to accentuate the form and characteristics of the subject with the aim of creating an illusion of space and three-dimensionality within the flat plane of the picture. This is achieved through light and shadow. Translated into terms of photography, light corresponds to white, and shadow to black. The stronger the contrast of light and shadow—of black and white—the stronger the illusion of three-dimensionality and depth. Conversely, the lower the contrast of light and shadow—the grayer the print—the flatter the appearance of the picture. Usually a strong feeling of depth is desirable, necessitating strong black-and-white contrast. However, there is a limit beyond which depth-effect becomes too strong and therefore undesirable. It is then up to the photographer to tone down the illumination to produce the desired degree of contrast. For example, direct sunlight is unsuitable for portraits because shadows tend to be too black. As a result, eye sockets no longer appear as depressions, but as holes, giving a "portrait" a skull-like appearance. Here we have evidence of the depth-effect becoming too strong—we don't want the effect of a "hole," we merely want the effect of a "depression." By reducing the contrast range, by "filling in" with auxiliary light until the shadows appear not black but gray, by "balancing" the illumination, the depth-effect can be reduced until it appears "just right."

Contrast with respect to both graphic black-and-white effects and the creation of a feeling of depth can be controlled through the illumination:

1. *Filling in.* By means of extra lights or reflectors, shadows that otherwise would print too dark can be lightened to any desired degree. Indoors, the best fill-in light is produced by softly diffused floods or by "indirect" light reflected from walls and ceiling. If several lamps are used, merely turning one against the ceiling is often sufficient to "balance" the illumination. Outdoors, when sunlight is too "hard," a "peanut" flashbulb at the camera, diffused by a handkerchief, makes an ideal fill-in. For close-ups, several thicknesses of handkerchief should be used to reduce the excessive brightness of the flash. If flash equipment is lacking, a reflector consisting of a plywood panel covered with crinkled aluminum foil makes an excellent "fill-in" which, furthermore, has the advantage of permitting the photographer to see the exact extent to which shadows are lightened.

A word of caution: the danger of every type of fill-in is not that they are not efficient enough, but that they are too efficient. Beginners, especially, excited by their new-found control of illumination, are apt to "fill in" so much that they inadvertently reduce contrast to such a degree that the picture appears "flat." Unfortunately, pictures that are too flat usually look worse than pictures that are too contrasty. Hence, when in doubt, "fill in" too little rather than too much.

2. *Type of light.* By selecting the most suitable type of light * to produce the desired effect, a photographer assumes complete control over the contrast range of his picture. For example: average portraits demand a softly diffused light of low contrast. Consequently, the best type of illumination for outdoor portraits is light from a hazy, overcast sky. If outdoor portraits must be made on a sunny day, an experienced photographer will pose his model in the open shade where the light is suitably diffused. On the other hand, "glamor portraits" derive their effect from the strong contrast of black and white. Consequently, a contrasty type of illumination such as direct sunlight, or spotlight illumination indoors, is the type of light most likely to produce the desired effect.

3. *Modification of light.* Every source of light can produce, within certain limits, illumination of different qualities. For example, on a clear day the sunlight can be exceedingly hard, and contrast extreme. A hazy, overcast sky considerably softens the light, and contrast is reduced. And, finally, light from a cloudy sky or light in open shade can be so evenly diffused that it is practically "shadowless." Discriminating photographers wait until conditions are right—and they get the type of illumination best suited to their work.

Indoors, matters are simpler: intensity of the illumination can be controlled merely by regulating the distance between the subject and the light source. Most spotlights can be "focused"—i.e., their spread and intensity can be adjusted to fit the demands of the subject. Floodlights can be made to produce light of softer or harder quality by means of different types of diffusers and reflectors (see pp. 57-58).

4. Exposure and Development

The ability of a negative emulsion to render contrast is not an unalterable factor (see pp. 44-45). It depends largely upon the way a film is exposed and developed. Deviations from standard produce changes in the contrast range of the negative which can easily be controlled and used to produce pictures with a specific contrast range.

Experienced photographers know that the simpler their equipment the easier their work. For this reason, they try to get along with as few different types of film as possible. Rather than carry a specific type of negative material for different purposes, they modify the characteristics of one emulsion to fit the requirements of many different situations in accordance with the following principles:

To increase contrast beyond "normal," the film must be exposed shorter than normal and developed longer than normal. Depending on the degree

---

* For complete information on the different types of artificial light, see pp. 54-57. How to make the best use of artificial light will be discussed on pp. 97-99.

80

to which contrast must be increased, exposure should be shortened by 30–50 per cent, and the time of development increased 20–50 per cent.

To decrease contrast below "normal," the film must be exposed longer than normal and developed shorter than normal. Depending on the degree to which contrast must be decreased, exposure should be increased by 50–200 per cent and the time of development shortened by 20–50 per cent.

The term "normal" always refers to the standard recommendations for exposure (in accordance with the rated film speed) and development (standard duration at a temperature of 68° F.) as stated in the instruction sheet that accompanies the film.

5. Paper Gradation

The "technically" easiest way to control the contrast range of the final picture is to print the negative on a paper of appropriate gradation.

To increase contrast, the negative must be printed on a paper of hard gradation.

To decrease contrast, the negative must be printed on a paper of soft gradation.

However, simple as this method of contrast control may be, it has one serious drawback: a negative that must be printed on paper of harder or softer than "normal" gradation will never produce a print as smooth in tone and rich in modulation as a negative so perfect in contrast that it can be printed on a paper of "normal" gradation. For this reason, it is definitely advisable to strive from the beginning for negatives that have the desired contrast range and consequently can be printed on paper of normal gradation. Of course, this does not always mean "negatives of *normal* gradation" since many subjects demand for best effect a treatment based upon either higher or lower contrast. In such cases, best results will always be produced if contrast control has been achieved by one or several of the means discussed above. Then the desired gradation is present in the negative and can be transferred to the print by using a paper of normal gradation.

6. Dodging

Every experienced photographer knows that there is hardly a negative from which a "straight print" can be made. Even though the print as a whole may look all right and contrast in general may be perfect, there usually are a few spots that can stand improvement: a shadow may print too black; a highlighted area may seem to have too little detail; or a corner of the print may be too light. By making the whole print lighter or darker, or by using a paper of different gradation, of course, a photographer can improve such details. But, on the other hand, the rest of the picture would suffer if such a change were made.

In such a case, the only way to improve the picture—and a very good way, too!—is by means of "dodging." Dodging means local contrast control, and works as follows:

To make a certain area lighter, it must be given less exposure than the rest of the picture during printing. This is done by inserting a piece of cardboard of appropriate shape and dimensions between the printing paper and the light-source for part of the exposure. In order to avoid sharp outlines in the print, such a "dodger" (as it is called) must be constantly moved slightly back and forth during the shading. Attaching the piece of cardboard to the end of a stiff wire permits the printer to reach any area within the picture without unnecessarily shading border zones. This type of dodging is called "holding back."

To make a certain area darker, it must be given more exposure than the rest of the picture during the printing. This is done by using a piece of cardboard through which a hole of appropriate shape and dimensions has been cut. The light is allowed to fall through this hole for an additional period upon the area to be darkened while the rest of the picture is shielded by the cardboard from overexposure. In order to avoid sharp outlines in the print, the dodger must be constantly moved slightly back and forth during the exposure. This type of dodging is called "burning in."

7. Combinations

Each of the six contrast controls discussed above works on a different principle. Therefore, the photographer can approach a particular problem in various ways. However, best results are usually achieved through combining two or more of these methods of control. At first, this may seem complicated and confusing. With growing experience and confidence, however, reaching for the right type of film or filter or light, etc., becomes as automatic as reaching for a knife, fork, or spoon at the dinner table.

The following chart presents a summing up of the different means for contrast control:

Means for increasing contrast	Means for normal contrast	Means for decreasing contrast
Contrasty (slow) film; Contrast color filters; Contrasty illumination, direct sunlight, spotlights; Shorter than normal exposure with longer than normal development; Contrasty printing paper; Dodging.	Medium fast film; Color correction filters; Well-balanced illumination; Standard exposure according to exposure meter in conjunction with standard development; Normal printing paper; Dodging.	Soft (fast) film; Diffused light, light in open shade, light from overcast sky, fill-in light; Longer than normal exposure in conjunction with shorter than normal development; Soft printing paper; Dodging.

How to "Stop" Motion

Every subject that moves while being photographed will appear blurred in the picture, however slightly. This is a natural consequence of the exposure, for as the lens projects the image of the moving subject onto the film, the motion is likewise recorded in the projected image. The result is comparable to making an imprint with a rubber stamp while moving the stamp sideways: naturally, the impression will be blurred—becoming increasingly so the faster the motion (the higher the speed of the subject) and the longer the duration of contact between stamp and paper (the longer the duration of the exposure).

That pictures of subjects in motion appear "sharp" is nothing but an illusion, similar to the illusion of sharpness discussed on p. 62. If enlarged enough, the sharpest picture will show innumerable overlapping circles of confusion. Similarly, if sufficiently enlarged, subjects whose motion appears completely "stopped" will reveal unsharpness in the direction of the motion. The picture "appeared" sharp only because the resolving power of the eye is not great enough to detect the degree of blur.

Out of these facts evolve the two principles according to which motion in a photograph can be "stopped":

1. The image of the moving subject must be "immobilized" on the film for the duration of the exposure.

2. The motion of the image on the film must be restricted to such an extent during exposure that the unavoidable blur remains below the resolving power of the eye.

Here is how this can be accomplished in practice:

1. *"Immobilizing" the image of the moving subject.* This method of stopping motion has the advantage of being within the range of any camera from the simplest "box" to the most expensive instrument, regardless of the speed range of the shutter. There are two different ways to stop motion of the subject:

1(a). USE THE CAMERA LIKE A SHOTGUN. Look through the finder at the image of the moving subject, follow through with the camera, and release the shutter while the camera is in motion. In this way, the image of the moving subject remains practically stationary on the film during exposure and consequently is rendered sharp, while the less important background becomes blurred owing to the motion of the camera. It is pictorially more effective than any other method of "stopping" motion since it preserves the "feeling" of motion through contrast between sharpness and blur. It re-creates the impression one gets when watching a moving object.

1(b). CATCH THE PEAK OF THE ACTION when movement is practically at a standstill. For example, photograph an athlete as he crosses the bar at

83

the peak of a high jump; a golfer completing the follow-through when the club is over his shoulder; a diver at the start of his downward plunge, etc. . . . Figuratively speaking, photograph the pendulum at the end of its swing before it goes into reverse—and motion will then appear "stopped" even when "seen" through the lens of a "box."

2. *Restricting the motion of the image on the film.* There are four different approaches, each of which can be used either separately or in combination with any of the others:

2(a). HIGH SHUTTER SPEED. The higher the shutter speed, the shorter the exposure, the less the image changes its position on the film, the smaller the degree of unavoidable blur, and the sharper the final picture. Whether or not shutter speed is high enough to produce the desired result depends on the speed of the moving subject: the faster its motion, the higher the shutter speed must be to "stop" image movement on the film. This shutter speed, however, is determined not only by the *actual speed* of the moving subject but to an even higher degree by its *"apparent" speed relative to the camera.* Technically, it makes a great difference whether a train traveling at 60 mph. is photographed in side view as it passes the camera at right angles or in front view at a very narrow angle when traveling at the same speed toward the camera. In the first case, the "effective" speed of the train in relation to the camera is very high; in the second case it is almost zero, even though *in both cases* the train speed is 60 mph. The following table lists the shutter speeds that are necessary to obtain sharp pictures of subjects moving at various speeds.

SUBJECT	DISTANCE: OBJECT-CAMERA	DIRECTION OF MOTION	FOCAL LENGTH OF LENS					
			2 in.	3 in.	4 in.	5 in.	6 in.	10 in.
Pedestrians walking, or children playing, or slow-moving animals	25 ft.		1/60	1/75	1/100	1/125	1/150	1/250
			1/40	1/50	1/75	1/85	1/100	1/150
			1/25	1/30	1/40	1/50	1/60	1/80
Horses galloping, bicycles racing, or automobiles moving 30 mph	50 ft.		1/180	1/275	1/360	1/450	1/550	1/900
			1/120	1/180	1/240	1/300	1/360	1/600
			1/60	1/90	1/120	1/150	1/180	1/300
Horses trotting, bicycles coasting, or children racing	25 ft.		1/200	1/300	1/400	1/500	1/600	1/1000
			1/120	1/180	1/240	1/360	1/450	1/750
Automobiles, trains, etc., at 40-60 mph	100 ft.		1/75	1/100	1/126	1/160	1/200	1/330
Fast athletic events	25 ft.		1/300	1/425	1/550	1/700	1/850	1/1400
			1/200	1/300	1/400	1/500	1/600	1/1000
			1/100	1/150	1/200	1/250	1/300	1/480

If a camera doesn't have the exact shutter speed recommended here, the one that is closest to it should be used. When indicated distances are doubled, exposure times may be twice as long; when distances are halved, shutter speeds have to be twice as fast.

2(b). DIRECTION OF MOTION. It sometimes happens that the range of available shutter speeds does not include speeds high enough to take sharp pictures of fast-moving subjects. In such cases, image motion on the film can be reduced considerably, and sharp pictures can be obtained at comparatively slow shutter speeds, if the moving subject is photographed coming toward or going away from the camera instead of passing at right angles. How slow shutter speeds can be is shown in the above table. Provided that such a "head-on" or "rear view" of the subject is pictorially acceptable, this method for "stopping motion" is recommended especially for simpler cameras with relatively limited shutter speeds.

2(c). SUBJECT-DISTANCE. The farther the moving subject is from the camera, the lower its "angular velocity"—i.e., its "apparent" speed relative to the observer (and the film!). Seen from a distance of several miles, a fast plane seems to crawl across the sky; while flying close at a low altitude, the same plane appears as a mere blur. By making use of this phenomenon—i.e., by increasing the distance between subject and camera—photographers who have cameras equipped with insufficiently fast shutters can still produce sharp pictures of fast-moving objects. For example, if the distances in the table on p. 84 are doubled, shutter speeds only half as fast as those listed are required to "stop" the motions in question.

Incidentally, in this respect, subject-distance is the equivalent of image scale. Doubling the subject-distance, or shooting with a lens of half the focal length, produces an identical result: the subject is rendered only half as large on the film. Consequently, "angular velocity" can be reduced either by increasing the distance between subject and camera or by photographing the subject from the same distance with a lens of shorter focal length. For example, if the 6-inch standard lens of a 4-by-5 camera requires a shutter speed of 1/600 sec. to stop a given motion, the motion can be stopped satisfactorily at a shutter speed of 1/200 sec. by using a miniature camera equipped with a 2-inch lens. Since the focal length of the lens of the miniature camera is only one third that of the 4-by-5 camera, a shutter speed one third as fast is sufficient to produce the same result. This fact is established in the table on p. 84 in which minimum shutter speeds are listed for lenses ranging from 2 to 10 inches in focal length.

2(d). SPEEDLIGHTS. An exposure can be timed in two different ways: by opening and closing the shutter; by turning the illumination on and off. Mechanical shutters permit exposures ranging to a thousandth of a second. Beyond this speed, inertia and insufficient strength of the shutter material make higher speeds impractical. But there is almost no limit to the shortness of duration of an illuminating electric spark, such as is used in the tube of a speedlight (see p. 56). Commercial and amateur speedlights operate at speeds of around 1/1000 sec.; for scientific purposes, speedlights with flash durations as short as 1/1,000,000 sec. are available. Exposures of this order, of course, will "stop" any kind of motion, no matter how fast, and have been used successfully to get tack-sharp pictures of bullets leaving the muzzle of a rifle, and of fragments of material shattering under the impact of an exploding shell.

With speedlights, furthermore, it is absolutely impossible to get unsharp pictures resulting from camera motion. As far as motion rendition is concerned, if a speedlight is used, a needle-sharp photograph can be taken inside a truck jolting at high speed over a bumpy road.

Since speedlight exposures are timed by the duration of the spark, and not by the speed of the synchronized shutter, which is usually set at 1/100 or 1/250 sec., such photographs can be taken successfully only if "local" illumination is so low that it will not permit objects to register noticeably on the film. Otherwise, since the shutter is open for a comparatively long time, a secondary picture would be superimposed upon the sharp image produced by the speedlight, and the resulting photograph would appear unclear and confused owing to motion of the subject.

Summing up: Motion can be "stopped" in many different ways, and best results will usually be produced by combining two or more of the methods discussed above. The basis for any motion photograph should be a fast film, since fast films alone permit utilization of high shutter speeds. Shutter speeds should be as high as light conditions permit. If necessary, in order to use a larger diaphragm stop to permit use of a higher shutter speed, depth must be sacrificed. If a combination of these factors is not sufficient to "stop" the motion in question, following the moving subject with the camera (1a) and/or catching it at the peak of motion (1b) should be considered. If motion is so fast that this is not sufficient to produce sharp pictures, the "angular velocity" must be reduced by shooting from a different direction (2b), from farther away (2c), or by using a lens of shorter focal length (2c). In cases of extremely fast motion, especially at very short subject-distances, speedlights will aid the photographer to succeed where other methods failed.

The following survey lists the different means and methods for "stopping" motion:

High-speed film (for practical utilization of highest shutter speeds).

High shutter speed (2a), if necessary in conjunction with large diaphragm.

Exposing while following the moving subject with the camera (1a).

Shooting at the peak of a motion (1b).

Shooting in the direction of the motion (2b) instead of shooting at right angle.

Increasing the distance between moving subject and camera (2c).
Using a lens with shorter focal length (2c).
Speedlights (2d).

A word of advice: "Technically," it is possible to "stop" any kind of motion and render the subject extremely sharp. Whether or not this always leads to the best result pictorially, however, is another question. In a black-and-white photograph, "motion" as well as color can be depicted only in a symbolic form. For color, this form is graphic black-and-white contrast. For motion, it is blur. There is, for instance, absolutely no difference between the sharply rendered picture of a car standing still and a car in motion. If it is important to indicate the fact that the car is moving, motion must be "symbolized" in the form of a blur. In other words, the picture must be shot at *a shutter speed low enough* NOT *to "stop" the motion of the car.* Of course, the degree of blur must be "just right." If it is too great, the car is unrecognizable; if too little, the car appears to be at a standstill and no feeling of motion exists. One must choose between the "literally true" and "emotionally true" rendition. Which of these offers the better solution depends on the particular circumstances and the intent of the photographer.

How to Expose Correctly

At the moment of exposure, the first and most important step in the making of a photograph is completed. Prior to this moment, the photographer has the chance to create, arrange, select, reject—to make the picture just as he wants it. This chance is gone the instant he releases the shutter. After that, he can do little to influence the result as far as composition, distribution of light and dark, color rendition in terms of black and white, symbolization or "stopping" of motion, etc., are concerned. Consequently, it is necessary to fully consider all these aspects *before* the exposure is made.

The basis for any "technically perfect photograph" is a correctly exposed negative. "Exposing correctly" means admitting to the film the amount of light necessary to produce negatives with the right degree of density and contrast. There are a number of different factors that must be considered when computing an exposure (they are listed in the following paragraphs), but the basis for any exposure should be a reading taken from a good exposure meter.

Correctly used, an exposure meter guarantees correctly exposed negatives. The corresponding saving in film alone should within a reasonable time be enough to pay for the cost of the meter. The gain in enjoyment and satisfaction that comes with improvement in one's work, of course, is quite incalculable and cannot be expressed in dollars and cents.

On the other hand, an improperly used exposure meter is potentially harmful and of less practical value to the photographer than any "fool-proof" exposure guide that can be bought for twenty-five cents. The following rules apply to the use of any exposure meter, regardless of type or make, which is designed to measure *reflected light:*

1. *The film-speed dial* must be set in accordance with the rated speed of the film. Some films (p. 42) have different speeds in different types of illumination. Set dial for the rated daylight speed when photographing in natural light; set dial for the tungsten speed when taking pictures by incandescent light.

2. *The brightness reading* must be taken of the most important object in the picture. Beginners often make the mistake of pointing the meter toward the horizon when taking an over-all reading for a landscape shot. This allows direct skylight to enter the photo-electric cell, and results in a reading that is too high and, consequently, causes underexposure. To avoid this, when measuring over-all brightness for a landscape shot, aim the meter at a point halfway between the horizon and yourself. Only when the subject of the picture is the sky—a sunset shot, or a "cloudscape" taken from a plane—should the meter be aimed directly at the sky. In such a case, the sky is the subject, and exposure should be determined by its brightness reading. If the ground is included, it can be permitted to go black through underexposure in the final picture.

3. *When taking a close-up reading* of, for instance, a face, be sure that your meter or hand does not cast a shadow on that part of the subject at which you aim the meter. Otherwise, the reading will be too low, causing overexposure. If necessary, in order to avoid measuring the shadow, take the reading from a slightly different angle.

There are three different methods of measuring the brightness of reflected light, each of which has a particular advantage over the others:

4. *The camera-position method* is the easiest and fastest (though not the most accurate) way of measuring light intensities. The reading is taken from the camera position by pointing the meter toward the subject. Outdoors, be sure that skylight does not falsify the reading (see above under 2).

5. *The brightness-range method* is the most accurate way to determine

correct exposure. Two different readings must be taken: one of the brightest and the other of the darkest part of the subject. These readings must be taken from such a short distance that *only* the brightest and darkest areas, respectively, are measured. To do this, the photographer must be able to get close enough to the subject, and he must take care not to measure a possible shadow cast by the meter (see above under 3). Exposure is determined by setting the pointer of the meter midway between the values that correspond to the highest and lowest readings. In case it is not possible to get close enough to the subject to accurately measure its brightest and darkest part (landscape photography), substitute readings can usually be taken from similar objects of similar brightness located near by. For example, instead of measuring the brightness of a distant tree, a nearby tree that is lighted in a similar way can be measured even though it may be outside the field of the camera. And instead of measuring the brightness of a face, the photographer can take a substitute reading from the palm of his hand, provided that it is lighted in the same way and that the reading is not falsified by the shadow of the meter.

6. *The close-up method* is a variation of the brightness-range method and produces the most accurate results in cases where it is important to get the best possible exposure for one particular subject of more or less uniform brightness, as, for example, the face of a person. Only one close-up reading of the object in question is taken (avoid a shadow cast by the meter), and all other objects, irrespective of their brightness, are disregarded. This method is recommended whenever one object is of particular interest while the rest is of negligible importance or background.

All the methods and rules discussed so far apply to the measuring of *light reflected by the subject.* However, exposure can also be determined by directly measuring the intensity of the illumination itself—the "incident light." Differences between the two methods are as follows:

Reflected-light reading: the common method according to which the meter is *aimed at the subject* from the direction of the camera. Most exposure meters work according to this principle. This is the most accurate method of determining correct exposure, more adaptable to unusual circumstances than the method of measuring incident light, though sometimes not as simple.

Incident-light reading: a comparatively recent method according to which *the meter is aimed at the camera* from the subject position. With the exception of the Norwood, which is expressly designed for this method, *other meters need special adapters before they can be used for measuring incident light, provided that they can be converted at all.*

This method is particularly useful for taking pictures with artificial light, since it integrates all the light from all the lamps regardless of their position and distance.

No matter how accurate a light-intensity reading is, it provides no more than a basis for the exposure, since some or all of the following factors must be considered in computing the final exposure:

1. Film speed
2. Depth of subject
3. Movement of subject
4. Contrast of subject
5. Color of subject
6. Distance of subject
7. Color filter factor
8. Slip-on lens factor
9. Type of developer
10. Time of exposure

1. *Film speed.* The film-speed dial of the exposure meter must be set in accordance with the rated speed of the film to be used (see p. 41). Different exposure meters may be calibrated for different systems of film-speed rating. Be sure that the film-speed rating you apply belongs to the same system for which the meter is calibrated. Some films have two different speed ratings: one for daylight and one for incandescent light (tungsten). The daylight speed is always higher than that of the incandescent light. When setting the meter dial, be sure to use the film-speed rating that corresponds to the type of illumination that will be used to take the picture.

2. *Depth of subject.* The greater the extension in depth that must be covered sharply, the smaller the necessary diaphragm stop. And the smaller the diaphragm stop, the longer the duration of the exposure (the slower the shutter speed). Usually, practical considerations force the photographer to compromise between a diaphragm stop that is small enough to produce sufficient sharpness in depth and a shutter speed that is fast enough to adequately "stop" motion. Whichever is more important —depth or motion—determines whether an exposure "for depth" (relatively small diaphragm in conjunction with slower shutter speed) or "for speed" (relatively fast shutter speed in conjunction with larger diaphragm) must be selected.

3. *Movement of subject.* Subjects at rest can be exposed for any length of time, provided the camera is firmly supported. To avoid unsharpness

90

caused by motion, pictures that must be taken with the camera hand-held should normally be exposed not longer than 1/25 sec. For the exposure of subjects in motion the table on p. 84 lists the minimum shutter speeds that are required to "stop" motion. However, a certain degree of blur often suggests a feeling of motion (see p. 87). As previously mentioned, a compromise between a relatively high shutter speed (to "stop" motion) and a relatively small diaphragm (to produce sufficient sharpness in depth) is usually unavoidable.

4. *Contrast of subject.* Exposure meters are calibrated to give correct data for subjects of average contrast. If subject contrast is very much higher than average, exposure should be doubled. If subject contrast is very much lower than average, exposure should be halved. This way, it is still possible to produce well-balanced negatives by correspondingly decreasing the time of development for the "contrasty" subjects and increasing the time of development for the "contrastless" subjects. (See p. 80 for detailed information.)

5. *Color of subject.* Exposure meters are calibrated to give correct data for subjects of medium color. In order to get fully exposed negatives of very light and very dark subjects, exposure as indicated by the meter must be increased by a factor of 1½ to 2.

6. *Distance of subject.* If subject-to-camera distance is shorter than approximately five times the focal length of the lens, discrepancies between the "listed" and the "effective" values of the diaphragm stops become so great that they must be considered in order to avoid underexposure (see p. 30). The formula according to which the necessary increases in exposure can be computed is given on p. 30. An exceptionally handy and practical device that simply "dials" the necessary data is the *Effective Aperture Kodaguide* made by The Eastman Kodak Company and available for a few cents at most photo stores.

7. *Color filter factor.* All color filters absorb a certain amount of light which would otherwise be available for the exposure. This loss of light must be compensated for by a corresponding increase in exposure in order to avoid underexposure of the negative. The amount of increase—the exposure factor by which exposure as indicated by the meter must be multiplied—depends on color and density of the filter, the type of film it is used in conjunction with, and the type of illumination (daylight or incandescent light). These filter factors are listed in the table on p. 51. For example, if the meter indicates an exposure of 1/100 sec. at f/11, and the filter to be used has a factor of 2, exposure must be doubled. This can be accomplished either by opening the diaphragm one stop and shooting at 1/100 sec. at f/8; or by halving the exposure time and shooting at 1/50 sec. at f/11.

8. *Slip-on lenses* (see p. 222) change the focal length of the standard

lens in conjunction with which they are used. As a result, the stop values engraved on the lens are no longer valid since they are computed for the focal length of the standard lens and *not* for the focal length of the lens-system "standard lens plus slip-on lens." Compared to the standard lens, the combination of standard-plus-positive-slip-on-lens is faster, and the combination of standard-plus-negative-slip-on-lens is slower. In practice, positive (wide-angle) slip-on lenses are used almost exclusively for close-ups to photograph small objects in a scale larger than that which would be possible with the standard lens alone. In such cases, discrepancies in the value of the stop numbers caused by the slip-on lens can be disregarded since the gain in lens speed is balanced by the loss in lens speed caused by the increase in bellows extension necessary for making the close-up shot.

The combination of negative (telephoto) slip-on lens and standard lens, however, is always considerably slower than the standard lens, and demands corresponding increases in exposure. The simplest way to compute such increases is to measure the distance between lens center and film after focusing, to measure the opening of the diaphragm that will be used to take the picture, and to divide the first by the second. The resulting figure is the "effective stop number," and its value is the same as that of the corresponding stop number on the exposure-meter dial.

9. *Type of developer.* Film-speed ratings are always based on negative development with standard developers. Special "fine-grain" developers (see p. 114) produce negatives with comparatively fine grain (see p. 43) because they only partially develop each individual negative grain. Furthermore, some do not penetrate the emulsion but confine their action more or less to the surface. As a result of this "incomplete development," fine-grain developers produce negatives that appear "underexposed" unless exposure has been increased accordingly. The amount of increase—the exposure factor—varies with the type of fine-grain developer. As a rule, developers producing the finest grain demand the greatest increases in exposure. Consult the manufacturer's instruction sheet.

The simplest way to provide for the necessary exposure increase is to deduct the speed loss from the "theoretical" film speed, and to set the film-speed dial of the exposure meter for the lower "effective" speed. Let us assume, for example, that a film with an ASA rating of 50 should be developed in a fine-grain developer that has a factor of 2. Instead of setting the dial for the full "theoretical" speed of 50, set it at 25, and diaphragm and shutter speed are thus automatically computed for correct exposure in conjunction with development in that particular fine-grain developer.

10. *Time of exposure.* Under normal conditions, decreasing the diaphragm by one full stop must be compensated for by doubling the time

of exposure if the result is to be the same in regard to negative density. However, when the light intensity becomes abnormally low, this ratio no longer applies and increases in exposure produce proportionally less and less density in the negative ("reciprocity failure"). This fact must be considered when taking time exposures at night with small diaphragm openings. For example, if an exposure of one minute at f/4.5 is correct, but the diaphragm must be stopped down to f/16 in order to produce sufficient sharpness in depth, exposure according to the meter would be thirteen minutes. Actually, however, because of reciprocity failure, a thirteen-minute exposure would be quite insufficient to produce a negative of the same density as the one exposed one minute at f/4.5. Depending on the type of film, an exposure of approximately half an hour would probably be needed. Since reciprocity failure manifests itself to different degrees with different types of film, no definite rule can be given, and information must be gathered through actual tests.

Practical application. To illustrate the degree to which a reading taken from the exposure meter may have to be revised before it can be applied to diaphragm and shutter, let us consider the following example: the subject—close-up in natural size of a dark red rose; the camera—35-mm. reflex with extension tubes; negative material—medium-fast panchromatic film; illumination—two photofloods; the filter—red filter for improved rendition of detail; the developer—fine-grain. Exposure according to meter should have been 1/10 sec. at f/20.

The following factors must be considered: rendition in natural size (p. 30)—4 times; unusually dark subject (p. 91)—1½ times; red filter (p. 51)—4 times; fine-grain developer (p. 114)—2 times. To get the final factor by which to multiply exposure as indicated by the meter, we must multiply the individual factors: $4 \times 1\frac{1}{2} \times 4 \times 2$ equals 48. Consequently, in order to get a fully exposed negative of the rose, we must expose—not 1/10 sec., but approximately 5 full seconds . . . which is quite a difference. . . .

Subjects that are too dark to register on the meter can be exposed according to the following tables. Data are computed for high-speed panchromatic film with an ASA speed of 400. However, if a slower pan-film with an ASA speed of only 200 or 125 is used, exposures must be doubled or tripled, respectively. If a super-fast pan-film such as Kodak Royal-X Pan (ASA 1250) is used, exposures can be reduced to one-quarter of the times suggested in the following tables. However, it is always advisable to take several shots at slightly different f-stops.

93

Subject	f/1.5	f/2	f/3.5	f/4.5
Movie entrances with people	1/300 to 1/100 sec.	1/200 to 1/50 sec.	1/50 to 1/20 sec.	1/25 to 1/10 sec.
Brightly lighted main streets	1/50 to 1/10 sec.	1/30 to 1/5 sec.	1/10 to 1/2 sec.	1/5 to 1 sec.
Ordinary city streets, neither exceptionally light nor dark	1/2 to 5 sec.	1 to 10 sec.	3 to 20 sec.	5 to 30 sec.
Very dark streets and corners, only occasional street lights	15 to 30 sec.	25 to 45 sec.	1 to 3 min.	2 to 5 min.
City skyline with lighted windows, long shots at 1/4 to 1/2 mile.........	1 to 3 sec.	2 to 5 sec.	5 to 15 sec.	10 to 25 sec.

EXPOSURE TABLE FOR CANDID THEATER SHOTS
(Computed for Tri-X film developed in Kodak D-76)

Brightness of stage lighting	f/1.5	f/2	f/2.8	f/3.5
Dim	1/20 to 1/10 sec.	1/10 to 1/5 sec.	1/5 to 1/3 sec.	1/4 to 1/2 sec.
Medium	1/50 to 1/30 sec.	1/30 to 1/25 sec.	1/20 to 1/15 sec.	1/15 to 1/10 sec.
Bright	1/300 to 1/150 sec.	1/200 to 1/100 sec.	1/100 to 1/50 sec.	1/60 to 1/30 sec.
Brilliant	1/400 to 1/200 sec.	1/250 to 1/125 sec.	1/125 to 1/80 sec.	1/80 to 1/50 sec.

Since determination of degree of illumination is subject to personal judgment, it is advisable to make several exposures with different shutter speeds or diaphragm settings to insure getting the best results.

CONCLUSIONS

Exposing can be reduced to a science. We can eliminate the greatest source of failure if, instead of relying on our eyes and "guessing" an exposure, we rely on dial readings, tables, and scientifically established exposure factors. If in doubt, take several exposures at different diaphragm or shutter-speed settings to be certain of at least one perfectly exposed negative. The best way of "bracketing" such a series is to shoot around an exposure that is likely to be correct, starting with an exposure that is probably slightly too short, and doubling the exposure with each consecutive shot. If, for practical reasons, only one exposure can be taken, one should remember that overexposure is always preferable to underexposure. For a quick checkup and recapitulation, here is a list of the most common causes of underexposure:

Incorrect use of meter (too much sky light!)

Film-speed dial incorrectly set (difference between daylight and tungsten rating!)

Filter factor not considered, or wrong factor used

Fine-grain developer factor not considered (exposure would have been all right if negatives had been developed in a standard developer)

If several factors are involved, one may have been forgotten, or a factor may have been added instead of multiplied

The close-up factor may have been forgotten (this applies only if subject distance is five times the focal length of the lens or shorter)

How to Use Artificial Light

Natural light is usually a more or less given factor over which the photographer has only limited control. By contrast, artificial illumination is completely subject to the photographer's control. Though it may often be inadequately "handled," natural light, because of its very "naturalness," can never be really "bad" as far as pictorial considerations are concerned. Artificial illumination, however, because of its flexibility that makes it adaptable to any imaginable purpose, positively invites misuse. With the aid of artificial light, the most unusual effects can be produced. But unless illumination—whether natural or artificial—is arranged and controlled by the photographer to express specific ideas or feelings, the result is apt to be confused, haphazard, or meaningless.

PURPOSE AND PRINCIPLES OF LIGHTING

Before he starts to take a picture, a photographer should know what he expects his "lighting" to do. A few moments of constructive thinking often make the difference between "knowing" and "guessing," planned experimentation and random "trial," success and failure, satisfaction and disgust. In photography, light plays a triple role:

1. Light Is the Photographic "Medium."

Light is to the photographer what color is to the painter; stone, clay, and wood to the sculptor; and sound to the composer. In perfect darkness, even the best photographer is helpless. With the aid of light, he can do almost anything. Light has as many nuances and degrees as "color" or "sound." "Light" and "dark" are essentially the same, being different manifestations of the same medium, infinite in their number of shades and transitions, and different in value only. Differences in value produce differences in impression and "mood." Illumination sets the "key" of a picture. Basically, lightness is gay, darkness is somber. Over-all lightness can make a photograph friendly, joyous, exhilarating. Over-all darkness tends to make it somber, sad, or depressing. Between these extremes, any mood

95

from objective documentation to subjective interpretation can be projected by a photographer who has a "feeling" for light and knows how to handle it.

For example: The interior of a night club must be photographed. The "mood" of the place is one of intimacy, darkness pierced by many tiny lights. In order to preserve this mood, which is the outstanding "quality" of the subject, a photographer with "feeling" for light will take the picture more or less "as is." He may use carefully subdued "fill-in lights" to indicate shadow detail—but no more light than is absolutely necessary to create the right "atmosphere" and avoid an impression of unrelieved black. On the other hand, a photo-reporter without much feeling for "mood," determined to get a "technically perfect negative," may simply take the picture with flash. Naturally, his picture will be sharper and more detailed than that of the first photographer, gradation will be better, contrast less abrupt, and the motion of the people will be "stopped." In short, he will get everything but the mood of the place, which he destroyed in a burst of uncontrolled light. His will be a beautiful negative but a bad picture.

2. Light as Creator of Volume and Form

Volume and space are three-dimensional, while a photograph has only two dimensions. Therefore, to directly "translate" volume and space into a photograph is physically impossible. All a photographer can do is to create an illusion of three-dimensionality. If he succeeds, his subjects acquire "roundness" and "volume," and his space has "depth"; if unsuccessful, his photographs appear "flat."

Light is the most important medium for creating an illusion of volume, roundness, and depth. If a face is illuminated from directly in front with "shadowless" light, it appears "flat." However, if the light is moved to one side to cast shadows, the same face then acquires volume and depth.

Any draftsman knows that "shading" adds depth to his drawing. This is true also of a photograph. Drowned in a flood of uncontrolled light, even a veritable "Venus" will appear as "flat" as a paper doll. On the other hand, properly lighted, even a shallow bas-relief can have volume and depth. It is the interplay of light and shadow that creates an illusion of three-dimensionality.

3. Light and Shadow as Black and White

In a photograph, brightly illuminated objects appear white, and objects in deep shadow appear black. In between lies a range of different shades of gray. These "graphic" qualities of an illumination are just as important pictorially as the space-effect-creating qualities of light. White is dominating and aggressive; black is passive and receding. In a picture, white areas attract attention first and can be used to lead the eye of the observer to points of major interest. Black induces a feeling of strength, solidity, and power. Gray is neutral. To make white appear "whiter" it has to be contrasted with black. To make black appear "blacker" it has to be contrasted with white. White or black contrasted with gray appear less pronounced than contrasted with each other.

Through selection of the right kind of illumination almost any subject can be photographed either as it appeared to the eye, or lighter, or darker. To convince yourself of this, make the following experiment: take a small black object and place it in front of a white background. Illuminate the setup evenly with a photoflood, then take a picture. It will show object and background in their natural values of black and white. Now place the light much closer and adjust it so that it strikes the object fully but leaves the background in shade. The resulting picture will show the originally black object as white against a background of black. As a third step, "balance" the illumination until both object and background appear as identical shades of gray. Such a series illustrates not only that light can be used to create different graphic effects but also the dangers that result from incompetently handled illumination.

HOW TO LIGHT A PICTURE

Anyone who wants to acquire more than a theoretical knowledge of the functions of different types of lights should repeat the following experiment in portraiture. It will teach him, step by step, how to build an effective illumination. For this experiment he requires a model and four lights.

Preparations: Pose the model comfortably and naturally in front of a neutral background. Darken the room illumination until there is just enough light left to see what you are doing, but not enough to interfere with the effect of your lights.

The Main Light

The first step: Place the "main light." Its purpose is to establish the form of the subject and to fix roughly the ratio of light to dark. It is the most important of your lights. The ideal main light is a large spotlight, approximating the effect of the sun. If you lack this type of light, a No. 2 photoflood can be substituted. Place the light approximately 45 degrees to one side and 45 degrees above the model. This position automatically produces a good illumination. Later, as your experience grows, you may try other positions for more spectacular effects. But at the beginning it is advisable to stick to a "safe" setup. The main light is placed correctly if what it reveals makes sense and does not merely consist of a number of unrelated meaningless spots of illuminated subject matter. It must accentuate the main forms of the subject, modulate its planes with "plastic" light, and throw strong and significant shadows. Regardless of how much or how little it reveals, what we see must be graphically pleasing in composition, pattern, and black-and-white effect. The ratio of light to shadow sets the "key" of the picture. Predominance of light makes a photograph gay and "light," predominance of shadow creates a more serious, "glamorous," or somber impression. Equal distribution of light and dark should normally be avoided because the effect is dull.

The Fill-in Light

The second step: Place the fill-in light. Its purpose is to lighten slightly the shadows cast by the main light—just enough so they will not print too black but will show indications of detail.

The fill-in light should be a well-diffused photoflood. It should be placed as close to the camera as possible and slightly higher than the lens. In this position there is the least danger of producing "shadows within shadows" —separate crisscrossing shadows cast respectively by the main and the fill-in light. Such double shadows are extremely ugly and must be avoided. Multiple shadows result because the fill-in light is either too strong or placed too far away from the camera. To attempt to "kill" a shadow within a shadow by using an extra light is futile since this only produces an additional set of shadows.

The fill-in light is properly placed if it does not change the character of the illumination produced by the main light. Its function is to reduce over-all contrast in the negative to a printable level.

The Accent Light

The third step: Place the "accent light." Its purpose is to enliven the rendering by adding highlights and sparkle.

The accent light should be a small spotlight that can be focused on definite areas. It is used as a backlight to highlight the outlines of the subject, to add catchlights, glitter, and sparkle. Since it must be placed somewhere in back and to one side of the subject, it cannot cast "secondary" shadows. However, care must be taken to prevent it from shining into the lens and producing flares and ghost images on the film. A sheet of cardboard between light and lens will prevent this.

The accent light should be used sparingly and with discrimination. Its

98

effects are the final touches that give a picture sparkling life and make a print colorful and rich. They are the seasoning that flavors the picture, and if we overdo it, the result is comparable to that of too much pepper in the soup.

The Background Light

The fourth step: Place the "background separation light." Its purpose is to separate subject and background graphically through contrast between light and dark.

This lamp can be either a spotlight or a photoflood. What matters most is not the quality of its light but its correct intensity and position, both of which must be adjusted carefully by placing it at the proper distance from the background it must illuminate. By lightening the background behind the shadow side of the model and leaving it in shade on the highlighted side, the photographer graphically separates model and background and introduces "air" into his picture. A well-placed background separation light creates that feeling of "roundness" and space without which the model seems to "stick to the background." Contrast between light and dark creates the illusion of space.

CONCLUSIONS

The lighting scheme described above produces what might be called a "standard illumination." It is always successful, and can be used equally well to light a girl or a grasshopper, a dahlia or a drill press. It applies to incandescent light as much as to flash or speedlight illumination. It can be varied in innumerable ways simply by varying the intensity or spread of the different lights. By changing the ratio of light to dark, one can produce pictures that are either gayer or more somber. By increasing the contrast until the shadows print pure black, one can achieve the typical "Hollywood glamor lighting," guaranteed to produce the most seductive effects. Once a photographer has familiarized himself with the purpose and effect of the different lights he can do anything he likes, and will succeed as long as he observes the following basic rules that apply to any type of lighting scheme:

1. Never add a second light until you are thoroughly satisfied with the effect of the first.

2. Crisscrossing shadows must be avoided at any price.

3. Too much light and too many lights will spoil any lighting.

99

ADVICE TO USERS
OF ELECTRIC POWER

Ordinary home wiring is dimensioned for average household needs. By comparison, photographic lights consume relatively large amounts of power. To find out how many photofloods, etc., can safely be connected to one circuit, multiply the voltage of the power line by the number of amperes of the fuse. The result is the number of watts that can safely be drawn from one circuit. For example, if the line carries 110 volts and the fuse can take a load of 15 amperes (this is the most common combination), multiply 110 by 15. The result is 1650 watts, the maximum load that you may draw from this circuit without danger of blowing a fuse. Divided among your photofloods, it means that you can use simultaneously either three 500-watt bulbs, or two 500-watt and two 250-watt bulbs, or one 500-watt and four 250-watt bulbs, or six 250-watt bulbs. In any case, the combined wattage of these lights amounts to 1500 watts, which leaves 150 watts available for other purposes (for example, ordinary ceiling lights).

To avoid blowing a fuse, additional lights must be connected to a different circuit. You can easily determine the different circuits in your house by connecting lamps to different outlets and unscrewing the fuses one by one. All the lamps that go out when a certain fuse is unscrewed connect to the same circuit, while the lamps that remain lit are controlled by a different fuse (and the outlets they are connected to belong to a different circuit).

The fuse is the safety valve of the power line. It is an "artificial weak link" designed to break under overload in order to protect the line and save it from destruction. If you accidentally blow a fuse, do not replace it with a stronger one, and don't ever use a penny instead of a fuse. If you do, the next time it will be the power line itself that melts, and the resulting short circuit may start a fire that can burn down the house.

HOW TO USE FLASH

While all the rules of good lighting apply to any kind of illumination, regardless of whether it is produced by incandescent light or flash, there is one practical difference between the two: incandescent light is constant and steady; flash bursts into light and is extinguished within a fraction of a second. This characteristic of flash (and speedlight) complicates its use in two respects:

1. *The effect of the illumination* cannot be studied before the exposure, and especially if several flashbulbs are used simultaneously (multiflash),

100

exact prediction of the over-all effect of the illumination is extremely difficult, if not impossible. To solve this problem, many photographers balance their illumination, compose, and focus, with the aid of photofloods. Then, when everything is set, they switch over from house current to battery (flash gun), replace the photofloods with flashbulbs without changing the positions of their lights, start the action, and flash the picture at a high shutter speed. Matters can be simplified if two independent sets of lights are used, photofloods and flashbulbs (in separate reflectors) mounted side by side on the same light-stands. In this way, no time is wasted in exchanging bulbs and reconnecting wires.

2. *The exposure cannot be determined* with the aid of an exposure meter. However, manufacturers have assigned special "guide numbers" for different types of flashbulbs and speedlights in conjunction with different shutter speeds. Tables containing such data are available at any photo store, usually free of charge. Exposure is then computed as follows: find the guide number that corresponds to the type of flashbulb, film, and the shutter speed you intend to use, then divide this number by the distance in feet from flashbulb to subject. The resulting figure is the diaphragm number that must be used to produce a correctly exposed negative.

Very important: The diaphragm number established in the procedure described above is correct only if the flashbulb illuminates the subject from directly in front, and only if a single bulb is used. In all other instances, the diaphragm number must be adjusted as follows: for sidelight, increase the diaphragm opening by one stop; for backlight, increase the diaphragm opening by two full stops—always provided that only a single flashbulb is used. If two or more flashbulbs are used simultaneously (multiflash), *only the bulb that acts as the "main light" should be considered* when computing the diaphragm stop; all others (for backlight, fill-in, etc.) must be disregarded. However, if "main-light illumination" is provided by a number of flashbulbs of the same size—all directed toward the same subject area—the diaphragm must be computed for only one bulb and then adjusted by decreasing the opening by one full stop for each two bulbs. If a number of identical flashbulbs are strung out in order to evenly cover a large area in an over-all shot—each bulb illuminating only its own section of the subject—the diaphragm stop must be computed as if the shot were made with only one flashbulb at a bulb-to-subject distance equal to the average distance of all the bulbs.

These few rules are all there is to flashbulb exposure. They automatically lead to correctly exposed negatives, regardless of the type of lighting or the number of bulbs used. If negatives turn out unsatisfactorily, but the photographer is sure that he observed all the rules, the cause of the failure must be some mechanical breakdown of the equipment. The following table will help him to locate its source.

101

TROUBLE-SHOOTER CHART FOR FLASH PHOTOGRAPHERS

WHAT'S THE TROUBLE?	SYNCHRONIZER	BATTERIES	WIRES	CONNECTIONS	SHUTTER	LAMPS
Nothing happens when you press the switch	Switch or release button does not make contact	Batteries may be dead or inserted wrong side up, or case isn't closed tightly	Wire is broken somewhere, or not connected	Worn-out plug does not make connection		Faulty bulb (try different bulb)
Flash fires, but shutter does not work		Weak batteries (Very common)	Faulty tripper cord	Tripper wire not connected, or worn-out tripper plug	Maybe you forgot to cock the shutter	
Shutter works only after flash has fired	Synchronizer out of synchronization	Weak batteries (Very common)		Check tripper connections for corosion		
First few shots all right then shutter clicks after flash or not at all		Load gets too heavy for batteries; use more cells, or fresher batteries, or booster				
Shutter clicks all right but flash does not fire	Flash not pushed deep enough into socket		Broken wire	Bad connection		Faulty bulb (try different bulb)
Flash fires too late, after shutter has clicked	Corroded socket contacts			Corroded connections.		Solder on base corroded; rub base on emery cloth
Adding extensions causes shutter, which so far worked all right, to click after flash		Weak batteries; use fresher or more cells, booster, or flash with house current		Corroded connections		
Adding extensions causes both shutter and flash at camera, previously O. K, to go before extension flash		Weak batteries; use fresher or more cells, booster, or flash with house current	Try using heavier gauge wire	Corroded connections		
Extension flash does not fire		Weak batteries	Wire is broken	Extension not connected, or switch is off		Faulty bulb
Correctly exposed and developed negatives too thin in spite of apparently perfect working of flash	Synchronizer out of synchronization					Slow burning bulbs that go off like fireworks are "leakers" due to cracks or untight bulb-socket connection. They give off very little light only, cause underexposures.
Correctly exposed and developed negatives are blank in spite of apparently perfect working of flash and shutter					Forgot to cock shutter, to remove slide, to open the other shutter, to remove lens cap	
Flashbulb goes off the moment you insert it into the socket	Short circuit Switch is stuck		Wire plugged into remote-control outlet, or short circuit in cable	Short circuit		

POINTERS FOR PHOTO-SOPHOMORES

Arrange your illumination step by step. Start with the main light. Never add an additional light until the previous one is placed to your satisfaction.

Shadows that crisscross each other signify the beginner, or the blunderer.

Flat front light, and single flash at the camera, produce the pictorially worst type of photograph.

Sidelight renders surface texture better than any other type of light.

Backlight is the most dramatic type of illumination. Even if several flashbulbs failed to fire, you may still have a picture if your backlight went off.

In portraiture, the most important shadow is cast by the nose. It should not touch or cross the lips. If it does, the effect suggests a mustache or a beard—even if the subject is a girl.

Watch for the "blind spots" in a face and make sure that they receive enough light. You find them in the corners of the eyes near the nose, in the angles between nose and mouth, and beneath the jaw.

Concentrate your light toward the background and keep the foreground darker. Dark foreground suggests a frame around a print and guides the eye toward the center of the picture where interest belongs.

If you like prints with snap and sparkle, make sure you have pure black and white somewhere in your photograph.

Light is the strongest creator of mood. Arrange your illumination to fit the mood of your subject.

Keep your fill-in light well diffused in order to avoid the danger of shadows that criss-cross each other.

Light parts in a photograph usually draw the attention of the observer first; use light to guide the eye to points of major interest.

However, be careful when placing spots of brightness close to the edge of the picture; they may lead the eye out of your photograph.

Don't be afraid of pitch-black, detail-less shadows, provided such shadows are expressive in form and placed in such a way that they strengthen the pattern of the composition.

Place your fill-in lights high, so that their shadows will fall low.

Low-placed fill-in lights usually cast meaningless shadows and can completely mess up an otherwise clean background.

A fill-in light that is too weak is better than one that is too strong.

A fill-in light that is too strong produces almost the same flat effect as a single flashbulb at the camera.

Whenever possible, make use of natural light or local illumination.

PART FOUR

HOW TO DEVELOP AND PRINT

Introduction to the mysteries of the darkroom
—layout, equipment, methods, and techniques
—with special emphasis on simplicity, low
cost, and practical tips and suggestions

Photographer at the Crossroads—To Do or Not To Do

Having shot your pictures, you can do one of two things. You can take the exposed film to the drugstore or photo-finisher and have it processed. This is quite uninspiring, and so usually is the result: finished pictures that differ only little, if at all, from the average snapshot. Or you can do the finishing yourself. Doing the whole job of picture-making from start to finish literally doubles the pleasure you can get out of photography. And if you are ambitious, this is the only way to achieve your goal—to make pictures that have individuality—pictures that are enlarged, composed, and cropped according to *your* ideas; printed with the degree of contrast, lightness, or darkness that *you* visualized when you arranged the lights, selected the filter, calculated the exposure; "dodged," "burned in," or "held back" for most effective presentation of your subject.

To do all this you need a darkroom.

The Darkroom

To most beginners the concept of a "darkroom" is something rather formidable and expensive, the privilege of the "advanced amateur." Nothing can be further from the truth. A workable darkroom is literally nothing but a "dark room." It does NOT have to have running water, or built-in sinks, or waterproof floor. It does not even have to be "permanent" but can just as well be "improvised" somewhere in the corner of an ordinary room. Lack of a "real" darkroom is absolutely no excuse for sloppy workmanship or for doing no darkroom work at all. Many of our best photographers do some of their best work in improvised darkrooms which must be darkened each time before they can begin to work.

Qualifications

A workable darkroom must fulfill the following conditions:

1. *It must be dark.* If there are windows, they must be made light-tight by using opaque blinds. Black roller shades of the type used in lecture halls and auditoriums are ideal but expensive. Homemade blinds of masonite on wooden frames that fit tightly into the window casings are considerably less expensive and just as effective. If it is too difficult or too expensive to make special arrangements for darkening the windows, take the easy way out and develop and print at night when ordinary curtains are sufficient to keep out the feeble light of street lamps and sky. Minute amounts of stray light are usually harmless. To be sure, make the following experiment. Darken the room. Do NOT use the safelight.* Place a few

---

* A colored work light that will not affect emulsions (see p. 111).

coins on a sheet of film and a piece of sensitized paper, and leave them exposed on the worktable for three or four minutes. Then develop and fix both samples in darkness with the safelight turned off. Examine the fixed samples. If the film is perfectly transparent, and the paper perfectly white, your darkroom is dark enough, in spite of the slight amount of stray light. If the film is more or less gray except where it was protected by the coins, but the paper remains perfectly white, the darkroom is too light for developing, but dark enough for printing. If both film and paper are gray except where they were protected by the coins, the darkroom is too light for any kind of photographic work and the darkening arrangement must be improved.

2. *An electric outlet* is needed to plug in the safelight and the enlarger.

3. *The room temperature* should be anywhere between 65° and 80° F. If the room is colder or warmer, maintaining the correct temperature of solutions becomes too difficult. In winter, an electric heater can be used to raise the temperature. In summer, an exhaust fan built into the wall or door prevents a small (closet-type) darkroom from getting too hot. Special darkroom fans with light baffles are available at most photo stores.

4. *The water supply* should not be too far away. In the darkroom itself, a pail and a tray full of water are all that is needed. Negatives and prints can be washed later under a faucet anywhere outside the darkroom.

5. *The worktable* should be covered with linoleum, oilcloth, or have a plastic or wooden top impervious to water and photographic solutions. Several thicknesses of newspaper beneath the trays prevent accidentally spilled liquid from flooding the table or running down to the floor. However, a careful worker hardly ever spills any solutions, mainly because he does not fill his trays too high.

6. *The color of walls and ceiling* should be light to reflect a maximum of (safe!) light and thus improve visibility. The better we see, the more efficiently we work. The best wall and ceiling color is a light yellow-green, similar to the color of the Ansco safelight filter # A-6 or the Kodak Safelight Filter, Wratten Series 0A.

The fortunate photographer who has the run of the whole house should have no trouble finding a place to install a permanent darkroom of modest scale. The less fortunate apartment dweller, and especially one who lives in a furnished room, has to use a little more ingenuity to arrange a darkroom for his work. Arranged in order of suitability are the following suggestions for the location of permanent and improvised darkrooms:

The basement: A corner of a dry and finished basement which can be partitioned off is an ideal location for a darkroom. Advantages: fairly even temperature the year round; electricity and running water are usually near by; privacy and seclusion; permanency of the setup permits the gradual development into a first-rate darkroom.

A large closet: A closet of the type usually found only in old houses can easily be converted into an excellent darkroom provided the ventilation problem is solved by installing an exhaust fan with a light baffle. Negatives and prints can be washed in the bathroom.

The attic: Advantages are privacy and seclusion which permit a permanent setup. However, there are often serious drawbacks: it is too hot in summer, too cold in winter; and running water may not be available on the same floor.

An ordinary room: Advantages are plenty of space and even temperature the year round. Drawbacks: before he can start to work, a photographer must darken the windows, clean a table, set up his equipment, get water from the bathroom, unpack the enlarger, switch from desk lamp to safelight, etc. All this makes for extra work; but once it is done, operations should proceed just as smoothly and efficiently as in any permanent darkroom setup.

The bathroom: Despite certain advantages (running water, waterproof floor, light walls and ceiling), this is the least suitable location for a darkroom. Drawbacks: steam and moisture spoil equipment, chemicals, and sensitized material in a very short time; utter lack of privacy.

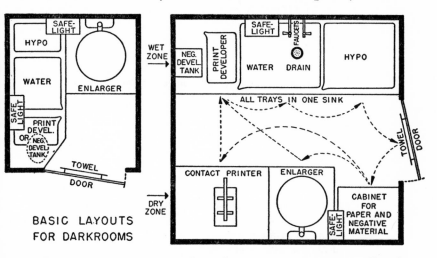

BASIC LAYOUTS
FOR DARKROOMS

The efficiency of any darkroom depends upon its organization. Cleanliness and order rank first. Strict separation of "dry operations" and "wet operations" follows in importance. On one side of the darkroom should be: negatives, paper, printer, enlarger; on the other side: developer, short-stop bath, hypo, water. In this way, negatives, which are the most valuable and vulnerable objects, are kept farthest away from liquids and chemicals, and the various steps in processing can be followed in logical and uninterrupted succession.

109

How much or how little he wants to spend on his darkroom equipment is almost entirely up to the photographer. Except for an enlarger, the essential pieces of equipment are relatively cheap. Expensive are those gadgets and accessories which mainly increase the comfort and ease of operations, as for example, electronic timers, motor-operated print washers, electric dryers, dry-mounting presses, and similar equipment. The following list contains only those items which are absolutely necessary for the successful operation of a darkroom.

General equipment
Safelight with interchangeable filters
Timer
Thermometer
2 graduates, large and small
Stirring rod
Several brown quart bottles for developers
Gallon bottle for fixer
Glass funnel
Apron
Towel

Material and equipment for negative development
Film developing tank
Negative developer
Short stop bath
Fixing bath (hypo)
Viscose sponge
Film clips

Material and equipment for printing and enlarging
Sensitized paper
Contact printing frame
Enlarger and paper easel
Developer trays in different sizes
Tray for stop bath
Deep tray for hypo
Two print tongs, black and white
Paper developer
Stop bath
Acid-fixing bath
Print washer and cork clips
Ferrotype tins and squeegee

The safelight. Special photographic darkroom lamps—Ansco, Kodak, etc.—with interchangeable filters are best. Colored incandescent bulbs are usually not "safe" and should be avoided. The color of the safelight filters depends on the type of work:

> *Dark green* * (Ansco #A-3; Kodak, Wratten Series 3) for panchromatic film development
>
> *Dark red* (Ansco #A-7; Kodak, Wratten Series 2) for orthochromatic film development
>
> *Yellow-green* (Ansco #4-6; Kodak, Wratten Series 0A) for paper development

Negative processing, and especially the loading of the developing tank with high-speed panchromatic film, should be done as much as possible in darkness in order to avoid accidental fogging. But successful printing and enlarging can be done only in a well-lighted darkroom. Ideal illumination is achieved as follows: suspend one large safelight turned toward the ceiling in the center of the darkroom for general illumination with indirect (reflected) light. Mount a small safelight next to the enlarger so that the light is directed onto the easel. Connect this safelight to the enlarger lamp by means of a two-way foot switch so that one light is on when the other light is off—the safelight goes off when you step on the switch to turn on the enlarger light for focusing and exposing, but goes back on when you take your foot off the switch. This arrangement makes focusing, calculation of exposure time, and dodging much easier than if the safelight were on constantly, for its light weakens the projected image. A third safelight should be mounted directly above the developer tray, its light shining on the developing paper for easy supervision of the developing print. Finally, a white light (with a 15-watt bulb) should be suspended above the hypo tray, its light directed downward and carefully shaded by means of a deep narrow reflector to prevent it from spilling beyond the fixing bath and fogging developing prints. It should be operated by means of a foot switch.

After a print has been in the hypo for about ten seconds, this light can safely be turned on by stepping on the foot switch, and the print can be examined. It is rather difficult to judge the exact shade and contrast of a print in yellow-green light, which tends to make the picture appear lighter than it actually is. Prints that appear "just right" under yellow-green light often appear too dark when dry and viewed by daylight.

---

* Since panchromatic film is sensitive to all colors, the recommended dark green filters are only "safe" if the lamp is at least four feet from the film. Its light is intended only for general darkroom illumination and NOT for close visual inspection of the negatives during development.

111

Timer and thermometer are indispensable for successful negative development. Excellent timers are made by General Electric and The Eastman Kodak Co. The thermometer should be accurate to within half a degree. Instruments with scales etched on the stem are most reliable. Separate scales which are not firmly anchored to the stem are apt to work loose in time and slide up and down, upsetting the accuracy of the thermometer.

Graduates are used for measuring definite quantities of developer stock solutions and diluting them with water in the prescribed proportions, and for dissolving chemicals. Glass graduates are preferable to enameled steel graduates, which rust when chipped, and to opaque porcelain graduates, which are more difficult to "read."

Stirring rods should be of glass or stainless steel, impervious to the action of chemicals. They must be cleaned immediately after use to avoid the contamination of one solution with chemicals from another.

Brown quart bottles with rubber stoppers should be used for storing developer solutions. Developers are sensitive to light, hence the brown-colored glass. Furthermore, developers are extremely sensitive to air, the oxygen of which affects and destroys the developing agent by oxidation, which gradually turns the almost colorless solution into an ugly dark brown fluid. For this reason, freshly prepared developer stock solutions should always be poured into several small bottles instead of being kept in a single large one. In this way, a small amount of developer can be withdrawn for use without the necessity of exposing the entire stock to the air. As a further precaution, bottles containing developer solution should always be kept completely filled. If there i not sufficient solution to make this possible, drop small glass marbles i to the solution until it reaches the proper height.

A gallon jug for storing hypo solution.

A glass funnel for pouring liquids back into their bottles after use, and for filtering solutions. Negative developers especially must be filtered each time before use to eliminate particles of emulsion resulting from previous development which otherwise may adhere to the developing films and cause spots. Filtering takes considerably less time than retouching spotty prints. To speed the filtering process, use absorbent cotton instead of filter paper.

An apron and a towel belong in every darkroom. Most developers cause indelible stains, and a single drop can spoil clothing. Non-absorbent plastic aprons are best. A towel should always be handy because wet fingers leave permanent marks on negatives and prints. Its degree of dampness is an indication of the manual skill of its user: an experienced craftsman hardly ever gets his fingers wet. Instead, he uses film hangers and print tongs for handling negatives and papers.

112

Film developing tank. Its size and construction depend, of course, upon size and type of the negative material. Some roll-film developing tanks have adjustable reels to accommodate different sizes of film. Some tanks for No. 120 and 35-mm. film can be loaded in daylight, eliminating the necessity for a darkroom, since printing and enlarging can be done at night in any ordinary room. All film reels and sheet-film hangers must be absolutely dry before they can be loaded; otherwise the film sticks the moment it hits a wet spot. Tanks and reels of stainless steel are more practical than those made of Bakelite, which may break when dropped. Plastic sheet-film hangers should be avoided.

Negative developer. Ready-mixed developers, prepared by the manufacturer either in powder or in the form of a stock solution, are more practical than developers which the photographer must make by combining the individual chemical components. Furthermore, they are generally more uniform and dependable, they can be stored almost indefinitely, and need only be diluted or dissolved in water to be ready for use. They eliminate the need for a scale and for storing a large number of different chemicals in space-consuming jars. They also eliminate a great deal of worry—about purity of chemicals, omission of an ingredient, inaccuracy of measuring and weighing, and waste due to deterioration, pollution, and incorrect storage of chemicals.

On the other hand, self-mixed developers are somewhat (though not much) cheaper than prepared formulas. Another advantage is that their exact composition is known to the photographer, who occasionally may want to modify the formula in order to vary the characteristics of the developer and to make it more suitable for a specific job.

While self-mixing has advantages for the more advanced amateur, beginners should use prepared formulas. Until more experienced, they should employ the brand of developer which the manufacturer of the negative material recommends. He made the film, he ought to know it best, and it is as much in his interest as in yours that *you* get the best possible results. After all, the manufacturer wants you to be satisfied so that you will buy more of his film.

113

Beware of all formulas that are advertised to produce a film grain "as fine as other fine-grain developers or finer" while simultaneously retaining the full speed of the film. Such a combination simply does not exist. Believe me, if such developers were possible, Ansco, Kodak, or any other big manufacturer would have made them long ago. So do not waste your money.

Do not overestimate the capacities of fine-grain developers. They can produce only a comparatively fine grain if they are properly used, if the film has an inherently fine grain, and if the negative is correctly exposed. Overdevelopment and overexposure always produce coarse grain.

Fine-grain developers have definite disadvantages: they require increases in exposure time up to three times "normal"—in other words, they cut the film speed by one half to two thirds—and they produce negatives of lower contrast than ordinary developers. This is not always desirable, and occasionally contrast must be increased by printing on a paper of harder gradation which, of course, once again emphasizes the grain.

Laboratory tests have shown that many standard developers will produce a film grain practically as fine as that produced by special fine-grain formulas if the developing time is somewhat shortened and negatives are developed to the same low contrast as those processed in fine-grain developers. The real advantage of fine-grain developers is the fact that they make it more difficult to overdevelop than standard developers.

Here are the characteristics of different types of developers:

1. *Standard developers* act fast and thoroughly, utilizing the full inherent speed of a film. They are intended mainly for processing comparatively large negatives (3¼ by 4¼ inches and larger). Typical examples are Kodak Developers DK-50 and D-76.

2. *Rapid developers* act more rapidly than standard developers and are widely used by professional photo-finishers and press photographers. They produce negatives of higher contrast and somewhat coarser grain. They are most suitable for the development of negatives with low-contrast subjects, and for "coaxing" the utmost out of underexposed films. Typical example: Kodak Developer HC-110.

3. *Fine-grain developers* produce negatives with a relatively fine grain and are mainly intended for the development of small-size films (2¼ by 2¼ inches and smaller). However, some fine-grain developers require certain increases in the exposure time of the negative. Individual factors depend on the type of developer and range from 1½ to 2 times normal exposure. Typical examples: B.P.I. Panthermic 777; Edward Minicol; FR X-33C; Kodak Developer Microdol-X.

4. *Ultra fine-grain developers* produce negatives with a finer grain than "ordinary" fine-grain developers. However, their exposure factors are higher and range from 2 to 3 times "normal" exposure. Typical example: Sease III, Windisch 665.

5. *Tropical development.* For high-temperature development, treat films in Kodak Prehardener SH-5 prior to development. This will harden the emulsion sufficiently to allow for normal processing procedures at solution temperatures up to 110°F. However, it is vitally important that all solutions including the wash-water have the same temperature.

6. *High contrast developers* produce negatives of more than ordinary contrast and are intended for the development of reproductions of black-and-white subject matter, line drawings, printed pages, etc. Typical example: Kodak Developers D-8 and D-11.

A number of useful and reliable developer formulas which the more advanced amateur can compound are reprinted on pp. 181-184.

The stop bath instantly terminates development by neutralizing the alkalinity of the developer retained by the emulsion of films and by sensitized papers. It furthermore protects the acidity of the fixing solution and prevents premature exhaustion of the bath. In conjunction with a hardening agent, the stop bath in warm weather serves to harden the gelatine of the film and to prevent it from curling, reticulating, and coming off along the edges. Formulas on p. 184.

The fixing bath ("hypo") serves to clear the negative by dissolving the undeveloped silver halides * which otherwise would in time darken and obscure the image. For practical reasons, most fixing baths contain an acid, a preservative, and a hardening agent. Such fixing baths are called "acid hardening fixing baths." They are available in prepared form or can easily be compounded by the photographer according to the formula reprinted on p. 186.

A viscose sponge is needed to wipe negatives carefully on both sides before they are hung up to dry. Otherwise, drops of moisture and adherent particles of emulsion would cause indelible spots on the film.

Film clips to hang films up to dry. Stainless steel is best. Each roll of film needs two clips, one at the top and one at the bottom to prevent the film from curling. For sheet film and filmpacks, hangers of stainless steel consisting of twelve clips attached to a rod are more practical than a great number of individual clips. In this way twelve sheets of film can be dried on each hanger.

---

* Light-sensitive particles of an emulsion.

Sensitized paper. All photographic papers, regardless of type or make, can be classified according to four different characteristics:

1. *Emulsion.* One must differentiate between two basically different types: slow-speed chloride and high-speed bromide papers. Between these are the medium-fast chloro-bromide emulsions. *Chloride papers* are used almost exclusively for contact printing for which they are especially suited because of their relatively slow speed. Faster emulsions would lead to impossibly short exposure times. *Bromide papers* are used exclusively for printing by projection (enlarging). Here, slow chloride emulsions would lead to impossibly long exposure times. The medium-fast chloro-bromide papers are equally suited to contact printing and enlarging.

2. *Gradation.* Gradation is the ability of a sensitized paper to render contrast. Most papers are manufactured in three to six different gradations, ranging from "soft" to "ultra hard." By selecting a paper with the appropriate gradation, the photographer can make drastic corrections of undesirable negative contrasts. For example, if a negative is too "hard" (contrasty), one can use "soft" paper, which reduces contrast, and produce a print in which contrast is normal. On the other hand, if a negative is too "soft" (contrastless, flat), the use of a "hard" paper, which increases contrast, will produce a normal print. Negatives in which contrast is normal should be printed, of course, on "normal" paper.

The gradation of photographic papers is usually designated by numbers: 1 designates soft gradation, 2 or 3 normal gradation, and 4 to 6 hard to ultra hard gradation.

3. *Surface.* The smaller the print is, the smoother should be the surface of the paper—if not, paper texture will obscure the fine detail of the image. Contact prints always look best on glossy paper. Larger projection prints can stand paper with rougher surfaces. Fancy surfaces, imitating the textures of canvas, tweed, silk, etc., are in bad taste. Prints intended for reproduction, regardless of size, must always be made on glossy paper, and should, preferably, be ferrotyped. Ferrotyping (see p. 138) gives glossy papers (other papers are not suited for this process) an extra smooth and shiny finish.

Glossy papers have a greater tone range than papers with rougher surface. Their whites are brighter, and their blacks richer and more lustrous. Prints on glossy paper always have more sparkle, and therefore give the

116

subject a more lifelike appearance than do prints on rougher surfaces. Glossy papers are most "typically photographic." Prints on very rough and fancy surfaces always look pretentious—as if the photographer were ashamed of his work, and had tried to improve it by imitating one of the "finer" arts.

The most commonly used color of photographic papers is white. The different shades of cream, ivory, buff, etc., in which some papers are available, in my opinion give a print a faded, sunburned, "yellow-from-age" appearance.

4. *Base weight.* One must differentiate between two thicknesses: Single Weight (Abbr.: SW.), which is relatively thin, and Double Weight (Abbr.: DW.), which is about twice as thick, corresponding in thickness to a heavy postcard. Single-weight papers are best suited for print sizes up to and including 8 by 10 inches, and for larger prints that have to be mounted. Double Weight papers are preferable for larger sizes. Single-weight papers are cheaper, wash and dry more rapidly, are easier to mount, and less bulky than double-weight stock. The latter, however, does not curl so easily, stands up better under rough treatment, and is generally preferable for prints that are exposed to much handling.

For final selection of all but glossy papers (which all look alike) consult the manufacturer's sample book of your dealer. When you order a specific paper, you must mention: the name of the manufacturer, the trade name of the paper, the gradation of the emulsion, the type and color of the surface, the weight of the stock, the size of the paper. Here is an example: Ansco Cykora—normal (No. 2), glossy, white, double weight, 11 by 14 inches.

Contact printing frame (or, if the higher price is no obstacle, a contact printer). Printing frames come in different sizes, corresponding to the different sizes of negatives. If negatives are contact-printed for record purposes only, printing all the frames of one roll together on a single sheet of paper has practical advantages. For this purpose an 8- by 10-inch printing frame is needed. It accommodates conveniently, on one sheet of 8-by-10 paper, twelve negatives 2¼ by 2¼, in the form of three strips of four frames each (or four strips of three frames each), or thirty-six miniature negatives 35 mm. in strips of six frames each, or four negatives 4 by 5 inches.

Enlarger and paper easel. An enlarger is nothing more than a camera in reverse. Any camera with a detachable back can be converted into an enlarger, simply by mounting a lamp behind it and shining the light through the negative and the lens onto a sheet of sensitized paper.

An enlarger, like a camera, has a lens that must be focused in order to produce sharp pictures, and a diaphragm that permits regulating the brightness of the projected image. Image size (the degree of enlargement) is directly proportional to the distance between lens and sensitized paper. But whereas a camera produces negatives by means of light from the outside, an enlarger produces prints with light that comes from within. There are three types of lighting systems:

1. *Condenser (specular) enlargers* are constructed like ordinary projectors. The lighting system consists of a projection lamp and a condenser (light-collecting lens). It produces extremely sharp, bright, and contrasty images. Advantages: shortest exposures, critical definition, excellent contrast. Disadvantages: owing to the extreme precision of rendition, blemishes of the negative—tiny scratches, abrasion marks, specks of dust, etc. —appear with utmost clarity in the print, and enlargements appear disproportionately "grainy."

Specular enlargers are excellent for photo-murals and reproductions, but they are not suitable for ordinary photographic work, especially not for the needs of the average amateur.

2. *Diffusion enlargers* represent the other extreme. The lighting system consists of an opal bulb (or a grid of fluorescent tubes) and a diffuser. It produces images that are relatively soft and contrastless. As a result, minor defects of the negative are suppressed in the enlargement to a surprisingly high degree, and prints appear grainless and smooth. On the other hand, prints often turn out too gray and flat unless negatives are rather contrasty. Diffusion enlargers are most suitable for large negatives from 5 by 7 inches up, for "pictorial" work of the more "romantic" type, and for "idealized" portraits of women and children. They are not recommended for amateur use.

3. *Diffuse-condenser enlargers* successfully combine most of the advantages of condenser and diffusion enlargers while avoiding their drawbacks. The lighting system consists of an opal bulb and a condenser. It produces images that are sharp but not painfully revealing, contrasty but not harsh, and prints that are relatively free from grain. *The majority of enlargers belong to this type, which is ideally suited to the needs of the average photographer and amateur.*

Combinations. Some of the more expensive enlargers, particularly in the larger sizes, provide interchangeability of lighting systems, and can be used alternately with either condenser, diffuser, or diffused condenser.

Manual focusing vs. automatic. Enlargers have to be focused just like cameras. This can be done in two ways: by hand or automatically. Manual focusing consists of racking the lens in or out while visually checking the sharpness of the projected image. In automatic focusing, the projected image is always sharp, regardless of the scale of the enlargement, because lens focusing is coupled mechanically with the vertical movement of the enlarger. Each system has its advantages and disadvantages. Manual focusing is more reliable, and accurate if done by a careful worker. On the other hand, manual focusing takes more time. Automatic focusing is much faster, but requires frequent checks to detect and correct unavoidable inaccuracies of focus caused by usage and wear. Moreover, auto-focus enlargers are naturally more expensive than manually operated instruments of the same type. As far as print quality is concerned, there need be no difference between the two.

The enlarger lens. Sharpness of definition and flatness of field are all-important. Speed is unessential. To get more manageable exposure times, most enlargements are made specifically with the diaphragm stopped down to approximately f/8. The best enlarger lenses are specially computed for short-distance work. Typical example: the Kodak Enlarging Ektar Lenses, which are available in focal lengths of 2, 3 and 4 inches.

The diaphragm of the enlarger lens should be equipped preferably with click stops which facilitate accurate stopping down in the semidarkness of the darkroom.

The negative carrier. Choose between two types: glass plates and glassless carriers. Glass plates always hold the film perfectly flat and in focus. However, dust and lint adhere to the four exposed surfaces, and the glass plates often produce "Newton rings"—irregular concentric shapes which are iridescent in all the colors of the rainbow, and which can drive a photographer "crazy.". . . Glassless negative carriers eliminate the danger of Newton rings and minimize the effects of dust and lint. However, they do not hold the negative as flat as glass plates, and consequently may cause partial unsharpness in the print. For negative sizes up to and including 2¼ by 2¼ inches, glassless carriers are more practical. For larger sizes, glass plates are preferable. Large negatives buckle more easily under the heat of the enlarger lamp than small ones, and need to be held more rigidly in focus.

The size of the enlarger. Many of the larger instruments permit interchangeability of lenses and condensers. By acquiring such a versatile instrument a photographer who owns two or more cameras for different film sizes can enlarge all his negatives by means of a single enlarger.

The scale of enlargement. Before one buys a specific enlarger, it is advisable to know by how many times it will enlarge a negative. Degree of enlargement is always measured "linear." For example, a 4- by 5-inch negative enlarged "twice linear" makes an 8- by 10-inch print; enlarged "four times linear," it makes a 16- by 20-inch print. Abnormally large prints, or exceptionally big enlargements of a small section of a negative, can be made by turning the enlarger head 180 degrees on its column and projecting onto the floor. Since not all enlargers permit such a backward turn of the enlarger head, it is advisable to check whether a particular instrument can be used in this way.

119

The light distribution must be uniform over the entire surface of the print. Some enlargers have "hot spots"—i.e., produce prints in which the center is darker than the edges. To check, expose a sheet of paper without a negative in the carrier. Select an exposure that will produce a medium shade of gray, develop, fix, and check for uniformity of tone. If the center of this test sheet is darker than the edges—showing a "hot spot"—light distribution is uneven and will cause subsequent trouble. Such an enlarger should be returned to the dealer and exchanged for a different make.

Distortion control. In a picture of a building taken with the camera tilted backward, the converging of verticals can be corrected during enlarging, by projecting the image on an easel that is not horizontal, but more or less tilted (see illustrations on p. 202). However, in order to create sufficient sharpness in depth to cover the entire enlargement, the enlarger lens has to be considerably stopped down. The result sometimes is impossibly long exposure times. This can be avoided if the negative carrier can be tilted independently of the lens. If the easel is then tilted correspondingly in the opposite direction, the converging verticals will be restored to parallelism, and the image will be sharp throughout, even though the diaphragm of the enlarger lens is wide open.

The easel. The best way to hold the sensitized paper flat and in focus is by means of an easel with adjustable masking strips that accommodate sheets up to and including 11 by 14 inches.

Developer trays. A good average size is 8 by 10 inches. Smaller trays are impractical, even for the development of smaller prints. Larger prints, of course, require larger trays. The best material is stainless steel. It outlasts any other material and is more economical in the long run than glass, which breaks, or enamel, which chips easily, rusts, and has to be discarded. Plastic trays should be avoided.

Stop bath tray. Same as above.

Fixing bath tray. It should be larger and, especially, deeper than the other trays. Again, stainless steel surpasses all other materials.

Print tongs. These are used for agitating and transferring prints from one solution to another. Touching prints with the fingers in processing usually causes spots and stains. Since hypo is "poison" to developers, two tongs are needed. One is used to agitate prints in the developer and to transfer them to the stop bath. Be very careful that the tongs do not touch the stop bath solution itself. The other tongs are used to transfer prints from stop bath to hypo and to agitate them during fixation. To prevent confusion, the developer tongs should be black plastic and the stop bath-hypo tongs white.

Paper developer. Such developer is different from negative developer in that it is faster and more contrasty in action. For best results, use the developer which the manufacturer of the paper recommends. Prepared

120

developers that need only be dissolved in water (or diluted if in liquid form) are most practical. Photographers who prefer to compound their own developer will find a good formula on p. 184.

Stop bath. Used as a short rinse between developer and hypo, it prevents prints from staining in the fixer because of insufficient agitation. Apart from this, it fulfills the same purpose as in the development of films (see p. 115; formula on p. 184).

Fixing bath. Acid hardening fixing baths are best for prints. Prepared fixers that need only be dissolved in water are most practical. A formula for self-mixing is reprinted on p. 186.

Print washer. A simple but extremely efficient print washer, in which the prints float on cork clips, can be built, according to the following sketches, by any roofer or tinsmith for a few dollars. Most commercial print washers are either less efficient or much more expensive.

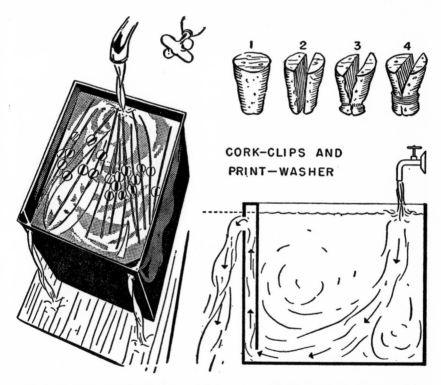

CORK-CLIPS AND
PRINT-WASHER

Ferrotype tins and squeegee. They are needed to give prints on glossy paper a high glossy finish. Matte and semi-matte prints are dried most conveniently in a *photo blotter roll*. Electric print dryers are much faster, but also much more expensive. The best models are "double-sided" and thermostat-controlled.

How to Develop a Film

Developing a film is hardly more difficult than boiling an egg. Anyone who can read a watch and a thermometer can do it successfully, for the time of development is determined by the temperature of the developer. If the developer is warm, the time of development must be shorter than if the developer is cold (the terms "warm" and "cold" used here cover a temperature range from 60° to 75° F.; "standard" temperature is always 68° F.). Naturally, different types of film, as well as different types of developer, require different "standard times" of development at 68° F. But these can be learned readily from the handy little tables and charts that film manufacturers provide for this purpose. One such chart is reprinted below for the purpose of demonstration.

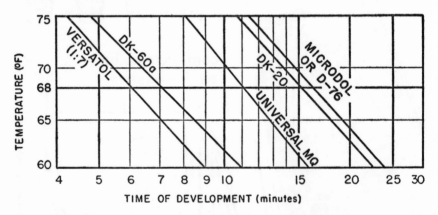

Time-Temperature Development chart for Kodak Plus-X roll film. It shows the developing times (for tank development) at various temperatures corresponding to recommended times at 68° F. Best results are obtained at 65° to 70° F.

To use this chart, find the diagonal that represents the developer you are going to use; find the horizontal that corresponds to the temperature of your developer; draw a vertical through the point of intersection of the two lines; find the correct time of development in minutes where this vertical intersects with the bottom of the chart.

Habits are easy to form but hard to change. It is important, therefore, that the photographic novice should learn from the outset correct methods of film processing. Specific instructions are given in the following sections. A few more general but equally important pointers are reprinted below.

Cleanliness is the first prerequisite for success—in the darkroom more so than elsewhere, because chemicals stain and solutions splash, and the resulting spots are "permanent."

Always perform the same operation in the same way. Standardize wherever you can. Develop a "system" for every step in processing films and prints—and stick to it!

Do not switch from one process or developer to another merely because someone else may have had success with it. Photography is as much a matter of individual taste and preference as any other art. Methods that are suited perfectly to someone else's way of working may be entirely unsuitable to you. Remember that there are about as many rumors in photography as in politics and war, and most of them are just as unfounded.

Without gauges and instruments, no airplane could fly, no car could be driven safely, no ship could be maneuvered. The same applies to photography if you wish to bring it under control and are not content with occasional success. These are the control instruments of our craft: EXPOSURE METER, TIMER, THERMOMETER. There are only these three, but they are indispensable. Use them constantly.

Do not try to "save" on material, least of all on developer, fixer, and chemicals. Most of them are comparatively cheap anyway. Before the developer and fixer are exhausted (see table on p. 177), replace them with fresh solutions. "Saving" on chemicals leads inevitably to the waste of much more valuable things, such as irreplaceable negatives, irrevocable opportunities, precious time. It always means that something must be done over—provided that you get a second chance.

Buy only products of well-known, reputable manufacturers. "Nameless" films, developers, and chemicals sold by certain chain stores are admittedly cheaper. Unfortunately they are often outdated stock bought up in bulk for quick resale to "suckers," or are so inferior in quality that they are practically valueless. After all, is it worth while to spend time, energy, money, and enthusiasm only to discover that it was all in vain because your material was inferior?

If you feel like "giving up" after comparing your pictures to the superior work of more famous and experienced photographers, remember that even Eisenstaedt and Bourke-White were once beginners, and that they depended on the friendly advice of authorities, or had to learn from their own mistakes.

123

A photographic emulsion consists of a suspension of minute crystals of light-sensitive silver halide in gelatine. Under the influence of light, the crystals of the emulsion undergo chemical changes: a "latent"—i.e., invisible—image is formed, its character depending on the intensity of the light that produced it. To transform the latent image into a visible one, the exposed emulsion has to be "developed"—i.e., reduction of the light-struck silver salts has to be completed by treating them with chemicals which separate the silver from the salts, and which deposit it in the form of minute, irregular tangles of metallic silver—the "grain" of which the image is composed. Such chemicals are called developing agents (see p. 179). To make the resultant image permanent, the remaining unexposed and undeveloped silver halides, which upon exposure to light would darken and obscure the image, must be converted into a soluble form so they can be washed out of the emulsion. This is the purpose of the fixing bath. Finally, the undeveloped salts, together with all the chemicals used in developing and fixing, have to be eliminated by washing the film in water.

PRACTICAL
FILM DEVELOPMENT

The exposure and development of films have been standardized so completely that the best results are obtained by the most thoroughly mechanized method. Intelligent use of the three control instruments, *exposure meter, timer, and thermometer,* enables a photographer to produce negatives that are technically far superior to those obtained by subjective methods. In my opinion, exposing negatives "by experience" and developing them "by visual inspection" is obsolete and inferior to the "time and temperature method" of negative development, which will be discussed below.

Preparations

Regardless of the type of film or developer, the preliminary steps are the same. Consult the chart on the opposite page as you go along.

Darken the room. See suggestions on p. 107. A simple test to determine whether a room is dark enough for negative processing has already been given on pp. 107-108.

How to develop a __film__ in a tank which must be loaded in darkness, but has a cover that makes the changing of solutions possible by ordinary light.

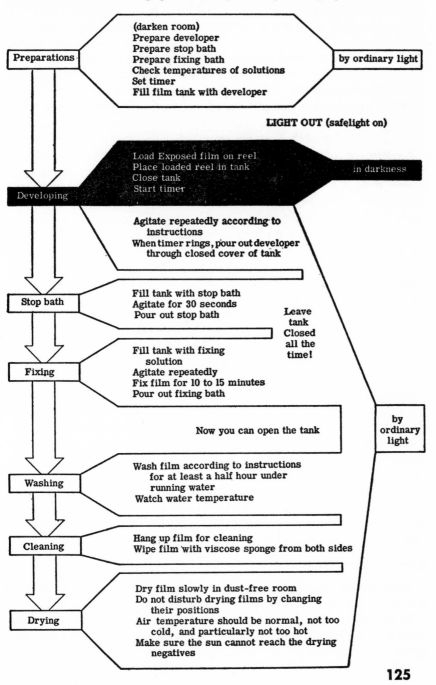

Preparations

(darken room)
Prepare developer
Prepare stop bath
Prepare fixing bath
Check temperatures of solutions
Set timer
Fill film tank with developer

by ordinary light

LIGHT OUT (safelight on)

Developing

Load Exposed film on reel
Place loaded reel in tank
Close tank
Start timer

in darkness

Agitate repeatedly according to
    instructions
When timer rings, pour out developer
    through closed cover of tank

Stop bath

Fill tank with stop bath
Agitate for 30 seconds
Pour out stop bath

Leave
tank
Closed
all the
time!

Fixing

Fill tank with fixing
    solution
Agitate repeatedly
Fix film for 10 to 15 minutes
Pour out fixing bath

by
ordinary
light

Now you can open the tank

Washing

Wash film according to instructions
    for at least a half hour under
    running water
Watch water temperature

Cleaning

Hang up film for cleaning
Wipe film with viscose sponge from both sides

Drying

Dry film slowly in dust-free room
Do not disturb drying films by changing
    their positions
Air temperature should be normal, not too
    cold, and particularly not too hot
Make sure the sun cannot reach the drying
    negatives

125

Prepare the developer. Decide what type of developer to use by consulting the survey on p. 114. When in doubt, follow the recommendations of the film manufacturer. Before using a fine-grain developer, see that the film was exposed accordingly, otherwise negatives will turn out too thin. Developer formulas appear on pp. 181-184. Instructions for compounding developers are on p. 180. It is always a good practice to filter a developer before using it—elimination of foreign matter reduces greatly the danger of spotty negatives. Simply pour the solution through a funnel that is loosely stopped with a wad of cotton. Do not filter developers that are too cold. (See p. 173.)

Prepare the stop bath. Formula on p. 184.

Prepare the fixing bath. In using a prepared fixer, follow instructions very closely in dissolving its components. Otherwise the bath may spoil immediately. A fixing bath formula is printed on p. 186; instructions for preparing fixing baths on p. 185. If the bath has been used before, make sure it has not been exhausted (see table on p. 177).

Check the temperature of all solutions. The normal temperature is 68° F. Differences of seven degrees, higher or lower, are harmless, provided that all solutions have the same temperature, wash water included. This is very important. Differences in temperatures of solutions can cause reticulation (see picture on p. 153). Solutions that are too hot may melt the emulsion of the film and cause it to float off its base. Solutions that are too cold act sluggishly and erratically, or do not act at all. If temperatures are higher than 75° F., or lower than 60° F., cool or heat by floating in the solutions a small aluminum cup filled with cracked ice or very hot water.

Set the timer. The time of development depends on the type of film and the type and temperature of the developer. Consult the manufacturer's charts (see example on p. 122). Determine the correct time of development in accordance with the temperature of the developer.

Fill the film tank with developer. Make sure it is filled neither too high (or else it will overflow when you immerse the film reel), nor too low (or else a strip along the edge of the film will be incompletely developed).

Arrange film, film reel, and film tank cover so you can find them easily in the dark. Then turn off the light. If you are working with panchromatic film, turn off the safelight also.

Roll Film Development

Load film on reel. Before you risk your first exposed film, use a roll of *unexposed* film and practice loading the reel—first in daylight, then in the dark. Loading a film reel is easy when you have the knack. However, the first time something may go wrong, so do not risk your first exposed film. Be sure that the film reel is *completely dry.* Otherwise, the film will stick the moment it hits a wet spot, will have water spots, kinks, and scratches, and you will have what is called in movie production jargon a "film salad."

Place the loaded reel in the tank. Tap it sharply a few times against the tank bottom in order to dislodge air bubbles trapped between the coils of the film. Place the cover on the tank.

Start the timer immediately.

Now you can turn on the white light provided, of course, that your tank has a lighttight cover.

Agitate repeatedly. Correct agitation is of the utmost importance for the production of uniformly developed negatives of correct density. It is essential to avoid mechanical uniformity of agitation, which may cause streaky development. For this reason, motor-driven agitators are not to be recommended. Their action is too even and is more likely to produce streakiness than to prevent it. After the film has been in the developer for approximately half a minute, start agitation by holding the tank in both hands and vigorously moving it backwards and forwards (in the manner of a cocktail shaker) while tilting and rotating it simultaneously. Continue this for approximately five seconds. Repeat at half-minute intervals during the entire period of development. If you use a daylight-loading tank, or a tank in which you can turn the reel by means of a rod inserted through the cover, rotate the reel back and forth for the first minute, and there-after for approximately five seconds every two minutes, until development is completed. In addition, every second time, *turn off the white light,* remove the tank lid, lift the reel completely out of the tank, and plunge it in again in order to stir the developer vertically as well as horizontally.

When the timer rings, without removing the cover of the tank, pour the developer back into the bottle and fill the tank with the stop bath.

Stop bath. Agitate for thirty seconds, then pour the stop bath out through the tank cover and discard it. It can be used only once. Pour in the fixing solution.

Fixing solution. Agitate at once for half a minute, repeat again several times during the next ten minutes.

Now you can take the cover off the tank.

Washing. Correct washing is of the utmost importance to the perma‑nency of the negative. Even minute traces of chemicals left in the emul-sion may in time produce discoloration and fading of the image. Roll film can be washed on the reel in the developing tank. First, put a piece of cork underneath the reel so as to raise it until the opening of the center core is higher than the edge of the tank. Then put the tank under the faucet and let a thin stream of water run directly into the center core of the reel. Another method, equally effective, is to connect one end of a piece of rubber hose to the faucet and put the other end in the hollow center of the reel. In both cases, water is forced through the core of the reel, out at the bottom, and up through the coils of the film, taking with it all the chemicals that have to be removed. Most other methods of washing are less efficient. Washing films in a sink or tray by simply letting water run into the vessel and out over the edge is less effective since hypo is heavier than water and sinks to the bottom, where it is more slowly removed by this method of "washing."

If a greater quantity of films have to be processed, time can be saved by suspending the negatives on cork clips and then washing them in the print washer described on p. 121. Position of the clips must be changed once during the washing.

The temperature of the wash water must be within five degrees of the temperature of the other solutions, otherwise the negatives may reticulate (see picture, p. 153). Occasional temperature checks during washing are recommended. Negatives must wash for at least half an hour under water running fast enough to fill the washing vessel every five minutes.

Cleaning. Remove the thoroughly washed film from the water, place a film clip on one end, and hang it up. With a well-soaked viscose sponge, carefully wipe both sides to remove water drops, gelatine particles, and other foreign matter. Thirty-five-millimeter films have to be cleaned especially well because the smallest specks of foreign matter will appear huge in the strong enlargements. Moreover, if the emulsion is very soft, it is almost impossible to rid the film completely of tiny particles of gelatine, because wiping only loosens more particles from around the edges of the perforation holes. To prevent this from taking place, rinse the thoroughly washed film briskly under the faucet, on both sides, immerse it for about two minutes in a 2 per cent solution of a wetting agent, take it out, and hang it up to dry without touching the emulsion again. The wetting agent will cause the water to run off smoothly, and the film will dry perfectly clean. Check the film after ten minutes. If a few drops have formed, remove them, not by wiping, but by absorbing them with the corner of a moist viscose sponge. Some wetting agents precipitate in the presence of calcium, and must be used with distilled water only. Consult the manufacturer's instructions.

Drying. Films must be dried slowly and evenly in clean air. Rapid drying seems to increase the size of the negative grain. Drying under a fan is the surest way of ruining a film, because the forced draft propels particles of dust and dirt, like tiny projectiles, into the emulsion—i.e., if unfiltered air is used. Films that were disturbed during the drying process may appear streaky, for changes in position usually cause changes in temperature and air currents, affecting the rate of drying. The part that dries faster will look different from the part of the negative that dries more slowly. To prevent drying roll films from adhering, space them far enough apart, and weight their lower ends with film clips.

Filmpack Tank Development

As far as the principle is concerned, filmpack is developed exactly like roll film, except that the individual sheets are developed in the compartments of a special "cage" instead of on a reel. Sometimes the film back tends to stick to the walls of the cage. This can be prevented by leaving the paper backing on the films to provide a separator between film and cage. Pound the loaded tank a few times on the table to dislodge air bubbles, then agitate at half-minute intervals by turning the tank once slowly end over end. After completion of development, take the sheets out—of course in darkness—tear off the paper backings, rinse the negatives for half a minute in the stop bath, and fix them in a tray. To insure complete fixation, leaf through the stack of film sheets two or three times immediately after immersion, then once every two minutes until fixation is complete. Suspend films at one corner on cork clips and wash for at least half an hour under running water in the tank described on p. 121. Take them out, wipe both sides carefully, and hang them up to dry, following the instructions given above.

Sheet Film and Glass Plate Tank Development

In darkness, load the developing hangers, lower them smoothly into a developer-filled tank, and start the pre-set timer. Strike the hangers down hard two or three times to dislodge air bubbles, then agitate vertically for approximately five seconds. Leave the hangers undisturbed for one minute, then lift the whole rack out of the solution, let the developer drain from one corner, then put the hangers back into the tank. Repeat this operation once every minute for the entire duration of development, draining the hangers alternately from different corners.

When the timer rings, lift the whole rack out of the tank, drain, and put into a second tank filled with a stop bath. Lift and drain four or five times, drain, and transfer the hangers to a third tank filled with fixing solution.

Agitate the negatives vertically in the fixer for half a minute, then lift and drain hangers once every two minutes for the entire duration of fixation. From here on, proceed by white light.

Wash the negatives in their hangers in a fourth tank, or float them suspended by one corner on cork clips in the tank described on p. 121. The negatives must be washed under running water for at least half an hour. Take them out of their hangers, wipe both sides carefully, and hang them up to dry according to instructions given above.

Filmpack and Sheet Film Tray Development

If up to six filmpack or sheet film negatives must be developed in a hurry, the following method can be used provided that the operator is careful, has short fingernails, and that the temperature of the developer

129

is not higher than 68° F., otherwise the film gelatine softens and becomes too vulnerable.

In darkness, immerse the exposed negatives, emulsion side up, one after another in a tray of water not warmer than 68° F. Be sure the first film is completely immersed before you place the next one on top of it, otherwise they will stick together permanently. After the last film is immersed, carefully draw the bottom film out and place it on top of the pile, touching it only at the extreme edges. Be careful that its corners do not scratch any of the other films. Similarly, take one film after another from the bottom and place it on top until the whole stack has been leafed through twice.

Start the pre-set timer and transfer the films to the developer, pulling one at a time from the bottom of the water tray. Repeat the operation of slowly leafing through the films from bottom to top for the entire duration of the development, turning the negatives sideways once in a while, but always keep the emulsion side facing up.

When the timer rings, transfer the negatives individually to the stop bath, leafing through them twice as described above.

Finally, remove the films one by one to the fixer and, immediately after immersion, repeat the performance of leafing through the pile twice, then continue every two minutes until fixation is complete.

Suspend films by one corner on cork clips, and wash for at least half an hour under running water in the tank described on p. 121.

Clean and dry as previously outlined.

How to Make a Print

One must differentiate between "contact prints" and "enlargements." The latter are also called projection prints or blowups.

A contact print is identical in size to the negative from which it is made. It is a true positive replica of the negative with most of its merits and faults. Contact prints are made with the aid of a printing frame (or a contact printer) on slow chloride papers (see p. 116).

An enlargement is, of course, always larger than the negative from which it is made. It is possible to a very high degree to control enlargements, and to extensively correct undesirable features of the negative. Enlargements are made with the aid of an enlarger (see p. 117) on fast bromide or medium fast chlorobromide papers (see p. 116).

Aside from these differences, the processing of contact prints and enlargements is identical.

130

How to make a contact print

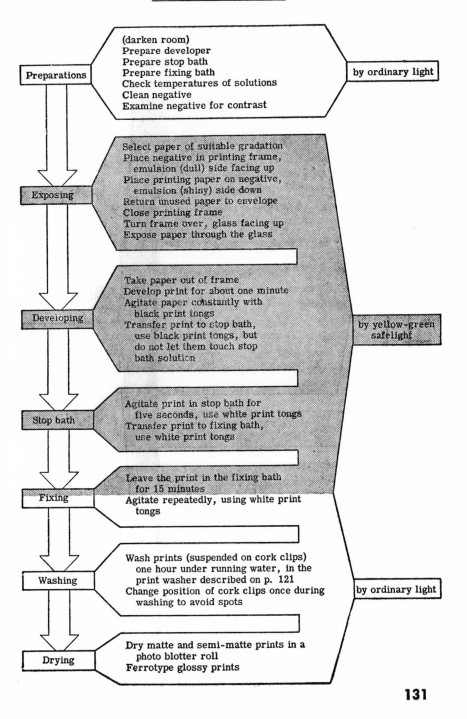

| Preparations | (darken room) Prepare developer Prepare stop bath Prepare fixing bath Check temperatures of solutions Clean negative Examine negative for contrast | by ordinary light |

Exposing
Select paper of suitable gradation
Place negative in printing frame,
  emulsion (dull) side facing up
Place printing paper on negative,
  emulsion (shiny) side down
Return unused paper to envelope
Close printing frame
Turn frame over, glass facing up
Expose paper through the glass

Developing
Take paper out of frame
Develop print for about one minute
Agitate paper constantly with
  black print tongs
Transfer print to stop bath,
  use black print tongs, but
  do not let them touch stop
  bath solution

by yellow-green
safelight

Stop bath
Agitate print in stop bath for
  five seconds, use white print tongs
Transfer print to fixing bath,
  use white print tongs

Fixing
Leave the print in the fixing bath
  for 15 minutes
Agitate repeatedly, using white print
  tongs

Washing
Wash prints (suspended on cork clips)
  one hour under running water, in the
  print washer described on p. 121
Change position of cork clips once during
  washing to avoid spots

by ordinary light

Drying
Dry matte and semi-matte prints in a
  photo blotter roll
Ferrotype glossy prints

131

How to make an enlargement

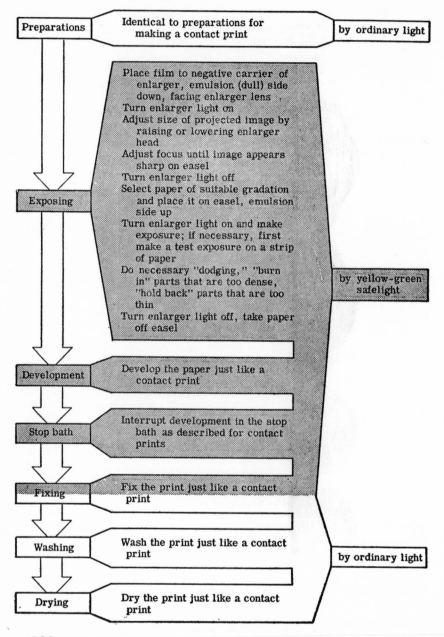

| Preparations | Identical to preparations for making a contact print | by ordinary light |

Exposing

Place film to negative carrier of enlarger, emulsion (dull) side down, facing enlarger lens .
Turn enlarger light on
Adjust size of projected image by raising or lowering enlarger head
Adjust focus until image appears sharp on easel
Turn enlarger light off
Select paper of suitable gradation and place it on easel, emulsion side up
Turn enlarger light on and make exposure; if necessary, first make a test exposure on a strip of paper
Do necessary "dodging," "burn in" parts that are too dense, "hold back" parts that are too thin
Turn enlarger light off, take paper off easel

by yellow-green safelight

Development — Develop the paper just like a contact print

Stop bath — Interrupt development in the stop bath as described for contact prints

Fixing — Fix the print just like a contact print

Washing — Wash the print just like a contact print

by ordinary light

Drying — Dry the print just like a contact print

132

The two preceding graphs show the steps involved in the making of contact prints and enlargements. Most of the necessary operations are so simple that no further explanation is needed. However, there are a few exceptions, and the additional instructions contained in the following paragraphs are intended to clarify these.

The Negative

A good print starts with a good negative. A "good" print signifies not only one that is correctly exposed and developed, but one that is also CLEAN. So before you put your negative into the printing frame or the enlarger, remove particles of dust and lint with a soft camel's-hair brush. Be sure that the glasses of the printing frame and negative carrier are also clean. Getting rid of dust can be quite a problem. The more you brush and rub, the more electrically charged negatives and glasses become, and consequently the more they attract other particles of dust. It is almost impossible to clean a negative properly on dry cold winter days, and brushing must be done very gently in order to prevent the film from becoming excessively charged. To determine whether a negative is clean, examine it under the light beam of the enlarger. If the negative is tilted at the proper slant, even the smallest specks of dust will appear glaringly white against the dark background of the film. Fresh fingermarks can sometimes be removed by wiping the negative with a tuft of cotton dampened in carbon tetrachloride. Old fingermarks cannot be eliminated. Minor scratches and abrasion marks can be minimized or temporarily eliminated by gently rubbing a light film of Vaseline into them. However, this is feasible only if the negative is used in an enlarger equipped with a glassless carrier; otherwise the Vaseline would stain the contact paper or smudge the carrier glasses. After the enlargement has been made, the Vaseline must be removed from the negative with carbon tetrachloride.

While for contact printing it does not matter too much if a negative is thin or dense, negatives that are extremely dense must be "reduced" (made more transparent; see p. 163) before they are enlarged. Otherwise, exposure times would be so long that accumulated heat from the enlarger lamp would buckle the film, and accumulation of stray light and reflected light would fog the paper. A negative is "too dense" if it requires an exposure that exceeds one minute. Before you reduce a negative that is too dense, examine its gradation: if it is too contrasty (usually as a result of overdevelopment), reduce with potassium persulfate (p. 164); if it is too contrastless (usually as a result of overexposure), use Kodak Farmer's

133

Reducer R-4a (p. 163). If a negative is so thin that it requires an "impossibly" short exposure, stop down the diaphragm of the enlarger lens; if this is not adequate, enlarge the negative on slow contact printing paper.

> The first prerequisite for successful printing and enlarging is a clean negative of correct density and contrast!

The Paper

Unfortunately, not every negative is "technically perfect" as far as gradation (contrast range) is concerned. There may be many reasons for this: either the exposure was too long or short, the developer too warm or cold, the development too long or short, or simply that subject contrast was abnormally high or low and the photographer failed to take corrective measures in time. In all such instances, negatives with "abnormal" gradation result. Luckily, such faults can usually be corrected in the print by selecting a paper of appropriate gradation in accordance with the following table:

Character of the negative	Extremely contrasty	Contrasty	Normal	Soft	Extremely contrastless
Recommended paper gradation (contrast grade numbers in brackets)	Extra soft (No. 1)	Soft (No. 2)	Normal (No. 2) or 3)	Hard (No. 4)	Extra hard (No. 5 or 6)

In analyzing a negative to determine the most suitable paper gradation, do not confuse gradation with density. One has nothing to do with the other. A very thin negative can be extremely contrasty (as a result of underexposure in conjunction with overdevelopment), or extremely lacking in contrast (overexposed and underdeveloped). And a very dense negative that appears almost uniformly black can be very contrasty (if considerably overdeveloped) or extremely lacking in contrast (if considerably overexposed). When in doubt, make a test print on paper of normal gradation. If it is too contrasty, make the final print on softer paper. If it lacks sufficient contrast, change to a paper of harder gradation.

> The second prerequisite for successful printing and enlarging is the selection of a paper with a gradation appropriate to the contrast range of the negative.

134

The Exposure

The operation which is most likely to cause trouble is the exposure of the print. Unlike most films, which have a relatively wide exposure latitude—i.e., can stand considerable overexposure and even some underexposure and still produce usable negatives—sensitized paper must be accurately exposed to produce good prints. A negative is only an intermediary step in the process of picture-making, and mistakes made at this stage can largely be corrected during the making of the print. But a print is the final step, and mistakes made in printing can no longer be corrected.

The simplest way to find the correct exposure is by trial and error. The few available print exposure meters are impractical because they are either too unreliable, depend too much on the subjective interpretation of the user, or are too complicated and expensive. After he has successfully exposed a few prints, any beginner will rapidly acquire enough experience to judge the density of his negatives correctly.

Contact print exposure determination. Duration of exposure depends on: intensity of the light source; distance between the light and printing frame; sensitivity of the printing paper; and density of the negative. The first three factors can be standardized and eliminated as "hazards" by always printing on the same type of paper with the same light kept at the same distance. The only remaining "unknown quantity" is then the density of the negative. If the negative is small, simply make a few test exposures until you get the right one. Start by exposing a sheet of, for example, Kodak Azo or Velox Paper for nine seconds, using a 40-watt bulb at a distance of eight inches from the printing frame. If the negative is large, to save paper use a strip about one inch wide and as long as the negative for the test exposure. Develop the exposure for the time recommended by the manufacturer, fix, and examine it by white light. If the image is too dark, exposure was too long. If it is too light, exposure was too short.

Enlargement exposure determination. Theoretically, of course, exposure is determined by the same factors as those which exist in contact printing. In practice, however, matters are slightly more complicated by virtue of the fact that two additional variables have to be considered: the diaphragm stop of the enlarger lens, and the degree of magnification of the projected image. The more the lens is stopped down, and the higher the degree of magnification, the longer the exposure time required, and vice versa.

The simplest way to determine the exposure time for an enlargement is through utilization of a test strip exposed as follows: take a sheet of paper of appropriate gradation and cut it in strips about one inch wide. Place a strip on the easel, cover four fifths of it with a piece of cardboard, and expose for thirty-two seconds. Then uncover one fifth more, and ex-

135

pose for sixteen seconds. Repeat this operation, exposing the remaining three fifths for eight, four, and four seconds, respectively. In this way, the five sections of the strip receive exposures of sixty-four, thirty-two, sixteen, eight, and four seconds, respectively. Develop the strip for the time recommended by the manufacturer, fix, and examine it by white light. Decide which exposure is correct, and use it as a basis for the final print. Of course, the "best" exposure may be between two steps. If so, the necessary correction can be made when one is exposing the final print.

The crucial test for the correctness of an exposure is the reaction of the sensitized paper in the developer. The print must appear "just right" after the time of development recommended by the manufacturer, or shortly thereafter. If, beyond this time, the print is still too light, if highlights are chalky and shadows grayish, the exposure was too short. If the image appears within a few seconds after immersion, and rapidly turns too dark, exposure was too long. In both instances, the print is a total loss. In the first instance, prolongation of development would only produce over-all grayishness resulting from fog, and yellow stain from the oxidizing developer. In the second instance, if the paper were prematurely taken out of the developer, the result would be a brownish print with mottled and streaky tones. Examples of such faulty prints are shown on p. 157.

> The third prerequisite for successful printing and enlarging is correct exposure of the paper!

The Development

Exposure of the sensitized paper produces a latent image which must be developed exactly like the latent image in a negative, except that the type of the developer, and the time of development, are slightly different. A number of excellent paper developers are available in prepared form. For those who like to compound their own developer, a formula that can be used with any kind of paper is reprinted on p. 184.

The temperature of the developer. This factor influences not only the duration of the development but also the tone of the print. Relatively cold paper developers are unpredictable, act sluggishly, and produce prints with an underexposed look, chalky highlights, and grayish shadows. Developers that are too warm produce prints brownish in tone resembling the results of overexposure.

> The fourth prerequisite for successful printing and enlarging is a developer temperature of 68° F.

The time of development. As mentioned previously, prints must be fully developed within a certain time—usually from fifty to one hundred and twenty seconds—to bring out the full inherent richness of tone. The only way to regulate the developing time is to adjust the time of exposure accordingly. Prints that appear fully developed before this time, and those that have not yet acquired their full strength within this time, are improperly exposed—and will always look it.

> The fifth prerequisite for successful printing and enlarging is maintenance of a developing time between fifty and one hundred and twenty seconds!

Practical Print Development

Never touch the emulsion side with your fingers. Slide the paper edgewise into the developer with the emulsion side facing up. Be sure to immerse the paper smoothly without interruption, or developing streaks may result (see picture on p. 157). Agitate continuously. If the developer tray is small, agitate by gently rocking it alternately from side to side and from front to back. If the tray is large, agitate the print by moving it around in the developer with the aid of the black tongs. Do not dip your hands into the solution—for the developer may become contaminated by the residue of another solution, be spoiled in a very short time, and produce prints with brown and yellow spots or streaks. Always use print tongs. Stop bath and fixing solution are "poison" to developers—be careful to keep your black print tongs from becoming contaminated with them.

Stop bath. When the print is fully developed, transfer it to the stop bath (formula on p. 184). Use the black tongs, but be sure that they do not touch the stop bath solution. Slide the print edgewise into the bath and "dunk" it with the white tongs. Agitate for five seconds. The stop bath not only stops development instantly but also prevents the print from staining in the fixing bath. Such staining happens frequently if prints are transferred directly from the developer to the hypo without sufficient agitation in the fixing bath.

Fixing. Remove the print to the fixing bath (formula on p. 186). Agitate thoroughly for ten seconds. Use the white tongs. Fixing takes from five to ten minutes, during which time the accumulating prints must be separated and agitated occasionally.

Washing. Wash prints (suspended on cork clips) for one hour under running water in the print washer described on p. 121. Stir occasionally to prevent them from sticking together. If running water is not available, soak the prints in a large tray for five minutes, change the water—repeat this process twelve times. Agitate and separate the prints repeatedly during washing.

Drying. Remove excess water by suspending the print for a few seconds by a corner, then dry matte and semi-matte prints in a photo blotter roll. After cleansing the ferrotype plate by wiping it under a stream of water with a soft cloth, ferrotype glossy prints by rolling them onto a ferrotype tin with a squeegee. Let the print dry thoroughly at room temperature. Do not remove prints from ferrotype plate prematurely, or the emulsion will crack. Prints that are perfectly dry strip off easily. Just lift one corner and draw the print diagonally off the plate. If sticking occurs, the plate is not clean enough. To prevent sticking, wash plates from time to time with Kodak Ferrotype Plate Polish. Yellow stains on the print are a sign of insufficient agitation during fixing, or of insufficient washing. Matte spots in the glossy finish are caused by air between the ferrotype plate and the paper. They can be avoided as follows: transfer the print dripping wet to the ferrotype plate; stand the print on its short edge, then let it down gradually in such a way that the water running down from the print forms a cushion between print and plate, driving all air ahead of it and preventing the formation of bubbles. Then roll the print down with a squeegee.

Finishing. The effect of a print depends to a surprisingly high degree on the way in which it is presented. If it is perfectly flat or faultlessly mounted, evenly trimmed, clean, and free from dust specks and spots, then the observer is much more likely to overlook or excuse small faults of composition, definition, or contrast. He senses that the photographer did his best—and will give him credit for that.

On the other hand, a picture may be really exciting subject-wise—but if it is badly dried, bumpy and curling, spotty from dust specks on the negative, sloppily trimmed, with corners worn from careless handling, then one must conclude that it was made by an untidy person, and in criticizing its obvious faults would probably overlook its attractive features.

Straightening. Papers that have a tendency to curl can be straightened by dampening the back of the photograph with a cloth moistened with a mixture of equal parts of alcohol and water, and keeping the print under pressure until it is perfectly dry. Separate prints from each other with sheets of white blotting paper.

Trimming. To get a perfectly straight, clean edge, trim the print with a single-edge razor blade and a steel straight-edge on a piece of glass. The glass, of course, dulls the blade within a relatively short time, but no other support produces an equally crisp cut. If a narrow white edge is left around the print, be sure that it is kept even. Personally, I prefer to trim off the white edge since I feel that its pure white tends to make the near-white tones of a photograph look grayish by comparison. On the other

138

hand, a white edge offers a certain protection to prints that must be handled frequently. If corners get ragged, just trim off a bit, and the photograph will look like new without the necessity of making the image smaller.

Spotting. This is the moment when many a photographer becomes annoyed that he neglected to clean his negatives more carefully before printing them. To spot a print, first remove dark spots with a knife—an etching knife or a razor blade which can be kept sharp by breaking off worn corners. Work very lightly. Carefully shave off the emulsion layer by layer until the spot is light enough to blend with the surrounding tone. Be careful not to dig through to the paper base—a common mistake of the beginner. Practice on inferior prints before you start on a good one. If you have overdone the shaving and the spot is therefore too light, darken it with pencil or water color when you retouch the light spots on the print.

Light spots must be darkened with pencil or water color. For glossy paper, special retouching colors are available at photo stores. Apply a shade of water color somewhat lighter than the area which surrounds the spot you are eliminating because as the water color dries it darkens. Mix the proper shade from black and white and apply it with the tip of a fine water-color brush. Work as dry as possible, applying the color in very thin layers, gradually blending the spot with the surrounding area. If necessary, apply a slightly darker coat of paint after the first one has dried. If a spot appears too dark after drying, shave it off before you apply a lighter tone to avoid a raised spot of paint on the picture.

Mounting. Prints can be mounted * on exhibition boards in many different ways—most of which are bad. Water-soluble glues and pastes distort the paper stock, causing prints and mounts to buckle. Only a professional bookbinder can do a competent job with glue. Rubber cement is temptingly easy to use, but will in time discolor and stain the print and cause irreparable damage. The only "professional" way to mount a print is to use dry-mounting tissue. Do not use the rubber wax-base type, which does not last because of early decomposition of the organic rubber component. Use instead the resin-base type, which lasts practically indefinitely and offers the further advantage of protecting the back of the photograph from the deteriorating effects of chemically aggressive glues and other components of the mount, and from humidity. Resin-coated dry-mounting tissue is chemically inert, is not affected by humidity and water, does not warp the print or mount, and is applied by heat. The mounting process itself is very simple and can be done with an ordinary flatiron according to the instructions that accompany the tissue.

---

* Incidentally, prints intended for submission to magazines should not be mounted.

The normal position of a print on its mount is slightly above center with equal side margins. To find this position, place the print in the upper left corner of the mount (see sketch); divide the space to the right of the print in two equal parts and draw the line A-B; divide the space underneath the print in two equal parts and draw the line C-D; connect the lower left corner of the print with point D; where this last line intersects with line A-B find point E. Place the print on the mount with its lower right corner at E and its sides parallel to the sides of the mount. Finally, write the title of the picture beneath the lower left corner of the print and sign your name at the right as shown in the accompanying sketch.

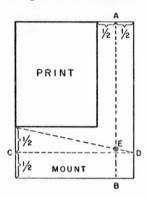
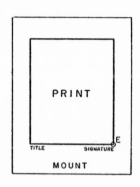

PRACTICAL POINTERS FOR ENLARGING

The previous instructions described the customary processing of both contact prints and enlargements. Out of such a routine, most photographers gradually develop methods of their own, based on improvements they have made, short cuts they have discovered, personal preferences they have acquired—and the sum total of such deviations from, and additions to, the ordinary routine of print processing eventually forms a valuable part of their "technique." In this sense, the following suggestions are offered as helpful additions to the ordinary routine of enlarging.

Cleaning. In cold dry weather, removing dust from negatives and glass plates becomes quite a problem. The more one brushes and rubs, the greater their charge of static electricity, and the more they attract dust and lint. Under such conditions, brush only once very slowly. Then use a rubber syringe and blow off dirt with a series of short, sharp puffs.

Cropping. One of the most valuable advantages of enlarging over contact printing is the possibility of utilizing only the most interesting part of a negative and presenting it in a pictorially effective size. Analyze your contact prints and decide which parts of the picture are important and which are superfluous. With the aid of two L-shaped pieces of cardboard,

140

mask off the margins of each contact print, slowly decreasing the rectangle within the L-masks until you find the most effective section of the photograph. Mark it with a grease pencil (which later can easily be removed with cleaning fluid). Ruthlessly eliminate unsharp foreground, wires cutting through the sky, untidy background, and superfluous detail, until nothing remains but the subject proper in its most concentrated form. Then enlarge it to a pictorially effective size.

Masking. When enlarging only a section of a negative, the rest of the film must be masked with thin black paper. Otherwise, stray light that passes through the marginal parts of the negative may fog the sensitized paper, make highlights appear a dirty gray, and lower the contrast range of the print. Neglect of this precaution is one of the most common reasons for the flatness typical of many amateur prints.

Reflections. In making enlargements of great magnification, be sure that light from the enlarger does not hit the chromium-plated enlarger column and reflect back onto the sensitized paper. If it does, cover the column temporarily with black paper held in place by scotch tape. Otherwise, dark parabolic marks will appear in the print.

Unsharpness. If you use a glassless negative carrier, heat from the enlarger lamp may buckle the negative and snap it out of focus before you are ready to expose the print. This is especially true if the negative is large, and if arriving at the best composition takes time. To prevent this, refocus just before you make the exposure.

Focusing. Focusing can be rather a problem if negatives are very dense, or if they do not contain sharply defined detail. If such is the case, focus on a minute blemish, a tiny scratch in the gelatine, a white mark left by a particle of dust, or the grain of the emulsion itself. Special focusing magnifiers are available which greatly facilitate critical focusing under conditions that provide nothing specific for the naked eye to focus upon.

Distortion. One of the greatest advantages of enlarging over contact printing is the possibility of correcting "converging verticals" in the negative to parallelism in the print. Simply tilt the paper easel according to sketches and pictures on p. 202, focus on the center of the image, and stop down the diaphragm until both upper and lower edges of the picture are sharp. Some enlargers have negative carriers which can be tilted independently of the lens. With the aid of these carriers (see p. 120), distortion can be corrected, and entirely sharp images can be produced, even when the diaphragm is wide open.

Dodging. Local contrast control as described on pp. 81-82 is one of the most valuable and indispensable techniques for the making of more effective enlargements. It may sound like a paradox—but the more a photographer learns, the more discriminating he becomes, and the more he improves "technically," the more he realizes that there is hardly such a thing as a negative that is "technically perfect" in every respect. Consequently, the more he makes use of the potentialities of "dodging." He hardly ever makes a print in which he does not "burn in" or "hold back" some part of the image in order to present his subject in the most pictorially and graphically effective form.

Diaphragm. Stopping down the diaphragm of the enlarger lens serves a triple purpose: (1) To regulate the time of exposure. If negatives are very thin, exposures are too short to be accurately timed, and "dodging" becomes virtually an impossibility. Stopping down decreases the intensity of the enlarger light and thus increases the exposure time. (2) To improve the definition of the lens. Wide open, most enlarger lenses do not cover the entire picture area sharply since their "speed" is not intended to shorten the exposure but to facilitate focusing and composing by making the image brighter. Most enlarger lenses are sharpest when stopped down to $f/6.3$ or $f/8$. (3) To increase the depth of field when working with glassless negative carriers. If the film buckles under the heat of the lamp, stopping down provides sufficient sharpness in depth to prevent partial unsharpness in the print.

Newton rings. These beautifully colored rings that appear at times are very annoying. The best way to avoid them is to use a glassless negative carrier. Sometimes a piece of clear cellophane between film and glass plates is effective, but it increases the hazard of spots from dust. Films that have been rolled for a long time are more likely to produce Newton rings than films that have been stored flat—a good reason for cutting up rolls of 35-mm. negatives into sections and filing them flat in envelopes.

Test strip data. When making a test strip for exposure determination, pencil the exposure times used on the back of the paper before developing it. In this way they cannot be forgotten—something which happens surprisingly often and forces the photographer to go through the whole rigmarole again.

Check for pure white. The best way to determine whether highlights and whites in a print are a true white or somewhat gray is to bend back a corner of the sensitized paper when in the developer and hold it against the image. Since the back of the paper is always pure white (unless a tinted paper is used), even the slightest degree of grayishness in a seemingly white highlight can be detected. Otherwise surprisingly dark shades of gray can, under the safelight, pass unnoticed as "white" if the eye has nothing really white with which to compare.

Check on darkness. Prints in hypo or water always look lighter than when they are dry. If a wet print looks just right under the safelight, one can be quite sure that it will look too dark after it has dried. Make allowance for this by developing prints slightly lighter than you want them to look when dry.

PART FIVE

LEARNING FROM MISTAKES

A "negative" approach to photography—
showing you how NOT to do things. Pro-
fusely illustrated with the products of hap-
less photographers whose misfortunes can
be your luck if you heed them as warnings

Double exposure—two pictures shot on the same film. To prevent double exposure, always be sure to transport the film or pull the filmpack tab, immediately after each exposure. However, if shutter and film transport are coupled (and double exposures impossible), do not leave the shutter cocked for any great length of time (not even overnight) since this is bad for the springs inside the shutter mechanism.

Dirt on film prior to exposure produces black marks similar to those in the sky of this picture. To prevent this, clean inside of camera regularly with a camel's-hair brush. If camera has bellows, extend bellows completely, open back of camera, hold camera vertically, and tap bellows gently but firmly from all sides. (left)

Dirt on negative during printing and enlarging produces white marks. To prevent this, carefully clean negatives and glass plates of printing frame or enlarger before printing (see p. 119). Furthermore, be sure that underside of condenser in enlarger is also perfectly clean since dust adhering to it will show up in the print. (right)

Faulty focusing—lens was focused on the trees in background instead of subject in foreground. This fault can be recognized by the fact that unsharpness is confined to a certain zone in depth, while the rest of the picture is sharp.

Subject movement—shutter speed was too slow to "stop" motion of the subject. This fault can be recognized by the fact that only the moving subject appears unsharp, while stationary objects in the photograph appear perfectly sharp.

Unsharpness and its most common causes

Camera movement—camera was not held perfectly motionless during the exposure. This fault can be recognized by the fact that every part of the picture appears equally blurred in the same direction, and nothing is really sharp.

utter failure—shutter stiff from cold which failed to close completely after the exposure was sponsible for these mistakes. Transporting the film while the shutter was still partially open used the light to trace parallel lines, straight (left) because camera was stationary on a pod, wavy (right) because camera was hand-held and moved during the winding of the m. To prevent this, have your shutter "delubricated" by a competent repair man before you ke pictures in extreme cold (around zero temperatures and below). It is "sticky" oil or just ain dirt which causes the shutter mechanism to act so sluggishly.

atic marks, caused by friction generated during the winding of the film. This danger is eatest during cold dry weather, least apparent under warm and humid atmospheric con- ions. To avoid such marks, wind film slowly and evenly and keep the camera grounded. ooden tripods, or metal tripods with rubber tips, for example, prevent grounding and facili- e accumulation of static charges on the film.

Light-struck negatives like these can be avoided: Never leave camera exposed to bright light longer than necessary. Do not load and unload camera in bright light. If there is no shade, turn away from the light and use the shade cast by your body. Be sure that film rolls are wound tight. Hold filmpacks by edges only and do not press on their flat sides since this may partially open them to light. Check camera periodically for light leaks which occur most often in corners of the bellows folds, and along sides of hinged or detachable camera backs. Check sheet film holders and filmpack adapters for worn light traps and worn and cracked slides.

Flares caused by strong direct light striking the lens. Their shapes depend on the position of the light source and the construction of the lens. The more complicated the lens, and the greater the number of its glass-to-air surfaces, the more the danger of flares increases. If the light source does not have to appear in the picture, flares can be prevented through shielding the lens from direct light by using a correctly constructed lens shade or a screen interposed between light and lens. If the light source has to appear in the picture, use of a coated lens minimizes the danger of flare but does not always eliminate it.

Diaphragm stars caused by light reflected from the blades of the diaphragm. These star patterns, which appear only around strong lights, become more pronounced as the diaphragm opening decreases. They can often be used to "symbolize" in a most pictorially effective form the radiance of strong direct light.

149

Fingermarks and scratches are unmistakable signs of carelessness. To prevent these, do not touch the flat sides of dry negatives with your hands (or marks like those above may result); handle negatives instead by the edges only. Use print tongs for handling paper during printing and enlarging (if hands and fingers are used, marks like those below left, which were caused by touching the unexposed paper with hypo-contaminated fingers, may result). In developing films according to the method described on p. 129, be sure that your fingernails are short (otherwise, scratches and digs like those below, right, are unavoidable).

Cinch marks caused by winding roll film too tightly. Cinch marks occur particularly often during the last stage of rewinding exposed 35-mm. film when the photographer tries to pull the tail end out of the take-up spool. To avoid these, rewind film only until sudden resistance indicates that the end of the film is reached, then open camera, take out both spools, and disengage the tail end of the film gently from the take-up spool.

Scratches caused by sand inside the camera or scratches on the film guides. Such scratches are the almost unavoidable result of carelessly exposing a camera to sand. Tiny grains of sharp-edged sand get into the camera and scratch the film directly, or by being trapped between film and film guides, cut into the metal, and cause bur, which in turn scratches the film as it passes across the guides. To avoid such scratches, protect camera from sand, clean inside of camera each time after use on a beach, have burs removed by a good camera repair man.

151

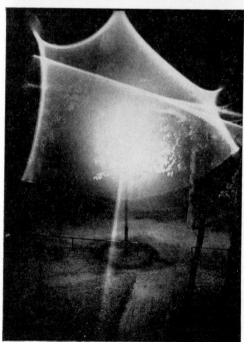

Different manifestations of damage caused by water

Drops of rain on the lens caused these strange halations. To prevent these, shield lens with an adequate lens shade, use an umbrella, or take the picture from a sheltered place—a doorway, the interior of a car, etc.

ater drops that dried on the nega-
ve caused these unsightly spots. To
event such spots, wipe negatives
arefully on both sides with a damp
scose sponge before you hang them
p to dry (instructions on p. 128).

egative emulsion reticulated par-
ally because of insufficient harden-
g and excessive temperature of
lutions and/or wash water. This
anger is particularly acute in warm
eather. To prevent this, use only
esh acid hardening fixing bath; be
re that temperature of solutions
es not exceed 75° F. If tempera-
res cannot be kept at 75° or lower,
se method for tropical development
escribed on p. 182.

← **FILM EXPOSURE** →

Too short   Correct   Too long

← NEGATIVE DEVELOPMENT →

Too short

Normal

Too long

Underexposed and underdeveloped	Correctly exposed but underdeveloped	Overexposed and underdeveloped
Over-all density: extremely low	Over-all density: too low	Over-all density: almost normal
Contrast: much too low	Contrast: too low	Contrast: too low
Shadow detail: completely lacking	Shadow detail: present but thin	Shadow detail: abnormally strong
Highlights: much too weak	Highlights: too weak	Highlights: too weak
Remedy: none; such negatives are total losses	Remedy: print on paper of hard gradation	Remedy: print on paper of extra hard gradation

Underexposed but normally developed	Correctly exposed and correctly developed	Overexposed but normally developed
Over-all density: too low	Over-all density: normal	Over-all density: too high
Contrast: too great	Contrast: normal	Contrast: too low
Shadow detail: practically non-existent	Shadow detail: normal	Shadow detail: abnormally strong
Highlights: too weak	Highlights: strong but still transparent	Highlights: too dense, graininess rather pronounced
Remedy: none; no intensifier can produce shadow detail that is not there	Negatives intended for enlarging should generally be slightly thinner, more transparent, than those intended for contact printing	Remedy: reduce in Kodak Farmer's Reducer R-4a (p. 163); print on paper of hard gradation

Underexposed and overdeveloped	Correctly exposed but overdeveloped	Overexposed and overdeveloped
Over-all density: about normal	Over-all density: too high	Over-all density: extremely high, negative appears practically black
Contrast: much too high	Contrast: somewhat higher than normally desirable	Contrast: about normal
Shadow detail: too weak	Shadow detail: strong	Shadow detail: much too strong
Highlights: rather dense and black	Highlights: very black and blocked; pronounced graininess	Highlights: perfectly black and detailless; graininess extremely pronounced
Remedy: if extremely dense, reduce with potassium persulfate (p. 164); print on paper of extra-soft gradation	Remedy: reduce in potassium persulfate (p. 164); print on paper of soft gradation	Remedy: reduce in Kodak Reducer R-5 (p. 164); print on paper of normal gradation

Uniform up-and-down agitation which pumped developer in always the same way through the perforation holes of the 35-mm. film caused streaks in the sky. Similar effects often result when sheet films are developed in hangers and agitation is mechanically up-and-down, pumping developer through the holes in the sides of the sheet film hangers.

Incorrect development can irrevocably damage a negative. Most disastrous in this respect are the consequences of incorrect agitation which cause unevenness and streaks. To avoid these, follow the instructions given on p. 127.

Insufficient agitation. Some of the components of stagnant, insufficiently agitated developer separated and thereby caused the two dark streaks and the light edge at the right side.

A "perfect print." Compare with the following faulty prints and notice evenness of grays, long scale of tonal gradation.

Uneven immersion of the exposed paper into the developer, a frequent result of insufficient solution, caused these streaks.

The three most common mistakes in print processing

"Forcing" an underexposed print in the developer produces nothing but a washed-out, harsh, contrasty and often yellow-stained print similar to this. . . .

"Pulling" an overexposed print prematurely from the developer produces a mottled, contrastless, and often brownish print similar to this. . . .

← PAPER GRADATION →

Too soft Correct Too hard

← PRINT EXPOSURE →

Too short

Correct

Too long

he commonly used method of exposure determination—test strips—has the disadvantage
that it allows solely for the comparison of different images in different degrees of light-
ess or darkness. A more practical method for making comparative test exposures is
rough use of a template—four different exposures of an identical negative section are
ius produced and therefore comparison of the results becomes much easier.

Test strip with four different exposures. Different sections of the negative must be compared. In this particular instance, comparison is fairly easy since, subject-wise, the different sections are almost identical. In other instances, however, variations in subject
matter make accurate evaluation of test strips almost impossible. It then becomes advis-
ble to make test exposures through the template illustrated below.

Exposure determination for enlargements

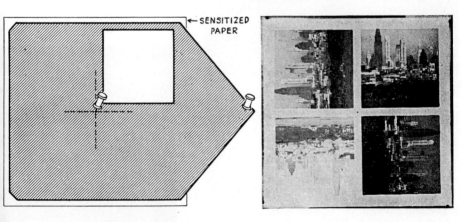

Cut template according to sketch at left out of thin, hard, cardboard or thin sheet metal,
making hole about 1½ inch square. Cut a supply of squares of sensitized paper (in
different gradations) ⅛ of an inch larger than the template. Put template on enlarger
easel so that the most important section of the picture appears in the window. Place test
paper beneath template and pin it down at center so it can be rotated around the pin.
Through the window in the template, expose test paper four times at different exposures,
rotating the paper 90° for each consecutive exposure. Develop, fix, and examine in white
light, use best exposure for making final print.

Solarization. Left: photograph of a sunset, short exposure. Right: same subject, photographed with longer exposure to produce more shadow detail. As a result, the sun appears black. Such a reversal of tone-values into the negative form caused by enormous overexposure is called "solarization." The rest of the picture remained unaffected since because of its darker subject matter, it was proportionally less overexposed than the sun.

Vignetting caused by a lens with insufficient covering power which, in an effort to improve perspective, was raised too high. If a lens with greater covering power had been used (see p. 33), this mistake would not have occurred.

Forgetting to pull the slide of the film holder or filmpack adapter would produce a picture like this.

Success—at a Price

Modern photographic materials are generally of such uniform high quality that failures due to faults in manufacturing are extremely rare. Out of the hundreds of unsuccessful photographs that I have seen during recent years, the failure of only two or three was caused by faulty material. In all other cases, the fault lay with the photographers—and mistakes could have been avoided if they had followed instructions more carefully. While it is human to try to avoid blame, before you blame the manufacturer, retrace your steps carefully under the assumption that there is a possibility that you did something wrong. The chances that you did are overwhelming. However, if you cannot find a likely explanation for a mishap—Kodak maintains a service for just such occasions. Simply send them your Kodak films and prints (preferably both), addressed to the Sales Service Division, Eastman Kodak Company, Rochester 4, N. Y., and they will provide the answer. There will be no charge—no obligation.

No one is infallible—and mistakes are nothing to be ashamed of as long as one tries his best. There are many times when we do not even suspect a pitfall, and avoid it only by sheer luck—until a subsequent time when we happen to fall into it. Actually, a mistake is "a blessing in disguise." Once made and its cause recognized, the same mistake can in the future be avoided. A photographer who has made "all the mistakes in the book" ought to be a perfect craftsman, provided that he has learned from his mistakes. Regarded in this spirit, each mistake made and understood is a milestone on the hard road to perfection, which leads to success.

In photography, unfortunately, there are only a few mistakes that can be corrected, and most of these only incompletely. Usually a mistake means "curtains"—no picture. However, because of their educational value, I have saved every "mistake" I could lay my hands on, with the result that on the preceding pages I can give my reader the benefit of other people's errors. I always advise photographers to save their "mistakes" and mount them in an album together with an explanation of their causes, incorporating them into a photographic library for reference of things to avoid. They paid for such in terms of money, material, time, and disappointment—they may as well reap the reward by never having to make the same mistakes again.

Since most photographic mistakes cannot be corrected satisfactorily, I do not even attempt to give instructions for their correction. However, the following are two exceptions: negatives that are too dense can easily be made more transparent by reduction, and some (but not all!) negatives that are too thin can be strengthened by intensification. Aside from this, all one can do is to salvage what is still usable—which normally means enlarging the undamaged sections from negatives that are spoiled because of scratches, spots, or streaks, and to give the rest up as lost. Or, as they say, "write it off to experience." If the negatives still exist, faulty prints should, of course, be made over again. If not—there are professional photograph-restorers who, with the aid of airbrush and copy negative can do miraculous things with unspeakable prints, and present you with perfect copies. However, the methods involved in this require a degree of skill and knowledge beyond the scope of this book.

CORRECTION OF MISTAKES

For successful reduction and intensification of negatives, the following rules must be strictly observed:

1. Negatives must be thoroughly fixed in *fresh* hypo and washed for at least half an hour under running water.

2. Negatives must be hardened in the following solution:

Kodak Special Hardener SH-I

For Aftertreatment of Films and Plates

	Avoirdupois U. S. Liquid	Metric
Water	16 ounces	500 cc.
Kodak Formaldehyde, about 37% solution by weight . . .	2½ drams	10.0 cc.
Kodak Sodium Carbonate, mono-hydrated	90 grains	6.0 grams
Water to make	32 ounces	1.0 liter

This formula is recommended for the treatment of negatives which normally would be softened by a chemical treatment as for the removal of stains or for intensification or reduction.

Immerse negatives in this solution for three minutes, then rinse and fix for five minutes in a fresh acid fixing bath. Wash thoroughly before attempting any further chemical treatment.

3. The best moment for reduction or intensification is immediately after the final washing of the developed negative. Dry negatives must be soaked in water for about ten minutes before they can be subjected to further chemical treatment.

4. Treat only one negative at a time. Some reduction processes are very rapid and require constant observation. Accurate control by time is not possible. Agitate constantly. Wash thoroughly after treatment, and wipe negatives carefully before hanging them up to dry.

5. The best way to reduce or intensify negatives is in a clear glass tray

with a weak light underneath. In this way, progression of the process can be easily watched and terminated at the proper moment.

How to Reduce Negatives

While most negatives that are too dense appear black and, therefore, similar, they actually may be quite different in regard to gradation. Some may be too dense and too contrasty, others too dense yet lack much contrast, while some negatives may be too dense and yet have "normal" contrast. There are three different types of reducers—"subtractive" reducers, which increase contrast; "super-proportional" reducers, which decrease contrast; and "proportional" reducers, which preserve the existing contrast. Therefore, a correct estimate of the contrast of a negative is necessary so that the right type of reducer can be used for the reduction of a particular negative. Since it is sometimes difficult to form a correct opinion about the contrast of a very dense negative, it is advisable to first make a test print on paper of normal gradation, and to judge the contrast of the negative from the appearance of the print: if the correctly exposed and developed print seems too flat, the negative lacks contrast; if the print seems too contrasty, the negative is too contrasty; and if the print seems "just right," the contrast of the negative is "normal" in spite of its density.

Dense negatives that lack contrast (usually as a result of overexposure) must be reduced with the following "subtractive reducer" which *increases contrast* while decreasing density:

Kodak Farmer's Reducer R-4a

Stock Solution A

	Avoirdupois U. S. Liquid	Metric
Kodak Potassium Ferricyanide .	1¼ ounces	37.5 grams
Water to make	16 ounces	500 cc.

Stock Solution B

Kodak Sodium Thiosulfate (Hypo) . .	16 ounces	480.0 grams
Water to make .	64 ounces	2.0 liters

For use take: Stock Solution A, 1 ounce (30 cc.), Stock Solution B, 4 ounces (120 cc.), and water to make 32 ounces (1 liter). Add A to B, then add the water and pour the mixed solution at once over the negative to be reduced, which preferably should be contained in a white tray. Watch closely. When the negative has been reduced sufficiently, wash thoroughly before drying.

For less rapid reducing action, use one-half the above quantity of Stock Solution A, with the same quantities of Stock Solution B and water.

Solutions A and B should not be combined until they are to be used. They will not keep long in combination.

Dense negatives that are too contrasty (usually as a result of over-development) must be reduced with the following "super-proportional reducer" which *decreases contrast* while decreasing density:

Kodak Persulfate Reducer R-15

Stock Solution A

	Avoirdupois U. S. Liquid	Metric
Water	32 ounces	1.0 liter
Potassium Persulfate	1 ounce	30.0 grams

Stock Solution B

	Avoirdupois U. S. Liquid	Metric
Water	8 ounces	250 cc.
°Sulfuric Acid (dilute solution)	½ ounce	15 cc.
Water to make	16 ounces	500 cc.

For use, take 2 parts of Solution A, and add 1 part of Solution B. Only glass, hard-rubber, or impervious and unchipped enamelware should be used to contain the reducer solution during mixing and use.

Treat the negative in the Kodak Special Hardener SH-1 for 3 minutes and wash thoroughly before reduction. Immerse in the reducer with frequent agitation and inspection (accurate control by time is not possible) and treat until the required reduction is almost attained. Then remove from the solution, immerse in an acid fixing bath for a few minutes, and wash thoroughly before drying. Used solutions do not keep well and should be promptly discarded.

Dense negatives of normal contrast must be reduced with the following "proportional reducer" which decreases density *without changing contrast:*

Kodak Reducer R-5

Stock Solution A

	Avoirdupois U. S. Liquid	Metric
Water	32 ounces	1.0 liter
Kodak Potassium Permanganate	4 grains	0.3 gram
°Sulfuric Acid (dilute solution) .	½ ounce	16.0 cc.

Stock Solution B

	Avoirdupois U. S. Liquid	Metric
Water	96 ounces	3.0 liters
Kodak Potassium Persulfate . .	3 ounces	90.0 grams

° To make, take 1 part of concentrated sulfuric acid and, with caution to avoid contact with the skin, add it slowly to 9 parts of water while stirring. *Never add the water to the acid* because the solution may boil and spatter the acid on the hands or face, causing serious burns.

For use, take 1 part of Solution A to 3 parts of Solution B. When sufficient reduction is secured, the negative should be cleared in a 1% solution of sodium bisulfite. Wash the negative thoroughly before drying.
CAUTION: Prepare the 10 per cent solution of sulfuric acid by *slowly* pouring one part of acid into nine parts of water, stirring constantly. DO NOT REVERSE THE PROCESS—otherwise acid will spatter over your hands and face!

How to Intensify Negatives

Before intensification is attempted, it is well to remember that first of all there has to be something in the negative that can be strengthened. Normally, negatives are too thin for two reasons: because of underexposure, and because of underdevelopment. Underexposed negatives are characterized by "shadows" that are as clear as glass—obviously, all that intensification can accomplish in such a case is to build up density (fog!) without building up detail. By this, of course, nothing would be gained. On the other hand, provided that they were correctly exposed, underdeveloped negatives, while generally too thin, are characterized by well-defined shadow detail which can be strengthened through proper intensification. However, before one intensifies a negative, the following should be considered:

All methods of intensification are delicate processes which are not always reliable. Unless negatives are absolutely free from hypo, and the necessary chemicals are absolutely pure, unevenness and indelible spots and streaks which permanently damage the negative may result.

Some of the most effective methods of intensification involve the use of deadly cyanides, and for this reason alone should be avoided. No negative is worth risking death from inhaling cyanide fumes.

In the opinion of the author, the most practical way to approach intensification is to make a duplicate negative. This method neither involves loss of a negative through faulty intensification, nor does it require the photographer to be in contact with dangerous chemicals. If a negative is fairly large, contact-print it, and if it is small, enlarge it, on contrasty process film. Fine-grain-develop the film 20 per cent longer than "normal," fix, wash, and dry in the usual manner. Then contact-print this positive replica of your original negative on the same type of contrasty process film, fine-grain-develop, etc., as before, and you will have a duplicate negative different only in that it will have much greater contrast and density. Try this method before attempting chemical intensification—if for no other reason than to have a duplicate in case the original gets spoiled.

165

For chemical intensification of a negative, proceed as follows:

Harden the gelatine for three minutes in the Kodak Special Hardener SH-1, the formula for which is reprinted on p. 162. Immerse for five minutes in a *fresh* acid fixing bath. Wash thoroughly for at least half an hour under running water. Then bleach the negative in the following solution:

Kodak Chromium Intensifier In-4

For Films and Plates

Stock Solution

	Avoirdupois	Metric
	U. S. Liquid	
Kodak Potassium Bichromate . .	3 ounces	90.0 grams
Hydrochloric Acid (concentrated) .	2 ounces	64.0 cc.
Water to make	32 ounces	1.0 liter

For use, take 1 part of stock solution to 10 parts of water.

Harden the negative first in the Kodak Special Hardener SH-1. Bleach thoroughly at 65° to 70° F. (18° to 21° C.), then wash 5 minutes and redevelop fully in artificial light or daylight (not sunlight) in any quick-acting, nonstaining developer which does not contain an excess of sulfite; for example, about 10 minutes at 68° F. (20° C.) in Kodak D-72, diluted 1 to 3. Then rinse, fix for 5 minutes, and wash thoroughly. Greater intensification can be secured by repeating the process.

Warning: Slow-working developers, such as Kodak D-76, Kodak Microdol, and Kodak DK-20, should not be used since they tend to dissolve the bleached image before the developing agents are able to act on it.

Negatives intensified with chromium are more permanent than those intensified with mercury.

Kodak Chromium Intensifier is supplied in prepared powder form. It is equally as satisfactory as Kodak In-4, and is ready to use simply by dissolving in water.

Stains and Spots in Negatives and Prints

Most stains and spots are caused by carelessness. Their prevention is as simple as their later correction is difficult. Usually they result from overworking the developer, contamination of the developer by hypo, insufficient fixation, exhaustion of the fixing bath, lack of agitation, inadequate washing. If tongs are not used in developing and fixing prints, direct handling must sooner or later cause brown or white fingermarks. If negatives and prints are subjected to humidity or light for a prolonged time, a yellowing and fading of the image invariably results. If prints are mounted with rubber cement or other chemically aggressive adhesives, spots will appear sooner or later.

The removal of spots and stains from negatives and prints involves techniques which are beyond the scope of this book. Many of these methods are risky and, unless performed by an expert, result in the loss of a negative or print. For this reason, before attempting any of the remedies that are published in photo-magazine articles or other textbooks, the photographer should take the precaution of making a duplicate negative or print.

Stained negatives can sometimes be cleaned with a special stain remover solution (e.g., Kodak Stain Remover S-6) followed by redevelopment. Stained prints should be discarded. If such prints are valuable and cannot be replaced because the negatives are not available, make a copy negative of the print by using a dark yellow filter and panchromatic film. Prints made from such a copy negative usually do not show the stain.

The following survey lists some of the most flagrant but most easily avoidable causes for mistakes:

Forgetfulness	False Economy	Carelessness
Forgetting to wind the film after each exposure	Expensive camera but no exposure meter	Fingermarks on lens and negatives
Forgetting to draw the slide when using filmpack or sheet film	"Unknown" brand of negative material bought cheaply	Sand or dust in camera which has been left "sunbathing" on the beach
Forgetting to pull out Leica or Contax lens before making exposure	Working with insufficient quantities of processing solution	Bottles not labelled, chemicals in paper bags
Forgetting to change focus when switching from long shot to close-up	Overworking developer and fixing bath in order to save on chemicals	No apron, thermometer, or towel in darkroom
		Hypo solution spilled
Forgetting to consider filter or other factors that influence exposures	Cheap colored bulb instead of proper safe-light in darkroom	Using hands instead of tongs; fingernails too long —negatives scratched

The pictures on pp. 145-160 illustrate most of the more common photographic accidents and mistakes, with the exception of stains and deposits on emulsions, which cannot be reproduced adequately in black and white.

PART SIX

PRACTICAL PHOTO CHEMISTRY

A postgraduate course for the ambitious amateur who has finished his apprenticeship by familiarizing himself with the basic techniques given in the preceding chapters. A short introduction to the chemistry of developing, fixing, and print permanency, with instructions for the handling and use of chemicals, and the preparation of formulas

A Postgraduate Course in Photo Chemistry

The previous chapters contained in concentrated form *everything* a photographer needs to know in order to make pictures that are "technically perfect." However, while there is a definite "lower limit" of knowledge—a minimum amount of know-how, rules, and skill without which photography cannot be practiced successfully—there is no "upper limit." A "complete" book on photography would need to have many thousand pages because it must deal with everything from basic to special techniques, discuss the fields of sensitometry, optics, and chemistry, touch upon electronics and radiology, go into physics and higher mathematics, and fade out—without ever reaching a definite end—with speculations into the nature of matter, light, and energy. But while all this is of the highest importance to the future of photography and the production of better photo material and equipment, it is, with very few exceptions, *absolutely valueless* to the practical photographer whose interest, aim, and ambition are to make good pictures.

One exception is a certain amount of knowledge pertaining to chemistry, enough to enable a photographer to understand the workings of developers, fixers, and other photographic solutions, and to help him to compound them in accordance with specific formulas. Such knowledge, while definitely not indispensable, can help the more advanced amateur to occasionally achieve better results, and will, for this reason, be dealt with in the following.

Advantages of Self-mixed Solutions

While it is always *more practical* to buy developers, fixers, etc., in prepared form, especially for the beginner who is concerned with other things that are more important at the start of his career, self-compounding of solutions may eventually become preferable for the following reasons:

Economy: Self-compounded solutions mixed from chemicals bought in bulk are less expensive than prepared developers, fixers, etc. This is particularly true of fixing baths and fine-grain developers.

Versatility: A great number of different formulas can be compounded from only a small number of chemicals simply by varying the number and proportions of their components. Often a slight change in the characteristics of, for example, a developer is desirable for producing a certain result. Self-mixed formulas can easily be modified to fit such special needs because their exact composition is known to the photographer, while altering a prepared formula usually ends in disaster.

Availability: A number of useful formulas, especially some developers and correction baths, are so unstable that they are not available in prepared form. Unless a photographer wants to abstain from using these sometimes "life-saving" formulas, he has to compound them himself.

169

The Equipment for Mixing Formulas

It is simple and not expensive. Savings made through the self-mixing of formulas should soon amortize the initial cost. You need:

One large and one small graduate. Pyrex glass is best.

One large and one small funnel.

A laboratory balance that must be accurate to within 0.1 gram, complete with a set of weights from 1 to 100 grams.

A set of spoons—glass or plastic—for taking chemicals out of their containers. Wooden or metal spoons are unsuitable because they are not chemically inert and are difficult to clean.

Two glass rods, large and small, with flat ends, for stirring solutions and crushing the residue of chemicals.

Glass beakers of Pyrex, in different sizes up to one gallon, for dissolving and mixing chemicals.

A number of mason jars, or wide-necked bottles with plastic screw tops, in different sizes, for storing dry chemicals. Some chemicals are sensitive to light and must be stored in brown bottles (see list on p. 172).

Ordinary quart and gallon bottles of brown glass for storing stock solutions.

How to Buy Chemicals

The cost of most chemicals constitutes only a fraction of the expense involved in making a photograph and is completely out of proportion to their importance with regard to the successful outcome of a picture. Chemicals that are not pure enough can unbalance a developer or a correction bath so completely that negatives are spoiled beyond repair. Consequently, only chemicals of guaranteed purity, uniformity, and freshness should be used, though actually they are somewhat more expensive than unguaranteed store brands, and they should be bought only through reputable photo supply houses or drugstores.

The degree of purity of chemicals is indicated as follows:

TECHNICAL—of comparatively low grade, generally not suitable for photographic work.

PURIFIED—of medium quality, suitable only for stop and fixing baths.

U.S.P.—of high quality, meeting the requirements of the United States Pharmacopoeia, satisfactory for photographic work.

A.R.—"Analytical Reagent," of highest purity, intended mainly for analytical purposes, unnecessarily pure and expensive for most types of photographic work.

PHOTOGRAPHIC GRADE—these chemicals comply with the specifications outlined in the standards issued by the American Standards Association (ASA).

The ending "ate" indicates that a chemical contains a relatively high amount of oxygen (for example: sulfate).

The ending "ite" indicates that a chemical contains a relatively small amount of oxygen (for example: sulfite).

The ending "ide" indicates that the chemical is a hydracid salt (for example: sulfide).

How to Store Chemicals

The majority of chemicals used in photographic work are sensitive to either moisture, air, light, heat, or cold. Exposed to these influences, in time they deteriorate and become useless. The best way to store chemicals is in glass containers, the worst in paper bags. Cardboard containers are unsuitable because they attract and retain moisture. Mason jars are excellent for all non-light-sensitive dry chemicals. Brown quart bottles with rubber stoppers are best for solutions. Glass stoppers have an annoying tendency to get stuck. To loosen, with one or two matches heat the neck of the bottle slightly from all sides, then gently tap the sides of the neck with a piece of wood and twist stopper counterclockwise. When replacing the stopper, do not forget to give it a light coat of Vaseline to prevent future trouble.

Chemicals should be stored in a dry, dark, cool (but not cold) place. Do not store sensitized material (film and paper) close to chemicals, for some chemicals give off fumes that fog the emulsion. To avoid mistakes, attach printed permanent labels to all bottles and jars. Poisonous chemicals must be clearly marked POISON. Do not leave chemicals unnecessarily exposed to air, from which many substances attract moisture.

All developers are highly sensitive to oxygen, which they absorb from the air. For this reason, completely fill bottles with stock solution to keep out unnecessary air. If a bottle is not completely filled, fill the empty space by dropping small glass marbles into the solution until capacity is reached. Large amounts of developer stock solution should be kept in a number of smaller bottles rather than in a single large one. Whenever a solution is used, therefore, only one bottle containing a small amount of liquid (which probably will be used within a short time) has to be opened and exposed to air, and the bulk of the stock remains undisturbed.

Fumes are given off by ammonia water and ammonium sulfide, for which reason they must be stored separately from all other chemicals, and from films and sensitized papers.

Sensitive to moisture to an excessively high degree are the following chemicals which, despite use of glass-stoppered bottles, must be stored in a perfectly dry moistureproof place: amidol, ammonium persulfate, caustic soda, pyrocatechin, glycin, hydroquinone, metol, potassium carbonate, pyrogallol.

171

Sensitive to light to an excessively high degree are the following chemicals, which, despite use of brown glass bottles, must be stored in darkness: ferric oxalate, gold chloride, potassium ferricyanide, potassium iodine, potassium permanganate, silver nitrate.

Unusually sensitive to heat are the following chemicals, which must be dissolved only in cold water and added only to other cold solutions: ferric oxalate, potassium metabisulfite, sodium bisulfate.

POISONOUS are the following chemicals, which must never be touched and must never come in contact with the skin: caustic soda (developer alkali), potassium bichromate (intensification), sulfuric acid (cleanser for developer trays, gives off poisonous vapors extremely dangerous to the lungs), uranium nitrate (intensifying), potassium ferricyanide (reducing agent), pyrogallol (developing agent).

How to Mix Solutions

Prepared developers, fixers, etc., are always accompanied by printed instructions for use which must be followed implicitly, otherwise failure may result. When compounding your own solutions, observe the following rules:

Containers of glass or stainless steel are most suitable for dissolving and mixing chemicals. Hard rubber absorbs certain chemicals and leads to contamination of subsequently prepared solutions. Enameled containers chip and rust and sometimes give off alkali (disastrous to fine-grain developers). Glazed stoneware sometimes has flaws through which chemicals can penetrate, and subsequently contaminate other solutions.

When compounding a printed formula, always dissolve its components in the order in which they are listed.

Never add a new chemical to a solution before the previous component has been *completely* dissolved.

When weighing chemicals, do not pour them directly onto the pan of the balance. Instead, place a piece of paper on each of the pans (to preserve the equilibrium), then pour the chemical onto the paper to avoid contamination with other chemicals. However, the same piece of paper may be used for weighing all the components that go into one formula.

Minute quantities of chemicals must be measured particularly accurately. When measuring liquids, hold the glass graduate so that the surface of the liquid is level with your eye, then take the reading at the bottom of the curve formed by surface tension at the top of the liquid. When taking a thermometer reading, keep your eye level with the top of the column of mercury, otherwise your reading may be off as much as two degrees because of the refraction effect of the cylindrical magnifier built into the thermometer rod.

Dry chemicals must always be poured into the water. If you pour the water on desiccated chemicals, they cake into a stony mass and take a very long time to dissolve. This is particularly true of prepared acid-fixing salts.

To speed up dissolution, stir vigorously while slowly pouring the chemical into the water or solution. However, be careful not to whip air into the solution when preparing a developer, for the oxygen contained in the air may prematurely corrode the solution (visible sign: brownish discoloration).

Write the date with a grease pencil on every bottle of stock solution immediately after preparation. It later enables you to estimate its freshness. If you intend to re-use a developer, with a grease pencil mark on the bottle the number of films developed in it to keep track of the degree of exhaustion. This is important for determination of necessary increases in subsequent developing times.

Filter developers before use by pouring them through a funnel loosely stoppered with a wad of cotton, to eliminate sludge and particles of gelatine and dirt which otherwise may settle on the developing films and cause spots. Before filtering, however, be sure that the developer is warmed to the correct working temperature (68° F.) for the following reason: the solubility of most chemicals decreases with decreasing temperatures. Consequently, if solutions have been stored at relatively low temperatures, some of their components may crystallize and precipitate to the bottom of the bottle. If such a solution is filtered at a temperature lower than 68° F., some of its most important components may be inadvertently filtered out, and the solution will then be useless.

When preparing or using a fixing bath, do not spill hypo crystals or solution. Hypo is "poison" to developers. Spilled fixing solution dries, and the fine powder subsequently contaminates the whole darkroom, leaving spots wherever it settles on films and sensitized paper. In many instances, tiny dots—supposedly caused by "air bubbles"—are actually caused by spilled hypo.

The Water for Solutions

Developer stock solutions must be prepared with boiled water. Boiling eliminates most of the free air contained in water, the oxygen content of which otherwise would prematurely oxidize the developing agent. Furthermore, it precipitates most of the suspended impurities and eliminates a large percentage of the calcium and magnesium salts.

Fine-grain developers must be prepared with distilled water, which must in addition be boiled. Distilled water is chemically free from impurities but still contains much free air which must be eliminated by boiling.

Stop baths and fixers can be prepared with any water that is pure enough for drinking purposes.

173

Intensifiers are extremely sensitive to chemical impurities and should be prepared only with distilled water.

Reducers can normally be prepared with ordinary tap water.

Impurities in the water can cause the following effects: calcium and magnesium can with other chemicals form soluble salts which dry on the emulsion in the form of fine crystals or white scum, showing as spots in the print; or they can form insoluble salts that settle at the bottom of the tank. These salts must be eliminated by filtration, since otherwise, if stirred up, they settle on the emulsion and adhere, causing spots. Iron increases the rate of oxidation of developers, causes rust spots on negatives and prints, and must be eliminated by filtration. Special water filters are available that can be attached directly to the faucet. Sulfur, usually in the form of hydrogen sulfide, combines with the silver of the emulsion to form silver sulfide and interferes with proper developing and fixing.

The Temperature of Solutions

The rate of chemical reaction increases with increase in temperature. As a result, all chemicals dissolve more readily, and in greater amounts, in warm than in cold water. However, some chemicals are so sensitive to heat that even moderate temperatures change their chemical properties to such a degree that they become useless for photographic purposes (see list on p. 172). Such chemicals, of course, must be stored, dissolved, and used at correspondingly low temperatures.

Developers can be prepared with water as hot as 125° F., but no hotter. Before use, of course, such a solution must cool down to the normal temperature of 68° F.

Hypo crystals can be dissolved in water as hot as it comes out of the hot faucet. When hypo crystals are poured into water of 140° F., the temperature of the solution is almost instantaneously lowered to around 50° F. Before use, of course, the temperature of such a bath must be raised to 68° F., or reticulation of the negatives may result (see p. 153).

The acid hardener component of an acid fixing bath is moderately sensitive to heat and decomposes at temperatures above 125° F. It should always be dissolved separately from the hypo in water not hotter than 100° F. Hypo and acid hardener should be mixed only when both solutions have cooled to the normal temperature of 68° F., otherwise the bath may turn milky and be spoiled by the formation of free sulfur.

The Concentration of Solutions

The strength of a solution can be indicated in two different ways: in terms of "percentage solution," used mostly in reference to solids dissolved in a liquid; and in "parts," used mostly when referring to a mixture of a solution and water.

174

A *percentage solution* is prepared by dissolving the specified quantity (in grams) of a chemical in a small amount of water, then adding sufficient water to make 100 cc. of solution. For example, to make a 5 per cent solution, dissolve 5 grams of the chemical in a graduate containing a small amount of water, then fill with water to the 100 cc. mark. The result will be 100 cc. of a 5 per cent solution.

PERCENTAGE SOLUTION

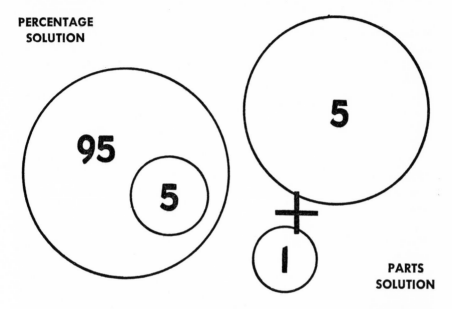

PARTS SOLUTION

A *parts solution* is prepared by mixing one unit of a specified stock solution with a specified number of identical units of water. Such units can be of any weight from grams to tons, provided that all quantities are reckoned in the same units of weight or volume. For example, to make a developer from one part of stock solution and five parts of water, mix one unit of stock solution with five units of water—one ounce of stock solution mixed with five ounces of water, or 100 cc. of stock solution mixed with 500 cc. of water—the result will be identical as long as identical units of measurement are used for both stock solution and water. If both liquids and solids are given in "parts," of course, equivalent units of measurement must be used. Thus, grams for solids go with cubic centimeters for liquids; and ounces for solids go with fluid ounces for liquids.

To convert a "parts solution" into a "percentage solution" proceed as follows: The developer mentioned above consisted of one part stock solution and five parts of water, in all six equal parts. In order to convert this ratio into percentage, divide 100 by 6, the result of which is 16.7 per cent. In other words, a solution of 1:5 is equivalent to a 16.7 per cent solution.

175

The crisscross method offers the easiest way of figuring the dilution of a high-percentage stock solution into a lower-percentage working solution. See the diagrams below:

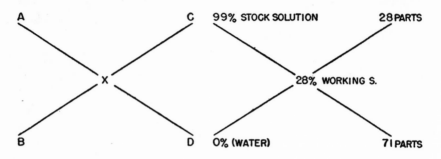

Place the percentage strength of the stock solution at A; place the percentage strength of the solution you dilute with at B (in the case of water, of course, this is 0 per cent); place the desired percentage strength at X; subtract X from A and write the result at D; also subtract B from X and write the result at C. Finally, take C parts of A and mix them with D parts of B, and you will get a solution of X per cent.

For example (see sketch above, right): to dilute a stock solution of 99 per cent acetic acid to a 28 per cent acetic acid working solution, take 28 parts of the 99 per cent stock solution and mix it with 71 parts of water (0 per cent solution).

The Keeping Properties of Solutions

To consistently produce high-quality negatives and prints that are uniform and reasonably permanent, it is necessary that solutions be maintained above the point of exhaustion. Exhausted developers act sluggishly. They produce negatives with less and less density and increasingly softer gradation (to the point of useless flatness), and prints with sickishly brownish tones. Exhausted fixers are even more dangerous because their exhaustion may not be immediately detected. They may still clear a negative and make a print insensitive to light (though this usually requires an abnormally long time), but such negatives and prints are not permanently fixed and will soon discolor and fade.

To avoid premature exhaustion of negative developers from oxidation, pour solutions back into the bottle immediately after use and keep the bottle completely filled (see p. 171 for method). Developers remaining in deep tanks must be protected from the air. For this purpose, float a piece of Kodapak Sheet on the surface of the developer in the form of a shallow boat, and keep cover on. Re-use of diluted paper developer (working solution) is definitely not advisable.

176

The figures in the following table, which are based on recommendations made by the Eastman Kodak Company for their products, give a rough idea how long certain solutions can be expected to last under different conditions.*

| Keeping properties and useful life of Kodak solutions | | | | | Useful Life 8" by 10" sheets per gallon | |
| Formula | Keeping properties without use | | | | | |
Developers	Tray	Gallon Tank	Stoppered bottle Full	Half full	Tray	Narrow and deep tank*
Kodak D-76	24 Hrs	1 Mo	6 Mo	2 Mo	20	30
Kodak DK-20	24 Hrs	1 Mo	6 Mo	2 Mo	20	30
Kodak DK-15	8 Hrs	1 Week	3 Mo	1 Mo	15	30
Kodak D-11	24 Hrs	1 Mo	6 Mo	1 Mo	20	40
Kodak D-72	24 Hrs	2 Weeks	3 Mo	1 Mo	20 (1:1) 15 (1:2)	40 (1:1) neg. 30 (1:2) neg.
Stop baths						
Kodak SB-3 (films only)	1 Day	1 Mo	Indef.	Indef.	25	
Kodak SB-1 (papers only)	3 Days	1 Mo	Indef.	Indef.	75	
Fixing bath			Stoppered bottle 65° F	75° F	Water rinse between devel. and fixing	Stop bath
Kodak F-6	1 Week	2 Mo	3 Mo	3 Wks	50	100

* Use of a replenisher (consult manufacturer's recommendations) considerably prolongs the useful life of negative developers used in deep tanks.

In this connection, one sheet of 8- by 10-inch film is the equivalent of:

1 roll of 35-mm. film, 36 frames per roll
1 roll 620
1 roll 120
2 rolls 127
4 sheets 4- by 5-inch film
6 sheets 3¼ by 4¼ inch film
11 sheets 2¼ by 3¼ inch film
1 roll 616 (116) = one and a half sheets of 8- by 10-inch film
1 roll 122 = two 8- by 10-inch sheets

If only a few films, or a single film, are developed at a time and solutions stand unused for some time, only a smaller quantity of film than that recommended above can be developed with good results.

If developers are used only once to develop a maximum number of films at one time, a slightly greater quantity than that indicated above can be processed with good results.

177

Weights and Measures

To convert avoirdupois measures into the metric form, and vice versa, use the following table:

CONVERSION TABLE FOR UNITS OF VOLUME AND WEIGHT*

To Convert From:	Multiply By								
	To Fl. Oz.	To Pint	To Quart	To Gallon	To C.C.or G.	To Ltr.or Kg.	To Grain	To. Oz. Av.	To Lb. Av.
Fluid Ounce	1.00000	.062500	.031250	.007813	29.5736	.029573			
Pint	16.0000	1.00000	.500000	.125000	473.177	.473177			
Quart	32.0000	2.00000	1.00000	.250000	946.354	.946354			
Gallon	128.000	8.00000	4.00000	1.00000	3785.42	3.78542			
Cubic Centimeter or Gram	.033814	.002113	.001057	$.0_3 2642$	1.00000	.001000	15.4323	.035274	.002205
Liter or Kilogram	33.8140	2.11337	1.05669	.264172	1000.00	1.00000	15432.3	35.2739	2.20462
Grain					.064799	$.0_4 6479$	1.00000	.002286	$.0_3 1428$
Ounce Avoirdupois					28.3495	.028350	437.500	1.00000	.062500
Pound Avoirdupois					453.593	.453593	7000.00	16.0000	1.00000

*Courtesy of E. I. Dupont de Nemours & Co.

Note: The small subnumeral following a zero indicates that the zero is to be taken that number of times: thus, $.0_3 1428$ is equivalent to .0001428.

For example: To convert 2-1/2 av. oz. to grams, multiply 2-1/2 by the factor 28.3495 or 70.87 grams.

To quickly change a formula from avoirdupois into the metric system, and vice versa, use the following conversion tables:

Compound Conversion Factors for Solids

Grains per 32 oz. multiplied by   0.06847 —grams per liter
Ounces per 32 oz. multiplied by   29.96   —grams per liter
Pounds per 32 oz. multiplied by 479.3   —grams per liter
Grams per liter multiplied by   14.6   —grains per 32 oz.
Grams per liter multiplied by   0.03338 —ounces per 32 oz.
Grams per liter multiplied by   0.002086—pounds per 32 oz.

Compound Conversion Factors for Liquids

Fl. ounces per 32 oz. multiplied by 31.25 —cubic centimeter per liter
cc. per liter multiplied by   0.032—fl. ounces per 32 oz.

For example: If a formula calls for 25 grams of an ingredient per liter of water, multiply 25 by 14.60 and the result is 365.00 grains per 32 ounces. In an emergency, United States coins can be used to weigh small quantities of chemicals. The following table lists their approximate weights:

Silver dollar	400 grains	26 grams
Half dollar	200 grains	13 grams
Quarter dollar	100 grains	6½ grams
Nickel	80 grains	5 grams
Cent	50 grains	3¼ grams
Dime	40 grains	2½ grams

To convert degrees Fahrenheit into Centigrade, subtract 32, multiply by 5, divide the result by 9.

To convert Centigrade into Fahrenheit, multiply by 9, divide by 5, add 32 to the result.

178

The process of development of a film or a sheet of sensitized paper involves three different operations:

1. Softening and swelling of the gelatine that permits the reducing agent to reach the exposed crystals of halide (silver bromide, silver chloride).

2. Disassociation of the silver and the bromide.

3. Transformation of the exposed crystals of silver halide into metallic silver—the "grain" of the emulsion.

To make this process possible, a developer must contain among its ingredients the following five components:

1. **A solvent**—water—without which dry chemicals can neither soften the emulsion nor reach the exposed halides (see chapter on "The water for solutions," p. 173).

2. **A developing agent.**[*] Its purpose is to transform as completely as possible the exposed silver halides into the metallic silver of the negative grain which forms the image, without attacking the unexposed silver salts. If these were also affected, the whole emulsion would turn uniformly gray or black, and no image could be formed. Only very few substances are known to possess those delicate selective qualities that are necessary for differentiation between exposed and unexposed silver salts. Most commonly used are: metol, Kodak Elon Developing Agent, Mallinckrodt Pictol, hydroquinone, glycin, paraphenylene diamine.

3. **An activator.** Most photographic reducing agents function properly only in an alkaline solution. For this reason, alkaline activators must be included in a developer. The higher the alkali content of a developer is, the more energetic, rapid, and contrasty will it develop. This content can occasionally be so high that the overactivated reducing agent also begins to attack the unexposed silver salts, producing over-all fog in the negative. Most commonly used activators are: sodium carbonate, Kodalk Balanced Alkali, borax, sodium or potassium hydroxide.

4. **A preservative.** All reducing agents have a natural affinity to oxygen. They readily combine with it, "rust" themselves away until they become photographically inactive, and discolor films and papers with brownish oxidation stains. Since water always contains free oxygen resulting from air dissolved in it, and since contact with surface air is unavoidable, reducing agents in developer solutions would oxidize rapidly unless a pre-

---

[*] Also called reducing agent.

servative were added to the developer. Such preservatives have the ability to combine with the oxidation by-products of the developing agent which otherwise would cause excessively rapid oxidation of all of the available developing agent. Most commonly used preservatives are: sodium sulfite and potassium metabisulfite. Used in large amounts, sulfite dissolves part of the silver halides and produces negatives with a finer grain.

5. A restrainer. To prevent the reducing agent from attacking the unexposed silver salts (which it might do if overly activated), and to counteract the effects of possible overexposure of the negative, a restraining agent is usually added to the developer solution. It prevents over-all fog and furthermore helps speed up development by making it safe to add larger quantities of alkali without the danger of harmful effects. Too much restrainer, however, slows down the effective speed of a film and necessitates prolongation of the exposure time. Most commonly used restrainer: potassium bromide.

RULES FOR THE PREPARATION OF DEVELOPERS

1. The preservative must be dissolved before the reducing agent. Otherwise, the reducing agent would oxidize excessively before the preservative took effect. However, there is one exception: In the case of formulas containing Kodak Elon Developing Agent, the Elon Developing Agent must be dissolved first since it is readily soluble in warm water but only slightly soluble in sulfite solutions without alkali. After the Elon Developing Agent is completely dissolved, the sulfite should be added immediately, then the other developing agents, and finally the alkali.

2. The alkali must be added after the preservative and the reducing agent have been completely dissolved. Alkali increases the natural affinity of the reducing agent to oxygen and would accelerate its rate of oxidation unless prevented by the preservative.

3. Always dissolve one chemical completely before adding the next one. Otherwise, discoloration of the solution and oxidation and precipitation of chemicals can occur.

4. Most formulas list the components in the order in which they must be dissolved. Follow instructions carefully to avoid undesirable reactions.

5. Use only boiled water of a temperature not exceeding 125° F. for the preparation of all developers, unless distilled and boiled water is specified.

180

Developers

Kodak Developer D-76

For Maximum Speed at Normal Contrast on Films and Plates

	Avoirdupois	*—U. S.*	*Liquid*	*Metric*
Water, about 125° F. (50° C.) .	24 ounces	96	ounces	750 cc.
Kodak Elon Developing Agent .	30 grains	115	grains	2.0 grams
Kodak Sodium Sulfite, desiccated . . . . 3 oz.	145 grains	13¼	ounces	100.0 grams
Kodak Hydroquinone	75 grains	290	grains	5.0 grams
Kodak Borax, granular	30 grains	115	grains	2.0 grams
Water to make	32 ounces	1	gallon	1.0 liter

Dissolve chemicals in the order given.

Average development time, about 12 minutes at 68° F. (20° C.). See individual recommendations listed for each material.

The useful life of this developer can be increased 5 to 10 times by use of the Kodak Replenisher D-76R. (See Eastman Kodak booklet, *Processing Chemicals and Formulas for Black-and-White Photography*, 50¢.)

A faster working developer can be obtained by increasing the quantity of borax. By increasing the borax quantity ten times, from 30 grains to 290 grains per 32 ounces (from 2 grams to 20 grams per liter), the development time will be about one-half that of regular Kodak D-76.

Kodak Fine Grain Developer DK-20

For Films and Plates

	Avoirdupois	*—U. S.*	*Liquid*	*Metric*
Water, about 125° F. (50° C.) .	24 ounces	96	ounces	750 cc.
Kodak Elon Developing Agent .	75 grains	290	grains	5.0 grams
Kodak Sodium Sulfite, desiccated . . . . 3 oz.	145 grains	13¼	ounces	100.0 grams
Kodalk Balanced Alkali . . .	30 grains	115	grains	2.0 grams
Kodak Sodium Thiocyanate (Sulfocyanate)	15 grains	60	grains	1.0 gram
Kodak Potassium Bromide . . .	7 grains	30	grains	0.5 gram
Cold water to make	32 ounces	1	gallon	1.0 liter

Dissolve chemicals in the order given.

Average development time, about 15 minutes in a tank at 68° F. (20° C.). See individual recommendations listed for each material. Increase development time about 15 per cent after each 8 × 10-inch film per 32 ounces or equivalent.

NOTE: Kodak Developer DK-20 and other developers containing silver halide solvents such as thiocyanates or thiosulfates may form a scum on the surface of the film, especially when partially exhausted. They should not be used with any of the new Kodak roll films, miniature films, or film packs; nor should they be used with the new Kodak sheet films, such as Royal Pan and Royal Ortho.

Ultra Fine Grain Developer

Sease III

Negative developer for ultra fine-grain development of miniature camera films. This developer requires 2 to 2½ times normal exposure.

Sodium sulfite, desiccated	90 grams
Para-phenylene-diamine base	10 grams
Glycin	6 grams
Distilled water to make	1 liter

Dissolve the sulfite and the para-phenylene-diamine in hot water (125° F.), then add the glycin. When completely dissolved, filter the solution while it is still warm.

Average development time is 25 minutes at 70° F., or 30 minutes at 65° F. Films having genuine fine-grain characteristics require only half of this developing time.

Kodak Developer DK-15

For Tropical Development of Films and Plates

	Avoirdupois—U. S. Liquid				Metric
Water, about 125° F. (50° C.) .	24	ounces	96	ounces	750 cc.
Kodak Elon Developing Agent .	80	grains	¾ ounce		5.5 grams
Kodak Sodium Sulfite, desiccated	3	ounces	12	ounces	90.0 grams
Kodalk Balanced Alkali . . .	¾ ounce		3	ounces	22.5 grams
Kodak Potassium Bromide . .	30	grains	115	grains	2.0 grams
*Kodak Sodium Sulfate, desiccated	1½	ounces	6	ounces	45.0 grams
Cold water to make	32	ounces	1	gallon	1.0 liter

---

* If it is desired to use crystalline sodium sulfate instead of the desiccated sulfate, then 3½ ounces per 32 ounces (105 grams per liter) should be used.

Dissolve chemicals in the order given.

Average time for tank development is about 10 minutes at 68° F. (20° C.) and 2 to 3 minutes at 90° F. (32° C.) in the fresh developer, according to the contrast desired. When working *below* 75° F. (24° C.), the sulfate may be omitted if a more rapid formula is required. Development time *without* the sulfate is about 6 minutes at 68° F. (20° C.). Develop about 20 per cent less for tray use.

When development is completed, rinse the film or plate in water for 1 or 2 seconds only and immerse in Kodak Hardening Bath SB-4 for 3 minutes (omit water rinse if film tends to soften); then fix for at least 10 minutes in an acid hardening fixing bath, such as Kodak Acid Fixer or Kodak Fixing Bath F-6, and wash for 10 to 15 minutes in water (not over 95° F. [35° C.]).

The use of developers containing Kodalk Balanced Alkali greatly reduces the likelihood of producing gas blisters, because this alkali does **not**

182

evolve a gas when treated with an acid. This is a distinct advantage, especially for summer work, when temperature control of solutions is often difficult.

Kodak Hardening Bath SB-4

For Use at 75° to 90° F. with Films and Plates

This solution is recommended for use in conjunction with the high-temperature developer, Kodak DK-15, when working above 75° F. (24° C.).

	Avoirdupois—U. S. Liquid		Metric
Water	32 ounces	1 gallon	1.0 liter
Kodak Potassium Chrome Alum . .	1 ounce	4 ounces	30.0 grams
*Kodak Sodium Sulfate, desiccated .	2 ounces	8 ounces	60.0 grams

* If crystalline sodium sulfate is preferred to the desiccated form, use 2¼ times the quantities.

Agitate the negatives for 30 to 45 seconds when they are first immersed in the hardener, or streakiness will result. Leave them in the bath for at least 3 minutes between development and fixation. If the temperature is below 85° F. (29° C.), rinse for 1 to 2 seconds in water before immersing in the hardener bath.

The hardening bath is a violet-blue color by tungsten light when freshly mixed, but it ultimately turns a yellow-green with use; it then ceases to harden and should be replaced with a fresh bath. The hardening bath should never be overworked. An unused bath will keep indefinitely, but the hardening power of a partially used bath decreases rapidly on standing for a few days.

Kodak Developer D-11

For High Contrast on Films and Plates

	Avoirdupois—U. S. Liquid		Metric
Water, about 125° F. (50° C.) .	16 ounces	64 ounces	500 cc.
Kodak Elon Developing Agent .	15 grains	60 grains	1.0 gram
Kodak Sodium Sulfite, desiccated	2½ ounces	10 ounces	75.0 grams
Kodak Hydroquinone . . .	130 grains 1 oz.	90 grains	9.0 grams
Kodak Sodium Carbonate, monohydrated	1 ounce	4 ounces	30.0 grams
Kodak Potassium Bromide . .	75 grains	290 grains	5.0 grams
Cold water to make	32 ounces	1 gallon	1.0 liter

Dissolve chemicals in the order given.

For process photography, use without dilution. For development of copies of continuous-tone subjects, dilute with an equal volume of water. Develop about 5 minutes in a tank or 4 minutes in a tray at 68° F.

Kodak Developer D-72

For Papers, Films, and Plates

Stock Solution

	Avoirdupois—U. S. Liquid				Metric
Water, about 125° F. (50° C.) .	16	ounces	64	ounces	500 cc.
Kodak Elon Developing Agent .	45	grains	175	grains	3.0 grams
Kodak Sodium Sulfite, desiccated	1½	ounces	6	ounces	45.0 grams
Kodak Hydroquinone . . .	175	grains 1 oz.	260	grains	12.0 grams
Kodak Sodium Carbonate, monohydrated . .	2 oz. 290	grains	10½	ounces	80.0 grams
Kodak Potassium Bromide . .	30	grains	115	grains	2.0 grams
Water to make	32	ounces	1	gallon	1.0 liter

Dissolve chemicals in the order given.

For dilution and development times, see individual recommendations listed for each material.

Stop Baths

The purpose of a stop bath (acid rinse) is threefold: to interrupt development instantly by neutralizing the developer trapped within the film and sensitized paper; to protect the acid fixing bath from premature exhaustion by neutralizing the alkalinity of the developer which is carried into the fixer with the film and paper; and to prevent prints from staining in the hypo, which might occur if sensitized paper were transferred directly from developer to hypo without proper agitation in the fixing bath.

Stop Bath for Films

A good acid hardening stop bath for negatives that has a greater hardening effect than ordinary hardening solutions.

Sulfuric acid 5% solution	30 cc.
Potassium chrome alum gran.	30 grams
Water to make	1 liter

Agitate negatives for a few seconds after immersion. To secure maximum hardening, leave them in the bath for 3 to 5 minutes.

Stop Bath for Prints

Acetic acid, 28%	50 cc.
Water	1 liter

To make approximately 28 per cent acetic acid from glacial acetic acid, dilute 3 parts of glacial acetic acid with 8 parts of water. Treat prints for at least 5 seconds. Capacity of the solution is approximately 20 prints 8 by 10 inches per liter.

184

Fixing Baths

After development is completed, the unexposed (and undeveloped) silver salts must be removed from the emulsion, since otherwise they would in time darken and obscure the image. These undeveloped silver compounds are readily soluble in a solution of sodium thiosulfate, commonly called "hypo."

A *plain solution of hypo* in water would remain efficient for only a short time, since it would soon become contaminated with chemicals carried over from the developer. As a result, negatives and prints would stain and fix incompletely or not at all. To prevent this, three more components are normally added:

An *acid*—acetic acid—which neutralizes the (alkaline) developer carried over into the hypo and prevents undesirable reactions between developer and hypo. However, addition of acetic acid to the hypo solution turns the bath milky and renders it useless by decomposing the hypo. This must be prevented by adding a preservative to the solution.

A *preservative*—sodium sulfite—which opposes the decomposition of the hypo by the acid and makes it possible to maintain a high enough degree of acidity of the fixer to neutralize all the alkali carried over by developer in films and sensitized papers. Furthermore, sodium sulfite combines readily with oxygen in the solution and absorbs it before it can react with the carried-over developer, preventing the developing agents (reducers) from oxidizing and staining the fixing negatives and prints.

A *hardening agent*—either white potassium alum or potassium chrome alum—is finally added to prevent excessive softening and swelling of the gelatine of negatives and prints, particularly during warm weather. These chemicals tan the gelatine and render it less vulnerable to mechanical injuries.

Boric acid is sometimes added to fixers to retard the precipitation of sludge (aluminum sulfite) and to prolong the useful life of the bath.

RULES FOR THE PREPARATION OF FIXING BATHS

Dissolve the sodium sulfite first, then the acetic acid.
Add the hardener (alum) to the sulfite-acid solution. Do not mix sulfite and alum directly with each other, for they will form aluminum sulfite, which precipitates as white sludge.
Dissolve the hypo by itself in hot water; then let it cool down.
Do not mix hypo and acetic acid directly with each other, for the acid will decompose the hypo and the bath will turn milky.
Acetic acid is sensitive to heat. Do not add it to solutions that are warmer than 85° F. Mixed with hypo in solutions over 85° F., it decom-

poses the hypo and the bath will spoil. *After they have cooled below 85° F., mix the sulfite-acid-alum solution with the hypo solution.* A fixing bath that has turned milky is spoiled and must be discarded.

RULES FOR THE USE OF FIXING BATHS

Leave negatives in the fixing bath approximately twice as long as is required to clear the emulsion. Normally, a fixing bath is exhausted when the time required to clear a negative is twice that required when the bath was freshly prepared.

An exhausted fixing bath will still clear a negative, but such negatives are not permanent and fade within a relatively short time. Consult the table on p. 177 with regard to the maximum number of negatives and prints that can safely be fixed in a given amount of fixing solution.

The safest way to fix negatives and prints is to use two separate fixing baths. First, fix in one for the prescribed time, then fix the negatives or prints for approximately five minutes in the second bath. Then, when the first bath begins to show signs of exhaustion, discard it, replace it with the second bath, and prepare a new bath for the second fixing.

Negatives and prints should not be left in the fixer more than twice the time which was required to clear them. Otherwise, excessive swelling of the gelatine (negatives), bleaching of the image (prints), and great difficulty in removing the fixation by-products from the paper base of prints may result.

Kodak Fixing Bath F-6

For General Use with Films, Plates, and Papers

	Avoirdupois	U. S. Liquid		Metric	
Water, about 125° F. (50° C.) . .	80 ounces	2¼ gallons		600	cc.
Kodak Sodium Thiosulfate (Hypo) .	2 pounds	7	pounds	240.0	grams
Kodak Sodium Sulfite, desiccated .	2 ounces	7	ounces	15.0	grams
°Kodak Acetic Acid, 28%	6 ounces	21	ounces	48.0	cc.
Kodalk Balanced Alkali	2 ounces	7	ounces	15.0	grams
Kodak Potassium Alum	2 ounces	7	ounces	15.0	grams
Cold water to make	1 gallon	3½ gallons		1.0	liter

---

* To make approximately 28% acetic acid from glacial acetic acid, dilute 3 parts of glacial acetic acid with 8 parts of water.

Dissolve chemicals in the order given.

Kodak Fixing Bath F-6 is recommended for general use. It is a nearly odorless bath and permits somewhat more rapid washing than Kodak Fixing Bath F-5. Kodak F-6 should be used in conjunction with a stop bath such as Kodak SB-1 or SB-1a, or an acid hardening bath (p. 184) to obtain the full useful hardening life.

186

Print Permanence

Prints processed as described in the previous sections will last for many years without discoloring or fading—provided they are protected from the influence of light—but they are not "permanent." Actually, of course, nothing is "permanent," and even the stars in time change. However, to have prints last as long as possible, they must not only be made with special care but must also be treated with special care and protected from all those influences which constantly threaten to decompose both paper stock and image.

Deterioration of photographic prints is most often caused by chemicals remaining in paper stock and emulsion, aggressive glues used in mounting, humidity, high temperature, and prolonged exposure to light.

An exhausted fixing bath cannot completely dissolve the unexposed silver salts, which in time decompose and bleach the print. The best way to prevent this is to use the two-bath fixing method recommended above, followed by extra long washing (up to three hours) in the tank described on p. 121, especially if double-weight paper is used. To make sure that washing has been as thorough as possible, use the following test recommended by the Eastman Kodak Company:

Kodak Hypo Test Solution HT-2

For Testing the Degree of Washing of Films and Papers

	Avoirdupois U. S. Liquid	Metric
Water	24 ounces	750 cc.
°Kodak Acetic Acid, 28% . . .	4 ounces	125.0 cc.
Kodak Silver Nitrate	¼ ounce	7.5 grams
Water to make	32 ounces	1.0 liter

° To make approximately 28% acetic acid from glacial acetic acid, dilute 3 parts of glacial acetic acid with 8 parts of water.

Store in a screw-cap or glass-stoppered brown bottle away from strong light. Avoid contact of test solution with the hands, clothing, negatives, prints, or undeveloped photographic materials; otherwise black stains will ultimately result.

Test for Washing: After washing, cut off a small strip from the clear margin of the film or print and immerse a portion of it in a small volume of the test solution for about 3 minutes. Any discoloration of the treated strip indicates the presence of hypo, and the degree of stain shows the relative amount of hypo. Well washed films usually show little or no coloration; with commercially washed films the tint may approach that of dark brown sugar. Well-washed prints usually show a slight tint corresponding roughly to that of light brown sugar. A darker tint indicates insufficient washing.

When the washing is known to be fairly thorough, a quick spot test can be made on the back of a print or the back of a blank piece of paper carried through the processing with the batch of prints. Remove excess water by wiping or blotting the back of the print, apply a drop of the test solution, allow 2 or 3 minutes for the solution to react, and judge immediately the depth of the stain as described above.

NOTE: The excess silver nitrate will darken on exposure to light. Therefore, even if the test shows adequate washing, return the print to the wash water for 2 or 3 minutes in order to remove as much as possible of the test solution.

Prepared test solutions for hypo are made by several laboratories, and by the Eastman Kodak Company.

A negative reaction of prints by the above test does NOT guarantee that the images may not ultimately fade. It only proves that prints are reasonably free from hypo. To insure *complete* removal of hypo, treat the prints with a hypo-eliminator solution. First, wash the prints thoroughly, then immerse them for six minutes in Kodak Hypo Eliminator HE-1 at 68° F., and continue to wash for another ten minutes before you dry the prints as usual.

CAUTION: The following solution must be prepared just before it is used, and must be kept in an open container during use.

Hypo Eliminator HE-1
For Professional and Amateur Use

	Avoirdupois U. S. Liquid	Metric
Water	16 ounces	500 cc.
Hydrogen Peroxide (3% solution)	4 ounces	125.0 cc.
*Ammonia Solution	3¼ ounces	100.0 cc.
Water to make	32 ounces	1.0 liter

CAUTION: Prepare the solution immediately before use and keep in an open container during use. Do not store the mixed solution in a stoppered bottle, or the gas evolved may break the bottle.

* Prepared by adding 1 part of concentrated ammonia (28%) to 9 parts of water.

Directions for Use: Wash the prints for about 30 minutes at 65° to 70° F. (18° to 21° C.) in running water which flows rapidly enough to replace the water in the vessel (tray or tank) completely once every 5 minutes. Then immerse each print about 6 minutes at 68° F. (20° C.) in the Hypo Eliminator HE-1 solution, and finally wash about 10 minutes before drying. At lower temperatures, increase the washing times.

Life of HE-1 Solution: About fifty 8 × 10-inch prints or their equivalent per gallon (4 liters).

188

Occasional Effects When Using the Hypo Eliminator HE-1

1. Slight tendency for prints to stick to belt on belt dryers. To prevent this effect, bathe the prints about 3 minutes in a 1 per cent solution of formaldehyde prior to drying.

2. An almost imperceptible change in the image tone. To prevent this effect, add 15 grains of potassium bromide to each quart (1 gram per liter) of the peroxide-ammonia bath (HE-1).

3. A very faint yellowing of the whites (undetectable on buff papers). To minimize this effect, bathe the prints in a 1 per cent sodium sulfite solution for about 2 minutes immediately after treatment in HE-1 and prior to the final wash.

To minimize the dangers resulting from exposure to light and air, prints that are expected to last as long as possible must be tightly packed and stored in darkness. For additional protection, they should be treated in the solution given below. This solution covers the silver image with a protective layer of gold, which is much less susceptible to atmospheric influences than silver.

Kodak Gold Protective Solution GP-1

For Increasing the Permanency of Silver Images

	Avoirdupois U. S. Liquid		Metric	
Water	24	ounces	750	cc.
*Kodak Gold Chloride (1% stock solution)	2½	drams	10.0	cc.
Kodak Sodium Thiocyanate . .	145	grains	10.0	grams
Water to make	32	ounces	1.0	liter

* A 1% stock solution of Kodak Gold Chloride may be prepared by dissolving the contents of 1 tube (15 grains) in 3¾ ounces of water (1 gram in 100 cc. of water).

Add the gold chloride stock solution to the volume of water indicated. Dissolve the sodium thiocyanate *separately* in 4 ounces (125 cc.) of water. Then add the thiocyanate solution slowly to the gold chloride solution, while stirring the latter solution rapidly.

For Use: Immerse the well-washed print (which preferably has received a hypo elimination treatment) in the Gold Protective Solution for 10 minutes at 68° F. (20° C.) or until a just-perceptible change in image tone (very slightly bluish-black) takes place. Then wash for 10 minutes in running water and dry as usual.

Approximate Exhaustion Life: Thirty 8 × 10-inch prints per gallon. For best results, the Kodak GP-1 solution should be mixed immediately before use.

Films and Plates: The above procedure may also be used with fine-grain images on films and plates when maximum permanency is desired.

189

PART SEVEN

LEARNING FROM EXPERIENCE

The beginning of a new and exciting phase
in any photographer's career—the first step
toward original work: to get away from
teacher's supervision and advertising claims,
and to find out for himself, by test and experiment, the potentialities and limitations
of his equipment, material, and techniques

Experimenting with Materials and Techniques

Many amateurs erroneously believe that anyone can become an accomplished photographer in a relatively short time. This view may be so prevalent because it is so easy to produce recognizable pictures. And, since this view is fortified by the you-push-the-button-we-do-the-rest kind of advertising, it is no wonder. What one overlooks is the fact that there is a world of difference between "recognizable pictures" and "good pictures." It is true that almost anyone can quickly master the rudiments of photo-technique and turn out "recognizable pictures." Out of the thousands of pictures entered in every photographic contest, most are "technically good," some are excellent. But—and any contest judge or editor will confirm this—despite their high technical standard, the overwhelming majority of these pictures are pointless, boring, and trite—in short, anything but "good." Why? For two reasons: (1) Lack of originality and imagination on the part of photographers who mainly imitated what others had done before. (We shall hear about this in Part VIII.) (2) Because the majority of photographers are satisfied with elementary techniques. As soon as they know how to focus, expose, develop, and print, they start out to make "finished pictures"—freshmen trying to do postgraduate work. Considering this, it is no wonder that so many photographs are meaningless and immature.

Photography is not quite as simple as that. If it were, it would be difficult to explain the fact that the work of some photographers is good while the work of others is poor. They obviously use the same equipment—Eisenstaedt, W. Eugene Smith, Mydans, and McCombe all use the same type of camera and identical brands of film that thousands of amateurs use. How then are their pictures so much better? Very simple: such photographers know how to "see" good pictures, or, in other words, what constitutes a good picture; and they know how to render their subjects in photographically exciting forms. To use an analogy from music: "run-of-the-mill photographers" use only one finger to play a tune, while "good photographers" use all ten. The piano and tune may be the same, but the rendition is different.

Having mastered the fundamentals of his craft, a photographer should then broaden his techniques. Learn how to play "with both hands." This applies both in practice and in theory. In practice—by attempting increasingly difficult subjects, such as photographs at night; candid indoor shots; extreme close-ups; wide-angle and telephoto pictures. In theory—by study-

191

ing the various methods by which things can be achieved in photography; how lenses of different focal lengths affect perspective; how filters of different colors translate colors into shades of gray; the interdependency of the times of exposure and development and their influence upon the contrast range of the negative; the characteristics of papers of different gradations and their effects upon the impression of the picture; the use of camera "swings" for controlling perspective and avoiding distortion; the effect of high key and low key as a method of creating predetermined "moods"; dodging, "burning in," and "holding back" for local control of contrast in the print; and so on.

What the amateur must realize as soon as possible is the fact that there are always many ways to photograph a given subject. First, of course, there is what one might call the "obvious way." It is the simple and easy way, never very "original," and seldom the "best." It is usually an imitative and unimaginative way. There are other approaches which, being creative, make common subjects appear exciting and new. By selecting an unusual point of view—literally as well as figuratively speaking—through use of a telephoto or wide-angle instead of a standard lens; by utilizing the close-up, a "dramatizing" filter, or backlight and silhouette, a photographer can produce pictures that intensely express an idea, feeling, or mood to the observer—pictures that make other photographers exclaim: "Why didn't I think of this! Where did I have my eyes!"

The following pictures are intended to stimulate the reader to perform experiments of his own. They should arouse his curiosity and make him eager to know more. They are photographic "finger exercises" designed to help him to explore the potentialities of his medium. They testify to the broadness of its scope. They are as "abstract" as the "scales" a music student must play in order to become a good musician. No one, of course, would photograph a given subject through filters of every color from red to blue. But to be able to select *the right type of filter,* a photographer must be familiar with the effects of all filters upon every color. The "scales" on p. 199 will help him to achieve this. This also applies to the other "exercises"—in exposure, perspective, contrast control, etc. In practice, of course, only one of the many different possibilities would be finally used to render a given subject. But to be able to select the most effective one, a photographer must know them all. And the only way of knowing is to have studied each in practice. This must be taken quite literally: take your camera, lenses, filters, etc., find some suitable test objects, and actually repeat all the following examples. To just read about them, and look at the pictures, is not enough. Remember, there is no short cut to success, unless it is by way of test and experiment. The hours spent on such "finger exercises" will save you incalculable time later.

192

Exposure too short

Development too short

"Normal" negative

Development too long

Exposure too long

To distinguish between overexposed and overdeveloped, and underexposed and under-developed negatives, is necessary for the production of "technically perfect negatives." Otherwise, one cannot correct such mistakes or avoid them. I recommend that my reader deliberately under- and overexpose, and under- and overdevelop, some negatives, to become familiar with their appearance, and to learn how to distinguish between them.

Appearance of the negative			Cause of the mistake	
Too thin	and too contrasty	=	Exposure	too short
	and too contrastless	=	Development	
Too dense	and too contrastless	=	Exposure	too long
	and too contrasty	=	Development	

1 Long exposure, short development, low contrast

2 "Normal" exposure, "normal" development, "normal" contrast

Print from negative 1 on normal paper. Notice wealth of detail in shadows.

Print from negative 2 on normal paper. Notice balanced rendition of contrast

These four pairs of pictures illustrate the extent to which subject contrast can be controlled in the negative by controlling exposure and development. Ordinarily, of course, only one such step would be used. However, to be able to produce negatives in which contrast is in accordance with the characteristics of the subject, a photographer must know how to produce any desired contrast—how to decrease, increase, or preserve the contrast of over-contrasty, contrastless, or "normal" subjects, respectively.

I recommend that my reader take a series of pictures of a subject with average contrast and try to produce a series of negatives with contrasts ranging from extremely low to extremely high.

3 Shorter exposure, longer development, higher contrast

4 Very short exposure, very long development, very high contrast

Print from negative 3 on normal paper. Notice high contrast, black shadows.

Print from negative 4 on normal paper. Notice absence of intermediate grays.

Subject contrast is preserved if	$\dfrac{\text{exposure is according to exposure meter}}{\text{development is according to "standard" rule}}$
Negative contrast decreases if	$\dfrac{\text{exposure is longer-than-normal}}{\text{development is shorter-than-normal}}$
Negative contrast increases if	$\dfrac{\text{exposure is shorter-than-normal}}{\text{development is longer-than-normal}}$

195

The light-accumulating ability of films

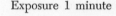

Exposure 10 seconds   Exposure 1 minute

Exposure 5 minutes   Exposure 30 minutes

These four pictures of an improvised darkroom were taken under identical conditions by the
light provided by the safelight and the weak illumination filtering through the partially open
door from an adjoining hall. To the eye, the setup corresponded approximately to the picture
in the upper right hand corner. Notice how increases in exposure bring out detail more and
more until, finally, the impression of a "darkroom" is completely destroyed.

To become familiar with the effects of the light-accumulating ability of films I recommend
that my reader take a similar series of pictures. Such "exercises" are important to successful
night photography in which underexposure results in complete failure, and overexposure
destroys the mood and mystery of night. The most important application of this phenomenon
is in astronomical photography in which hours and hours of cumulative exposure enables one
to photograph galaxies and stars that otherwise would be invisible.

Exposure 1/1000 sec. Bulb is completely underexposed and invisible. Interest is centered on the glowing filament.

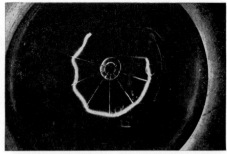

Exposure 1/250 sec. Bulb is still somewhat underexposed. Contrast is still high, emphasizing filament's white-hot glow.

Exposure 1/100 sec. Bulb is correctly exposed. Details in darkest as well as brightest areas are well defined.

Exposure 1/10 sec. Bulb is overexposed. Contrast begins to flatten out. Dark areas are abnormally rich in detail.

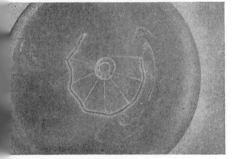

Exposure 1 sec. Bulb is enormously overexposed. Contrast is low. Reversal of the negative (solarization) has begun.

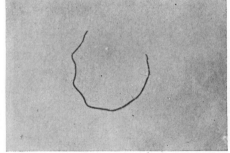

Exposure 10 sec. Bulb is overexposed beyond recognition. Solarization of brightest area is complete.

Six versions of an incandescent light bulb

In order to become familiar with the enormous exposure latitude of modern negative emulsions, and with the effect of decreases and increases in exposure, I recommend that my reader take a series of pictures of a contrasty subject in which exposures range from total underexposure to total overexposure. In the photographs above, notice how contrast increases as exposure decreases, and how shadow rendition improves with increased exposure. Notice, too, that the first and last pictures seem to be positive and negative in spite of the fact that both are positives.

Yellow filter

Red filter

Red filter and polarizer

Sky control through color filters

In the majority of outdoor photographs the sky is an important picture element. In order to make objects stand out in contrast against a blue sky, or to capture the beauty of clouds, control of the gray-tone rendition of the blue sky is necessary. For this reason, I recommend that my reader take a series of sky-and-cloud photographs through different filters in accordance with the instructions given in the table below.

Negative material	Filter	Tone of the blue sky
	blue	white
	none	lighter than it appeared to the eye
	medium yellow	as it appeared to the eye
Panchromatic film	dark yellow	slightly darker than it appeared to the eye
	light red	dark gray
	dark red	very dark gray
	red and polarizer	black

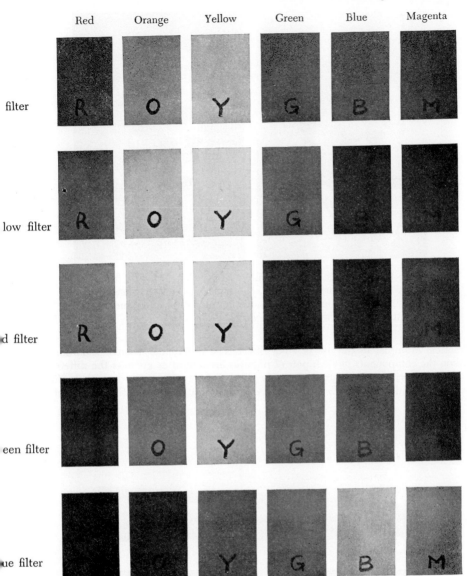

Red   Orange   Yellow   Green   Blue   Magenta

filter

low filter

d filter

een filter

ue filter

:olor translation into shades of gray can be controlled by means of color filters. To
ake a color appear darker in the photograph than it appears to the eye, a filter of a
omplementary color must be used. To make a color appear lighter, a filter of the same
olor must be used (see p. 49).

'o become familiar with the effect of different color filters on different colors, I recom-
end that my reader make a color chart containing red, orange, yellow, green, blue, and
iolet—by cutting swatches of colored paper and pasting them side by side—and photo-
raph the chart through different color filters.

he demonstration pictures above are photographs of the same type of chart taken on
anchromatic film through the four basic color filters yellow, red, green, and blue. They
ere printed on the same grade of paper (#2) for fair comparison of color translation.

Left: Panchromatic film, blue filter. *Right:* Panchromatic film, red filter. Sky and scarf were blue, the hat red, the hair blonde, and the suit gray. Notice the difference in color translation and subsequent change in "mood" produced by these filters.

Practical examples of the use of color filters. The differences in color rendition between the components of each pair of pictures are almost as great as the differences between positive and negative. But only photographers who have done their "finger exercises," and know which filter produces which results, achieve the desired effect.

Top: Panchromatic film, blue filter. *Bottom:* Panchromatic film, red filter. Sky was bluish-gray, upper front part of the locomotive orange, rear part of the roof dark blue, and lower part of the engine gray. Pictures taken under identical light conditions.

Left: "Ordinary" photograph. *Right:* Picture taken through a polarizer. Notice how disturbing reflections can be eliminated and the "hidden" subject brought out.

Polarizers and coated lenses are valuable aids in combating unwanted light manifestations. However, they are not always infallible, and there are things they cannot do. To become familiar with their potentialities and limitations I recommend that my reader shoot comparison pictures with and without a polarizer and a coated lens.

Left: Picture taken with uncoated lens. *Right:* Picture taken with coated lens. Notice how ugly flare—so common when one shoots against the light—can often be avoided by the use of a coated lens.

Control of perspective distortion

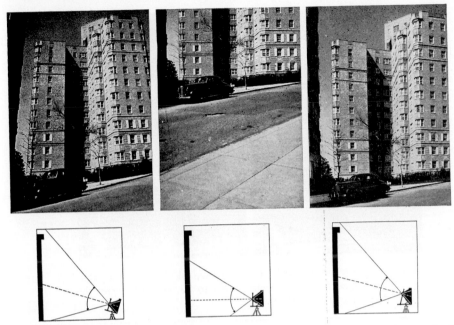

Distortion control by means of camera swings. *Left:* Tilting camera to include top of tall building produces "converging verticals." *Center:* Leveling camera so that film is parallel with building renders verticals parallel but cuts off top of building. *Right:* Keeping camera level but raising lens until all of building appears on groundglass, produces "normal," distortion-free photograph. For this purpose, a lens with sufficient "covering power" is needed.

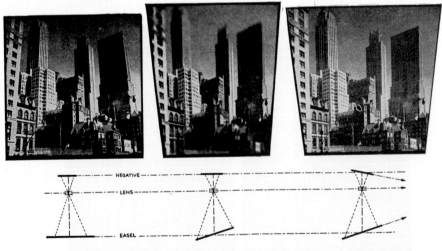

Distortion control by means of an enlarger. *Left:* Straight print from a "distorted" negative; verticals converge. *Center:* Tilting the easel restores verticals to parallelism; unsharpness must be corrected by stopping down enlarger lens. *Right:* Tilting negative and easel in opposite directions by means of a tilting negative carrier (see p. 120) produces distortion-free image that is sharp throughout even though the enlarger lens is wide open.

Left: **Wide-angle shot** from close-up. *Right:* **Telephoto shot** from far away. Use of lenses of different focal lengths enables a photographer to adapt the space impression of his picture to the demands of the subject. Here, photograph on left emphasizes the "endless" length of the row of houses, whereas picture on right stresses the narrowness of the individual buildings.

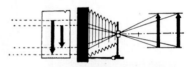

Wide-angle shot, camera close to subject. Depth appears exaggerated, proportions between subjects seem distorted, objects in foreground appear too big, objects in background appear too small. Notice great difference in size of images of arrows on groundglass in sketch.

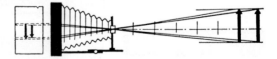

Telephoto shot, camera far away from subject. Depth appears shallow, proportions between subjects are well preserved, distortion is avoided. Notice small difference in size of images of arrows on groundglass in sketch.

Subject, setup, and distance between boxes are the same in both pictures (notice the folding rule); only the camera position and focal length of the lenses are different.

Perspective control by means of viewpoint and camera swings

Seven renderings of a cube—"finger exercises" in perspective control. To become familiar with the use of camera swings, I recommend that my reader take a similar series of pictures. Carefully note the following: (1) To give the most convincing impression of a cube or any three-dimensional form, a photograph must show three of its sides (lower row). Pictures showing only two sides of the cube suggest a hinged "screen." Picture showing only one side (top, left) suggests a flat surface without "body" or depth. (2) Converging of parallels can be made to suggest either "height" (top row, left of center), or "depth" (bottom row, left). (3) To avoid "distortion," the film must be parallel with the surface that has to be rendered distortion-free. To do so, the photographer must adjust the swing back of the camera accordingly. (4) If the swing back is correctly adjusted, the image on the groundglass will appear undistorted. If the image is partially out of focus, this unsharpness can be corrected to some extent by tilting the lens slightly. Remaining unsharpness must be corrected by stopping down the diaphragm. This type of work necessitates use of groundglass equipped view camera (p. 214).

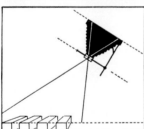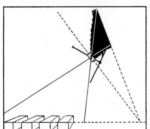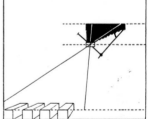

The extent to which perspective and extension of sharpness in depth can be controlled by using a swing-back and front is illustrated by these three pictures which were *taken from the same camera position with an identical diaphragm stop*—f/4.5.

Left: "Ordinary" photograph; notice limited extent of sharpness in depth.

Center: Adjusting camera front and back in such a way that imaginary lines drawn through the planes of subject, lens, and film meet in a common point produces a picture that is sharp throughout even though the diaphragm is wide open. Notice, however, the slight degree of distortion: parallel lines converge more sharply toward depth than in the undistorted but unsharp picture at the left.

Right: Readjusting camera front and back in such a way that imaginary lines drawn through the planes of subject, lens, and film are parallel produces a picture in which "inverted perspective" completely eliminates diminution toward depth: film box farthest away is rendered exactly as wide as the nearest one, parallels are rendered parallel, and do not converge toward depth.

Practical application of these principles is particularly useful in advertising and industrial photography in which undistorted rendition of objects is often necessary in order to create a correct impression of a product or a piece of machinery.

Direct front light produces "shadowless" illumination which obliterates "texture." This type of illumination must be avoided wherever texture rendition is important, for without shadows texture rendition is not possible.

Exercises i

Low-skimming, shadow-producing illumination brings out texture. Picture taken with a single floodlight. The diffused character of its illumination, however, produces shadows that are too weak for first-class texture rendition.

The concentrated beam of a low-skimming spotlight renders texture crisp and clean. Exaggerated contrast "dramatizes" the subject, but at the same time makes it appear too "harsh," unsuitable to the softness of bread.

xture-lighting

Combination of texture-producing, low-skimming spotlight and shadow-softening floodlight "fill-in" renders texture crisp but not harsh. In most cases, this setup gives the best illumination for "documentary" texture rendition.

207

Halo (non-antihalo plate)

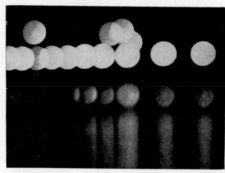

Out of focus

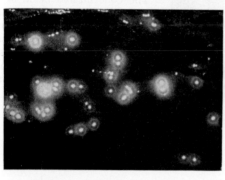

Halo (Duto diffusion disk)

Small diaphragm stop

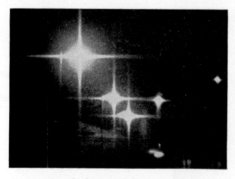

Single layer of fly screen

Two screens crossed at 45° angle

In a photograph, "light" and "white" are of necessity the same. Actually, however, "light" is radiant and active, whereas "white" is merely reflected light and passive. To render "light" in a photograph in the most effective form its radiance must be "symbolized." Some of the forms in which this can be done are illustrated above. To become familiar with the creation and use of such symbols I recommend that my reader experiment in this direction, studying and analyzing the "emotional" effects of different symbols, and learning how to use them for the creation of predetermined impressions.

The Great Confusion

The fledgling photographer, who goes out into the world to try his wings, immediately lands in the middle of a gigantic confusion—both literally and figuratively speaking.

Literally—because the moment he shyly enters a photo store to buy some equipment, he finds himself confronted with an overwhelming array of what at first seems like millions of different cameras, thousands of different lenses, and hundreds of different types of film and paper, not to mention the ten thousands of different accessories from photo-electric exposure meters and electronic flash guns to view finders that look around corners, and filters in all the colors of an expressionistic sunset.

Figuratively—because one day he hears that photography is nothing but a mechanical means of reproduction and the photographer just another technician: "the sooner you get off your high horse the better off you are"; the next day he reads in a photo magazine that photography is Art, that a photographer must be an Artist, and that photography is his "medium of expression." He reads about the "documentary photographers," the "Pictorialists," and the advocates of the "f/64 school," and he is confused by extreme differences in technique and approach. He is bewildered by an aggregate of pictures by amateurs and professionals representing all fields of photography. Which shall he choose? What shall he do?

Where does that leave our young photographer? And what is *he* going to do?

He can do one of two things: listen indiscriminately to anyone who "advises" him; toy with one camera and lens and film after another; consciously imitate the work of other photographers; identify himself with a "group" and thus forgo his individuality and limit his development.

Or he can make up his own mind by critically sifting advice given; by resorting to experiments and tests to verify certain claims, to expand his own knowledge and perfect his facility and technique; by learning from others—NOT by imitating them; by striking out on a path of his own to contribute the individuality and talent he possesses to express what are his aims.

In short, he can do what every man or woman did who ever accomplished anything worth while in this world: go his own way in his own manner and "be himself." And maybe—someday—he will become a great photographer.

Experimenting with Equipment

In the opinion of the author, the best way to select one's equipment is on the basis of two factors: quality and suitability.

Quality

1. Without *good quality tools* no craftsman—not even the best—can do a technically first-class job. A photographer is no exception. A cheaply made camera—equipped with a cheap, unsharp lens, film guides not truly aligned, front not properly squared and too weak, shutter speeds inaccurate and erratic—simply cannot produce the sharp, sparkling picture that anyone with a feeling for "graphic" qualities desires.

> RULE NUMBER 1: The higher the *quality* of his equipment, the more likely a photographer is to succeed in producing "technically perfect photographs."

Suitability

2. *Suitability of the equipment* is just as important as its quality. Many photographers overlook the fact that *their* equipment has to fit *their* temperament and ways of working. Too often they buy the type of camera that someone whose work they admire uses successfully, completely overlooking the fact that he might use a "technique" entirely different from that which they themselves use. To use an analogy: a heavy turret lathe is a wonderful precision-made tool—for the production of heavy engine parts; but it is completely unsuited to a watchmaker, who needs an equally precision-made but otherwise entirely different type of lathe.

> RULE NUMBER 2: The better suited the equipment is to your *personal* needs, habits, temperament, and character, the more it will facilitate your work, and the happier you will be with it. And—the less you have to worry about "technicalities," the better you can concentrate upon the more important *creative* problems of picture-making.

Your Own Contribution

3. Even the finest and most suitable camera, lens, accessory, etc., holds nothing but a promise. You, the photographer, are responsible; you alone can give your camera "life," can make it work, express your ideas, and create your photographs!

210

Photographers constantly keep asking me which camera, lens, or film, etc., I think is "best." This, of course, is a question which needs to be qualified: "Best for what purpose?" But even then it is very hard to give a definite answer, since there are always several brands of cameras, etc., that are equally well suited to do specific types of work. Which of them he should buy depends upon the preference and solvency of the photographer.

The more objectively a photographer approaches the problem of selecting a camera, the less he allows himself to be influenced by the glamor of brand names and the glitter of chromium trimmings, or by the impressive "records" made by certain makes of cameras, the better off he will be. Do not start by collecting catalogues and pamphlets describing various types of cameras. Start by asking yourself what kind of subject you want mainly to photograph (people, landscape, architecture, etc.); what kind of pictures you want to take (documentary, pictorial, snapshots, etc.); why you want to take them (hobby, record, profession, etc.); and what type of worker you yourself are (slow and careful, or temperamental and impulsive, etc.). Read the following paragraphs, which discuss these questions. Then make your decision, look at the camera of your choice, take it out for a trial period, use it, test it, see whether you like its "feeling" and the kind of pictures it produces, and—if you are really satisfied—buy it.

The Three P's.

Selection of a camera should always be governed by three factors: *the personality* of the photographer, the *purpose* for which the camera will be used, and the *purse* of the man who buys it. Everything else is immaterial.

---

1. **The personality** of the photographer determines the negative size of the camera.

Today, two markedly different trends exist in photography. One is characterized by a demand for the highest technical quality and precision of rendition; and the other is characterized by a demand for spontaneity, dynamic action, and human interest. The first trend has among its followers photographers such as Edward Weston, Berenice Abbot, Ansel Adams, and Paul Strand. The second, photographers such as Alfred Eisenstaedt, Ernst Haas, Art Kane, Gordon Parks, and Eugene W. Smith.

211

4 by 5 versus 35 mm.

Parallel with the development of these two trends, two types of cameras have been developed and perfected: large cameras which take 4- by 5-inch (or larger) sheet film or filmpack, and which produce photographs of unsurpassed technical quality and perfection; and 35-mm. miniature cameras, which combine extreme mobility with a minimum of size and weight. The best representatives of both types have such invaluable features as interchangeability of lenses; lens-coupled range finders for fast-action shots; groundglass focusing for parallax-free close-up shots; high-speed shutters with speeds to 1/1000 sec.; internal synchronization for flash and speedlights; double and triple extension for close-ups and renderings in natural and more-than-natural size. For both types different and often highly specialized negative emulsions are available.

However, though technically equal, each has its own characteristic advantages. In the 4-by-5 camera, which is admittedly heavy and bulky and comparatively slow to operate, the following advantages exist:

4 by 5 Advantages

1. *Highest sharpness and definition of rendition* in the final photograph. To make an 8- by 10-inch enlargement, the negative has only to be magnified twice linear; to make an 11- by 14-inch print, less than three times linear.

2. *Simple and fast processing.* Ordinary rapid developers can be used without danger of producing objectionable grain since negatives normally don't require a great degree of enlargement.

3. *Utilization of the full inherent speed of the film.* No increase in exposure is needed to compensate for speed losses since fine-grain development is not necessary (see p. 114).

4. *Easy processing and printing.* Specks of dust, abrasion marks, minute scratches and blemishes, etc., do not show nearly as much in prints made from 4 by 5 as those made from 35-mm. negatives because of the relative degree of enlargement.

35-mm. Advantages

On the other hand, the smaller size of the 35-mm. camera offers the following advantages:

1. *Smallness, compactness, and lightness*—invaluable when space is at a premium and weight a consideration—on canoe trips, hikes, mountain-climbing expeditions, or in war. A 35-mm. outfit with three different lenses, view finders, filters, and negative material for hundreds of exposures weighs less, and takes less space, than many a 4- by 5-inch camera without accessories or film.

2. *Maneuverability and inconspicuousness*—without which most "candid" shots are not possible to take. These advantages make 35-mm. cameras ideal for the reporter or documentarian who specializes in unposed pictures of people.

3. *Super-fast lenses*—with speeds of f/1.2 and f/1.5 are available *only* for 35-mm. cameras. Consequently, anyone who wants to specialize in candid theater, cabaret, or night photography must use a 35-mm. camera.

4. *Rapid-fire operation*—lens-coupled range finder in conjunction with film transport-coupled shutter-winding mechanism, backed up by film magazines containing negative material for thirty-six consecutive exposures (Robot camera: fifty), which with several cameras can be "fired" machine-gun fashion by means of a spring-driven motor, makes 35-mm. cameras ideal for every kind of sequence photography where up to five pictures per second have to be taken.

CONCLUSIONS

The choice between the two types of cameras should be based upon the temperament and interest of the photographer. If "graphic" quality and technical perfection are important to him; if he is a relatively slow, careful worker; if he wants to arrange his composition with care; if he is a perfectionist who would rather forgo a picture than lower his standards; and if he is willing to accept greater weight and bulk—then only a 4- by 5-inch camera will ever really satisfy him.

If, however, he is more interested in movement and action than in texture and definition; if he wants to travel light with a maximum of equipment which takes a minimum of space; if he is impulsive, acts quickly, and likes to shoot fast, catching his subjects "on the fly"; if he wants to carry his camera about, regarding it as a "photographic sketchbook"; and if he can tolerate a print quality of less sharpness and definition, face the problem of emulsion grain, forego smoothness of gray shades, and accept the fact that he must take great care in processing his films—then only a 35-mm. camera will ever really satisfy him.

However, the majority of amateurs, whose interests generally are not as specialized, will find the intermediate camera sizes, 2¼ by 2¼, 2¼ by 3¼, and 3¼ by 4¼ inches, more profitable. These intermediate camera sizes combine relative lightness and maneuverability with relatively large negative size and high degree of definition—qualities which in essence include some of the most desirable advantages of both the larger and the smaller cameras.

> **2. The purpose it must serve should determine the type of the camera.**

Having decided upon a definite negative size, the photographer should next decide what *type of camera* he needs. He has the choice of three different types:

1. The lens-coupled range-finder camera. This is the "fastest" camera type—the camera that is best suited to photographing action. Its disadvantages are that the small finder image makes composition difficult; that the extent of sharpness in depth is not directly visible; that photographers wearing glasses sometimes find it difficult to use a range finder.

Cameras typical of this group are: in the 4- by 5-inch size, the "press cameras" (Speed-Graphic, Linhof Technika, Burke & James Press, Busch Pressman D, etc.); in the 35 mm group the Kodak Retina, Leica, Fujica, Konica, Minolta, Voigtländer, etc.; and in the medium-format sizes the Linhof Press 70, Horseman Press 970, Mamiya 23, and Koni-Omega.

2. The view-type camera. This is the "slowest" camera type, but it offers several unique features not found in any other type. Its main advantage is its almost unlimited flexibility. The best cameras of this type provide "swings" both front and back in the vertical and the horizontal plane, so that full correction of perspective distortion is possible. The lens can be raised or lowered and moved sideways to right or left for further control of perspective. The back revolves to take either horizontal or vertical pictures, eliminating the necessity for turning the entire camera. Furthermore, these cameras permit the use of the greatest variety of lenses, from super wide-angle to super telephoto; and they are usually equipped with double- or triple-bellows extension for extreme close-up work. Extension of sharpness in depth can be observed directly on the large, negative-size groundglass. This makes it possible to get the utmost accuracy in focusing and in composing. Their disadvantages are slowness of operation, and the fact that they must be used on a tripod since they are not equipped with special view finders or range finders.

However, in the type of work to which they are best suited, such disadvantages are merely theoretical. View-type cameras are eminently suitable for architectural photography both indoors and outdoors, for every type of close-up, for photographing landscapes, technical and industrial subjects, objects of any kind, and copy work.

View-type cameras are available in sizes ranging from 3¼ by 4¼ inches to 8 by 10 inches, and larger. The most useful size is 4 by 5 inches. Typical representatives are the Linhof Color 4x5, Plaubel Peco, Sinar.

3. The reflex-type camera. This camera type combines the readiness

214

and maneuverability of the range-finder-type camera with the large nega-tive-size groundglass image of the view-type camera. It has in addition the advantage that the groundglass image remains visible until the mo-ment of exposure. (In twin-lens reflex cameras, which have a separate "finder lens," the image remains visible constantly—before, during, and after the exposure.) Its disadvantages are bulkiness and weight; the fact that wide-angle lenses normally cannot be used (some reflex cameras, however, permit the use of a moderate wide-angle lens); that correction of perspective is not possible because it lacks "swings" (exception: the British Soho Reflex permits a limited amount of perspective correction); and that stopping down the lens makes the groundglass image appear proportionally darker (exceptions: twin-lens reflex cameras, in which the image always remains bright because it is produced by a separate finder lens; and cameras equipped with an automatic diaphragm which at the moment of exposure closes down to a pre-set stop).

Reflex-type cameras are best suited to photographic work that demands speed of operation combined with accuracy in focusing and ease in com-posing. Consequently, photographers who want to specialize in portrai-ture, pictures of children, animals, and nature photography should first consider the different sizes of reflex cameras, of which they have the choice of two sub-types: (1) *the single-lens reflex cameras,* which permit inter-changeability of lenses and are easily adapted to close-up work of any kind; (2) *the twin-lens reflex cameras,* which show a constantly bright finder image but do not show the extension of sharpness in depth, do not provide interchangeability of lenses (exception: the Mamiyaflex) and are not particularly suited to close-up work either because their extension is limited or because of parallax problems.

Typical of the single-lens reflex-type camera are the 4- by 5-inch and 3¼ x 4¼-inch Graflex (discontinued), the 2¼ x 2¼-inch Hasselblad, Bronica, Kalimar, and Praktisix; and in the 35 mm size the Alpa, Topcon Super D, Contarex, Exa, Exakta, Pentax, Retina Reflex, Leicaflex, Miranda, Nikon F, Praktina, etc. Typical of the twin-lens reflex-type are the Rolleiflex and Rolleicord, Mamiyaflex, Minolta, Yashica, and in the 4 x 5-inch size, the Gowlandflex.

The beginner's camera. It is frequently said that a beginner in photog-raphy should start with a simple "box-type" camera—"because a more complicated camera is too difficult for the beginner to understand." Such a remark is no more justifiable than to say that the first radio one buys should be a crystal set, or the first car a Model T. Actually, a box camera might discourage a person who is seriously interested in photography, for no matter how hard he tries he cannot produce sharp and sparkling pictures with it. In my opinion, a 2¼- by 2¼-inch twin-lens reflex camera is most suitable for the beginner.

215

> 3. **The purse** of the buyer determines the quality of the camera.

Always buy the best camera that you can afford, but do not make the mistake of confusing the "best" with the "most expensive." The "best" camera is that most suited to *your* particular needs. For example, the "best" camera for one specializing in architectural photography is a comparatively inexpensive 4- by 5-inch view-type camera with "swings"; while for the candid night club and theater photographer a 35-mm. camera with 1.5 lens is "best"—an instrument which costs many times as much as a simple 4 by 5.

Secondhand Bargains

A good way of acquiring a fine camera at a reasonable price is to buy it secondhand. Thanks to that common amateur "disease" of constantly trading one camera for another after a brief period of use, the photo market is flooded with equipment classified "like new"—and such equipment sells for only one-half or two-thirds of its original price.

Whenever you buy a camera or lens, do not close the deal until you have had a chance to test the equipment under "field conditions" to find out whether you like its performance. Any reputable dealer allows a three-day trial period for this purpose, and will refund your money if you are not satisfied with your purchase. This procedure is especially recommended in buying secondhand equipment which is no longer covered by the manufacturer's guarantee. Following is a list telling you what particularly to look out for in buying a secondhand camera:

How to Test a Camera

Light-tightness of the bellows: take the camera back off, extend bellows completely, hold the camera up to a strong light or the sun. After covering both your head and the camera box with a focusing cloth to keep out extraneous light, look inside the bellows. Holes in the bellows, which occur mainly in the corners of the folds, will stand out like tiny pinpricks of light. Also be sure that the bellows connections at camera front and back are still tight.

Shutters: Click shutter repeatedly at all speeds. Listen to it; the sound should be clean and sharp on the short, and smooth and purring on the longer, exposure times, never grating or hesitating. Uneven sound indicates a dirty shutter that should be cleaned before acceptance.

Look for worn patches and pinprick holes in the curtain of a focal-plane shutter: take out the lens, hold camera up against the light, with your head under a focusing cloth, inspect curtain. A tiny pinprick can be

216

patched with black rubber paint; if worn spots show, the curtain is beyond repair and must be replaced.

Camera front: Check for excessive "play." In locked position, the front should be completely free from "waggle," even though it may bend slightly backward or forward under pressure of your hand. A loose front is a common defect of many secondhand cameras, and a frequent cause of unsharp pictures. In testing a view camera, also check stability of back.

The focusing mechanism: Check tracks or helical lens mount, respectively, for excessive play. They should work smoothly, be neither too tight nor too loose. Test a range finder for accuracy of synchronization by determining whether or not a certain subject appears "in focus" simultaneously on the groundglass and in the range finder. Be sure that the range finder is reasonably accurate at the three most often used lens-to-subject distances—six feet, fifteen feet, and infinity.

The lens board: In testing cameras with interchangeable lenses mounted on boards, be sure that the lens board fits tightly. Some lens boards fit so loosely that they can "jiggle" during the exposure and cause unsharpness. If a lens board is loose it can easily be taped to insure the necessary tightness. Sometimes a magnetic tripper is removed from a lens board, and a screw hole has not been plugged properly. Such a tiny hole in the lens board acts like the pinhole in a pinhole camera. It produces, in this case, a secondary image of the subject which, though weak, still causes double exposure of the negative.

How to Test a Lens

The simplest and most practical way to test a lens is to take a picture with it, enlarge the negative, and check the print for sharpness. However, in order to produce conclusive results, such a test must be conducted according to strict scientific rules since there are causes for unsharpness which are not related to the quality of the lens. Observation of the following recommendations will eliminate these factors:

1. *The lens must be perfectly clean.* A greasy film or fingermarks on the glass cause a slight degree of unsharpness. Cleaning a lens must be done very carefully to avoid scratching its surface. First, with a soft camel's-hair brush, remove all dust and traces of grit from the lens; then breathe on the glass and with a piece of lens tissue gently and lightly wipe it clean. Never touch the glass surfaces of a lens with your fingers.

2. *The camera should be supported* by a sturdy tripod to positively eliminate movement during the exposure.

3. *A cable release should be used* to trip the shutter as a further precaution against possible movement of the camera.

4. *A well-illuminated, flat, contrasty test object* which is rich in fine, sharp detail should be used. A square consisting of four pages from a

well-printed magazine will do very nicely. Test objects lacking in contrast and well-defined detail (such as people or a face) are unsuitable because in such subjects distinction between what is sharp and unsharp is almost impossible.

5. *Camera and test object must be at right angles to one another;* otherwise, one side of the image will be out of focus. If the camera has "swings," check to see that they are in "neutral" position. Sometimes a heavy lens pulls the camera front down slightly and throws the whole system out of alignment. This may cause considerable unsharpness which, however, is not the fault of the lens.

6. *Focusing has to be done extra carefully.* If a range finder is used, check first that it is "in synchronization" (see above under "focusing mechanism"). If "out of sync," the picture will be unsharp, no matter how good the lens is. When focusing a camera equipped with groundglass, check sharpness of image with a six-power magnifier to be sure that it is really "in focus."

7. *When shooting test pictures out of the window* (for checkup on sharpness at infinity), be sure that you do not shoot across a hot radiator —the rising warm air will blur your picture.

8. *Use a fine-grain film* for your test shots, and develop them in a fine-grain developer.

9. *Do not overexpose.* Overexposure causes halation within the emulsion of the film. Such negatives are always less sharp than correctly exposed shots.

10. *Make 11- by 14-inch enlargements* from your test negatives and check them for sharpness. After all, it is the final picture that counts, and not the appearance of the lens. If you are satisfied, the lens is all right— as far as your personal needs are concerned. If not—take your test shots, both negatives and prints, to your photo dealer and ask his advice.

CONCLUSIONS

Cameras should be treated with care as one would treat other precision instruments. But proper treatment should never approach fetishism—an attitude of those amateurs who get more pleasure from owning and fondling a fine camera than from using it to make photographs. It is a well-established fact that many amateurs own more and better equipment than some of our best professional photographers. But such amateurs pay high prices solely for the pleasure of owning such equipment. And as long as they insist on attributing so much importance to their equipment, their interest naturally centers around it instead of being concentrated on the photographs they might produce. When an amateur overcomes this "gadgeteer" stage, it is a sign that he has started to "grow up" as a photographer.

218

Most cameras are sold complete with lenses. This fact might seem to make a special section on lens selection superfluous. However, since many of these cameras are available in different models equipped with different types of lenses, a choice still remains with the photographer. In addition, there are cameras that provide for interchangeability of lenses, and at some time the owners of such a camera may wish to acquire another lens for a particular type of work which is beyond the scope of the original lens.

SUITABILITY

The most important quality of any lens is "suitability." Neither "speed" nor name nor price nor appearance is of the slightest aid if a lens is not suited to the particular kind of work to be done. A typical example of this is the mistake constantly made by amateurs in buying lenses that are too fast for their needs. They are either motivated by pure snobbishness, or they believe that "speed" is a valuable "reserve." Fast lenses *do* have serious disadvantages: aside from being heavier, bigger, and ever so much more expensive than slower lenses, *they are also generally less sharp*, even when stopped down! In order to produce sufficient sharpness in depth, the vast majority of photographs are taken with the lens stopped down to at least f/4.5. And since this is so, why not use slower, sharper lenses to produce sharper pictures with finer detail, rather than cope with the inferior sharpness of faster lenses merely because occasionally one expects to need their higher speed? It seems as impractical as driving about in a furniture van merely on the chance that someday one might need its capacity for moving to a new house.

Coated Lenses

The most important recent advance in lens development is "coating." I mentioned the fact (p. 29) that all lenses are subject to certain losses of light. And the more complex a lens, the greater the light loss. The chief cause of this light loss is reflection from the glass-air surfaces of the individual lens elements. This loss can now be eliminated almost completely through the use of certain chemicals which are vaporized in a high vacuum and precipitated on all glass-air surfaces of the lens to form an extremely thin "anti-reflection coating." "Coated" lenses can be recognized by their slightly bluish or purplish tinge. Such lenses are not only somewhat "faster" than uncoated lenses of the same type, because of improved light transmission, but are also "sharper" because lens flare and halation have been almost completely eliminated.

1. The standard lens is the photographer's "work horse"—the lens that "does a little of everything"; in short, the average lens for the average type of picture. A good standard lens combines, as far as possible, the advantages of the more specialized lenses and avoids their disadvantages. It is a compromise—sharper than a high-speed lens but not as fast; faster than a wide-angle lens but not covering as great an angle; covering a greater angle than a "process lens" * but not as sharp; sharper than a high-speed lens ... and so on.

A standard lens should have a focal length approximately equal to the diagonal of the negative it must cover, and a relative aperture from f/2.8 (for 35-mm. and 2¼- by 2¼-inch cameras) to f/4.5 (for 4- by 5-inch and larger cameras). As standard lenses, faster lenses are not suitable because they are not sharp enough, even when stopped down, and their superior speed is too rarely needed by the average photographer to compensate for this deficiency. Furthermore, standard lenses are always considerably less expensive than "high-speed lenses," and the difference in price can be invested more advantageously in a better camera, useful accessories, or even more film.

Excellent standard lenses for 4- by 5-inch cameras can be found among the old-fashioned f/6.3 anastigmats and double anastigmats made by several German manufacturers before World War I, and since discontinued. In comparison to "modern" lenses, usually their price is reasonable. Often they are either in "barrel mount" (i.e., without shutter) or mounted in an outmoded type of shutter. This should not be a source of discouragement, since any lens can easily be remounted in any modern shutter, with or without built-in flash synchronization. Some of the very best standard lenses ever made for 4- by 5-inch cameras are the old f/6.3 Carl Zeiss Tessar and f/6.8 Goerz Dagor lenses. Not fast according to modern standards—but what definition! Furthermore, they are sharp when "wide open" and need not, like many of our faster modern standard lenses, be stopped down to f/11 to become "really sharp." The large size of the 4 by 5 and the correspondingly narrow zone of sharpness in depth makes stopping down almost mandatory. In view of this, why waste money on useless "speed" and inferior "definition?"

2. Wide-angle lenses save the situation when distance between subject and camera is so short that a standard lens could render only part of the subject. Wide-angle lenses have more covering power than standard lenses

---

* A lens corrected for utmost sharpness, commonly used by engravers and for making reproductions.

of equal focal length. This means that a given negative size can be covered with a shorter-than-standard focal-length lens, and the picture it produces will have a wider-than-standard angle of view (from 65 to 140 degrees as compared to the standard 45 to 55 degrees).

Compared to standard lenses, wide-angle lenses have the following disadvantages:

Because of their shorter-than-standard focal length, they produce images in smaller-than-standard scale. As a result, photographers are often tempted to increase the image size of their subject by moving the camera closer. This, of course, not only increases the size of the image, but simultaneously produces the well-known wide-angle perspective which makes hands and feet appear ridiculously large, and heads unnaturally small.

The relative aperture is usually considerably smaller than that of standard lenses, and diminishes proportionately as the angle of view of the lens becomes greater (the greater its covering power). However, there are exceptions: the Nikkor 21 mm f/4, Biogon 21 mm f/4.5, Alpa Retrofocus 24 mm f/3.5, and many 28 mm f/2.8 wide-angle lenses for 35 mm cameras.

Some wide-angle lenses have a certain amount of curvilinear distortion— i.e., lines that are actually straight will be rendered slightly curved, becoming increasingly so toward the edges of the picture.

Some wide-angle lenses need to be stopped down to f/11 or more in order to cover the entire negative sharply.

When considering the purchase of a wide-angle lens, be sure that the bellows extension of your camera can be kept short enough to permit focusing the lens at infinity. In many reflex cameras, the mirror needs too much space for its upswing to permit the use of wide-angle lenses. Press-type cameras should be equipped with a "drop-bed"—if not, the front edge of the bed cuts off part of the image.

3. Telephoto lenses are indispensable when distance between subject and camera is so great that a standard lens would produce an image too small to be of use. Like a telescope, telephoto lenses magnify the subject. Relative to the negative size they must cover, their focal lengths are longer than standard; and correspondingly, their angle of view is narrower than that of a standard lens. They show less of the subject, but what is shown is rendered in larger scale. We must distinguish between two types of "telephoto lenses": (1) "Ordinary" long-focus lenses which, when focused on infinity, require a lens-to-film distance equal to their focal length. (2) "Genuine" telephoto lenses which, when focused on infinity, require a much shorter lens-to-film distance, corresponding to two-thirds or less of their focal lengths. This (from a practical point of view) valuable peculiarity of "genuine" telephoto lenses is due to their unorthodox construction, which includes a negative rear element that "magnifies" the image produced by the positive front element before it reaches the film.

For example, the 32-cm. Zeiss Tele-Tessar requires an extension of only about 20 cm. when focused on infinity, while on "ordinary" lens of identical focal length would require an extension of 32 cm. The rendering of both lenses, however, would be identical in "perspective" and image scale.

4. **Super-fast lenses** are indispensable when the light is too weak to permit correct exposure with a lens of "ordinary" speed. Such lenses are constructed with but one aim: speed! Consequently, other qualities have to be sacrificed somewhat. As a result, super-fast lenses are generally less sharp, considerably heavier and bulkier, and much more expensive than slower lenses of equal focal length. Furthermore, because of their complexity, they are more liable to produce flares and halation than an "ordinary" lens is. This fault, however, can be greatly reduced by "coating" (see p. 219). Super-fast lenses, for these reasons, definitely cannot be recommended as "all-round" lenses. They should be used only when light conditions make their use imperative.

Famous super-fast lenses—the Kodak Ektar f/1.9, the Zeiss Biotar f/1.4, and the Sonnar f/1.5 and f/2, the Leitz Summarit f/1.5 and 85-mm. Summarex f/1.5, the Schneider Xenon f/1.5, the Nikkor f/1.5 and the Fujinon f/1.2—are for 35-mm. cameras only. A few super-fast lenses have been made for larger cameras. But they are so heavy and big, and their cost is so exorbitant, that they are of no interest to the amateur.

5. **Soft-focus and portrait lenses** produce images in which contrast between sharp and unsharp is less pronounced than in images produced by "ordinary" lenses. Photographs taken with such lenses are in no part really sharp; but on the other hand, out-of-focus areas are never quite as fuzzy as out-of-focus areas produced by a normal lens.

Typical soft-focus lenses are the Thambar for the Leica; the Duto slip-on disks which transform the lenses of Rolleiflex and Rolleicord temporarily into soft-focus lenses. And for 4- by 5-inch and larger cameras, the Rodenstock Imagon "Depth-Image" lens which, with the aid of variable sieve-like stopping-down devices, makes it possible to produce pictures in which rendition is either critically sharp or soft to various degrees.

6. **Slip-on lenses** are single-element auxiliary lenses. Designed for cameras with permanently attached lenses, their use makes wide-angle and telephotography possible within the limits of the bellows extensions of these cameras. Slip-on lenses clamp onto the lens mount (Rolleiflex: bayonette-mount), and, if they are positive, shorten the focal length of the permanent lens; if negative, lengthen. If negative, they require considerable bellows extension and groundglass focusing control. To obtain satisfactory definition, small diaphragm stops should always be selected when slip-on lenses are used.

Typical of these lenses are the Kodak Portra and Telek Lenses, and the Zeiss Proxar and Distar.

222

PART EIGHT

HOW TO USE PHOTOGRAPHY

Now that you know "how to do it"—what are you going to do with it? The most important chapter in any photographic textbook—and the one most often neglected. Photography is a means to an end—the picture with purpose and meaning. This chapter shows you one approach—the rest is up to you

A Matter of Opinion

Photography is such a varied medium of visual communication that trying to establish rigid rules for the making of "good" photographs would be as ridiculous—and as worthless—as telling a painter exactly how to create and execute a good painting. Who is infallible enough to decide whether Rubens is a "better" painter than Renoir, or Cézanne "superior" to Van Gogh? Similarly, in photography: is Avedon "better" than Mili? Or Weston "superior" to McCombe?

Anyone can easily see that creative and "original" photographers—photographers who possess a style of their own—are different from one another. But no one can authoritatively say whether one photographer is necessarily "better" than another. If a photograph conveys something to the observer, if it is imaginative and original, filled with meaning, intent, and feeling—then it is automatically a "good" photograph, and its creator a "good" photographer. If not—the photographer who made it will just as automatically be considered a "poor" photographer, notwithstanding the "group" or "school" to which he belongs.

From this one may safely conclude that *the first requisite for a good photograph is that it have some meaning.* It must be the logical end result of (1) interest in a particular subject, (2) a personal feeling or opinion concerning it, and (3) a sincere desire to project this in a photographic form—coupled with the technical ability to do so, and a sufficiently imaginative approach to captivate the interest of the observer. If a photographer fails in this last respect—if he cannot "get his ideas across"—all his efforts are in vain, for his picture then has no meaning, at least as far as the observer is concerned.

Thus we can formulate a second prerequisite which a "good" photograph must meet: not only must it have a meaning, but this meaning must be expressed in such a form that *it becomes apparent to the observer.* As long as this is accomplished, it does NOT matter what final form the picture takes—whether it is sharp or fuzzy, "pictorial" or "documentary," or whether the subject is a landscape or a nude.

As far as form or technique are concerned, they should be determined by the mood or idea that is to be expressed in the picture. In consideration of this, I am, therefore, opposed to "groups" or "schools" as such, for I believe that rigid adherence to a "group" or "school" proves limiting. I dislike narrowness in any form. It is a deterrent to anything new and progressive. It stifles creative ability and promotes stagnation of the mind. Most adherents of "groups" and "schools" are too zealous. They ruthlessly condemn anything that does not "conform" with *their* opinions. Young inexperienced photographers are naturally eager to learn, and therefore are apt to be easily impressed, particularly by opinions uttered with "authority." If the reader is aware of this, listening to such set opinions can do him no real harm.

Conclusions: Be critical. Listening to others is often a good way to learn, but do not forget that you have a mind of your own and a right to your own opinion.

Now I am going to stick my neck out by voicing *my own opinions* on photography. I am well aware of the fact that I invite criticism, and that I may be accused of those things to which I objected in others. I take this "calculated risk" for the following reasons:

I firmly believe that anyone is entitled to voice his opinion and should have the courage of his conviction. I have no quarrel with followers of "groups" or "schools" because their approach is different from my own. I respect their opinions, even though I often disagree with them. What I resent is their narrow-mindedness and intolerance—their "conform—or be condemned."

I am not opposed to argument. I believe that any spirited discussion is stimulating, no matter how wide the disagreement. As a matter of fact, discussion without disagreement seems pointless to me because there is no possibility for constructive criticism.

Finally, I am stating my own opinions because I believe that what I have to say may contribute to my reader's becoming a better photographer.

A "PHILOSOPHY OF PHOTOGRAPHY"

There seem to be three different stages in the development of a photographer. Some photographers gradually pass from the first stage through the second to the third; others never get that far in their development; still others skip stage one. But the "naturals"—the "born photographers"—start at stage three.

First stage: At this stage the photographer is merely a collector, a "gadgeteer," one whose prime interest is in cameras and lenses, in the mechanics of photography. He usually possesses the finest equipment, the latest gadgets, and a full line of accessories. He is the delight of the owner of any photo store because he never keeps a camera for more than a few weeks. He always comes back to trade it in. He constantly "tests" his cameras and lenses, but he never gets around to taking a "real" picture.

Second stage: At this stage the photographer's prime interest is in "print

226

quality." He also owns a lot of fine equipment, but at least he takes pictures with it. However, he photographs purely for the purpose of taking pictures. The subject is more or less incidental. His ambition is to make a "perfect print." He lovingly talks about film grain and negative gradation, gamma and inertia, reciprocity failure and opacity, religiously buys each new brand of fine-grain developer as soon as it appears on the market, always hoping for perfection—the developer that will enable him to make "grainless" 16- by 20-inch enlargements from Leica negatives (with a contact print pasted in the lower left-hand corner).

Third stage: At this stage the photographer is akin to the painter or the novelist who is motivated by some kind of inner compulsion. He does not care what kind of camera he uses as long as it takes the kind of picture he wants. You may see him toting a battered Leica—model 1932—but his photographs get exhibited at the Museum of Modern Art. His "technique" may sometimes be questionable, but his sincerity is not. If a photographer definitely knows what he wants, even though he does not always know how to get it, he will eventually learn—through application and resourcefulness—ways to express better and more clearly on film and sensitized paper experiences he wants to share with other people.

The Mission of the Camera

To me, photography is a means to an end: a picture with purpose and meaning. *The purpose:* A photograph is a means of communication. A photographer takes pictures for other people to see. Every photograph is a message from photographer to observer. The purpose of such a message is to tell, in visual form, something that the photographer felt worth communicating to others. A picture that does not "say" anything is pointless. Of course, sometimes the "message" may not be of interest to others, or may not be "understood." This is particularly true of "experimental" photographs. In this respect, photographers share the fate of many other artists whose work was too "advanced" for their time, whose public was not "ready" for what they had to say. Such artists were ridiculed by their contemporaries, yet their work, once labeled as "radical" and worse, sets the style one generation later. It would be well for those who automatically condemn things "modern" and "advanced" to remember this. Even if such pictures do not always "come off"—a hazard which, incidentally, they share with every kind of pioneer work—they still are more stimulating than many "conventional" photographs. Of course, photographers who merely imitate the work of others, who indulge in "fads" for the sake of "being different," and who have nothing worth while to say—produce pictures that serve no purpose and justly invite criticism. But a photographer who is sincere in his work should always be respected. Sincerity and purpose are inseparable, and a sincere photograph is always a purposeful one.

227

The meaning: Any message has content. This content is its "meaning." The content of a photograph can be almost anything: educational, informative, satirical, entertaining. Even a picture taken merely for record's sake has a meaning—to provide a record for future reference. The majority of amateur pictures fall into this category, all the photographs of babies and sweethearts, of birthdays and picnics, are "records for future reference" to be looked at and enjoyed in times to come. Compare such photographs, which many a "serious" amateur derides as "snapshots," to the type of pictures one mainly finds in photographic salons: the snapshots at least mean something to the photographer and his family; the "salon pictures" often are completely meaningless.

Any meaningful photograph begins with an idea. The more original the idea, the more likely it is that the picture conveys something new to the observer, and the new or unusual is always stimulating. This automatically makes an *original* photograph an *interesting* photograph. And vice versa: a photograph based upon a trite idea can never in itself be anything but trite. All pictures that are imitations of other photographs are trite because they are repetitious. To me, imitating is a senseless waste of energy and time, but many photographers still seem to disagree. Otherwise, how can one explain the continuous production of such photographic clichés as pattern shots of rows of empty chairs, coils of heavy rope, bums with beards and battered hats, spectacles on open books, gnarled hands folded in simulated prayer, fake monks dressed up in burlap, and nude girls toying with rubber balloons? Aside from the hope of getting a "prize" at the local club contest, what is the purpose of such pictures? And why do such pictures deserve prizes?

With interesting motifs in existence everywhere, it is hard to understand why so many photographers waste their time on clichés. Perhaps it is lack of imagination. Or that they don't know how to "see." Perhaps they want to "play safe" by sticking to subjects that have been "done" successfully before. Possibly they feel they must compete with other photographers by making better pictures of the same subject. But whatever their motivation—unless they cease to imitate and begin to do "original" work, they will never make good pictures.

The first step on the road to original work is the realization that a camera is no more than an instrument for making pictures. Forget its appearance, its precision workmanship, its chromium trim, its shiny lens, and regard it in the way that you would, for instance, regard a typewriter. What the typewriter is to a novelist, the camera is to a photographer—a machine used only as a means to record his ideas. Anyone can learn to type, and similarly anyone can learn to make photographs. No one is concerned with the make of typewriter a novelist uses. Similarly, why should anyone care what brand of camera a photographer uses in making his pictures? The only thing that matters is whether his work is interesting and good, or pointless and bad.

A camera is an instrument potentially as versatile as a microscope or telescope. Similar to these, it can be used to record in picture form far more than a mere repetition of things seen before. Imaginatively used, a camera becomes an instrument for making discoveries in the realm of vision. Many of us have seen such photographs. But few amateurs realize how many such motifs are within reach of their cameras:

Extreme close-ups. This type of photograph of small objects of nature in more than natural size discloses a "new" world—faces of insects, grotesque as some of the masks of primitive tribes; tiny seeds of plants, revealing their ingenious arrangements for transportation, wings and featherlike devices, hooks, and spikes. Nothing seems more stationary than a weed or a tree; but in their earliest stages, many plants, in the form of seeds, wing their way with the wind as free as the birds, or travel for miles hooked to the fur of animals. Isn't it more exciting to photograph such aspects of nature than dressing your uncle in burlap, making him pretend to write with a "quill," and photographing him as a "monk"?

Telephotographs. Not only do they bring distance within your reach but they also render objects in their natural proportions. They eliminate "distortion." They make everything appear "monumental," and give one the feeling of being in the midst of things. Telephotograph your home town from a nearby hill and see how "impressive" it becomes. Photographed thus, in street scenes people seem as they "really" are, without that tense or frightened expression that is almost unavoidable when directly confronted with a camera. Use a telephoto lens if you want traffic to seem as congested as it is when you try to squeeze through it in a car. Photograph animals in captivity or in nature with your telephoto lens. Use it for any kind of subject—not only those that are too far removed for your standard lens, but also subjects that you never thought of telephotographing before. Step back until you get the necessary distance—and watch how your photographs will improve!

Infrared sensitized film. Have you ever thought of using it? Explore its possibilities, see how it "dramatizes" landscapes, penetrates dust and haze, unveils distance, makes well-known objects appear exciting and new. No "special equipment" is needed—even a "box" will do.

Pictures at night. The modern photographer's day has twenty-four hours. Part of your life is lived at night—so why not record some of it on film? Time exposures can be made with any camera, even with a "box." For instance, the pattern of traffic at night traced by the headlights of approaching cars produces diagrams in space and time that are seen only with the aid of a camera. Time exposures show the stars wheeling in the

229

sky as a profound cosmic spectacle. A lonely street lamp, a rectangle of light high up in a dark house, evoke the mystery of night, its darkness and quiet, which is an exciting field to explore.

Speedlights. Several reasonably priced good amateur models, which are light and small, are now available. Ideal for portraits of all kinds. The light is modulating and soft, the flash too short to blind the eye, and the tube is good for several thousand shots. The days of "hold it!" are over. There is no excuse now for "posing" and frozen smiles, no need for a tripod, blown fuses, or for pictures that are blurred because the subject or the photographer moved at the moment of exposure. You can "forget" your equipment and concentrate on what you want to photograph: the characteristic gesture, the fleeting expression, the natural, spontaneous smile.

To use the camera as a means for widening man's horizon, to explore the realm of the factual as well as the emotion, to show how people live and feel, seems to me one of the most exciting tasks a photographer can set himself. In my opinion, the man who most consistently uses the camera in this sense is W. Eugene Smith. Many of my readers have seen his work in *Life*. His picture stories on the Country Doctor (September 20, 1948), the Spanish Village (April 9, 1950), and the Nurse Midwife (December 3, 1951) are classics that will live in the history of photography. They should be seen and studied by anyone interested in photography. To the highest degree, they have those qualities that characterize great pictures: they have purpose and meaning; they are interesting and informative; they are sincere, moving, and deeply felt.

A camera is a responsibility—particularly in the hands of a man who takes pictures intended for publication. Photography has rightly been called a "picture language"—and if it misrepresents the truth, if it falsifies facts, and, by so doing, wrongly influences people in their opinion, then "shooting" with a camera becomes, in a sense, almost as dangerous and irresponsible as wildly shooting with a gun. Anyone knows the potential danger of a gun. But few photographers are aware of the damage that an irresponsibly used camera can do. This applies particularly to irresponsible photo journalism. To a lesser degree, this also applies to the pointless pictures inflicted upon the public via photo magazines and exhibitions. Many a young photographer believes that such pictures must be "good" since they are chosen to be printed or exhibited, and consequently takes them as a standard for his own work. Pictures of this kind have retarded the development of many amateurs and prevented them from recognizing the tremendous potentialities of their medium. Caught in the vicious circle of that society for mutual admiration called the "photo club," they never bother to look further for stimulation, for examples of good photography. And they never become "responsible photographers."

230

Photographers often justify the mediocrity of their pictures with remarks such as "If I only had this camera and that lens, I could take pictures like such and such a photographer. . . ." To them, it may come as a shock to hear that, for example, W. Eugene Smith never uses anything but a simple Leica—exactly the same type of Leica that countless amateurs use. And that, at a guess, 90 per cent of the photographs printed in *Life* are taken with either a 35-mm. camera (Leica, Nikon) or a Hasselblad 2¼ x 2¼". Obviously—it is not *what* camera a photographer uses, but *how* he uses it, that accounts for the merit of his pictures.

Photographers who believe that possession of a thousand dollars' worth of equipment automatically guarantees the production of "thousand-dollar pictures" are in for a disappointment. The basic operations of exposing, developing, and printing are the same for "thousand-dollar cameras" as they are for Box-Brownies. The same type of film is used in both. Negatives produced by both are printed on the same type of paper. And, apart from possible differences in size, the only difference between a "thousand-dollar camera" and a "box" is the optical and mechanical quality, which is mainly manifested in the degree of sharpness of the negatives. However, only a very good technician can practically exploit the superior quality of, for example, a four-hundred-dollar camera as contrasted to a forty-dollar camera. And even so, he would get only a slightly sharper picture—a fact which, of course, does not exclude the possibility that a more worth-while photograph may be produced by a photographer using the forty-dollar camera.

Expensive "special" equipment is needed only for "special" jobs. Such jobs are exceptional and rare, even among professional photographers. No amateur can convince me that he has exhausted all the possible sources for taking pictures with his own camera, and that he must advance to more "exceptional" cameras. If he is unimaginative enough not to be able to find motifs for his "ordinary" camera, he will not find them for his "specialized" equipment either.

In itself, a camera is no more creative than a lump of clay. But, like a lump of clay, in inspired hands it becomes a means for artistic expression. "Prize-winning cameras" and "cameras that can do everything" exist only in the imagination of publicity agents who are trying to promote their products. There are no prize-winning cameras, there are only prize-winning photographers! Any camera, from 35 mm. up to 8 by 10, can produce

231

inspiring pictures. As a matter of fact, great pictures have even been taken with a "lowly box"! In this respect, a camera is comparable to a car: any car that is in working condition will take you to your point of destination. Some, of course, will do so faster and with more comfort than others. However, it is still the driver who must steer the car and decide where to go!

Preoccupation with technicalities is one of the greatest obstacles to the taking of good pictures. This may seem contradictory in view of the fact that I recommended the development of added techniques as a means of producing better photographs. It is not, however. In developing their techniques, photographers too often become absorbed in the technicalities *per se*, and forget they are only a means to an end. To these photographers, they become the "end"—also the end to the possibility of careers as creative photographers.

Preoccupation with superficial technicalities is particularly evident in the importance most amateurs attribute to "technical data." Editors of photo magazines and annuals print them religiously below each picture, or in collected form in the back of the book. Save for a few special cases, such data are not only worthless but also misleading. To begin with, such data—as, for instance, the settings of diaphragm and shutter—can be furnished much more accurately, if needed, by any exposure meter. Moreover, statements referring to the brand of camera, lens, or film are of no practical value to anyone. They serve only as free publicity to the manufacturers of these items. The pains which some photo editors take in order to present their readers with "complete information" is really touching. For example, one reads, again and again, that a certain picture was "taken with a Rolleiflex 2¼ by 2¼ inch, equipped with a Carl Zeiss Tessar lens f/3.5." Anyone who knows what a Rolleiflex is also knows that its size is 2¼ by 2¼, that it comes equipped with either a Tessar or a Xenar, that all Tessar lenses are made by Carl Zeiss (unless *otherwise* specifically stated), and that the lens speed is normally f/3.5 (there are only a few f/2.8 Rolleis). But can anyone tell me what difference it makes, as far as the picture is concerned, whether it is taken with a Rolleiflex or any other twin-lens reflex camera of the same size, with a Tessar or a Xenar, or whether the lens has a speed of f/3.5 or f/2.8, especially since it was probably stopped down anyway? Upon being questioned, such editors always maintain "that their readers want such information," even though the editors themselves realize that it is of no practical value. Should not the editors then inform their readers to this effect? After all, aren't their magazines supposed to "educate" the amateur? What makes such "data" not only valueless but actually misleading is the fact that they never tell the full story. They do NOT tell whether the indicated exposure is right or wrong; and if the exposure is wrong, whether the negative is underex

232

posed or overexposed. Neither do they say anything about the illumination at the moment of exposure, which should be indicated in the form of a meter reading. Nor do they mention the time of negative development, the type of developer, the density and gradation of the negative, or the contrast grade of the paper. Furthermore, analysis of such data often reveals that they are obviously "fabricated." In many outdoor pictures, a shadow within a shadow discloses the use of a fill-in flash. No such flash is mentioned, however, in the "data," the purpose of which is supposedly to tell the amateur "how to do it." Or examination of the sharpness in depth gives the lie to the indicated diaphragm stop. But what else can one expect? How many photographers actually make notes on the "data" of every picture that they take, and how many photographers can later remember how they took a particular shot? As long as amateurs insist upon "data" with each picture that is printed, they must run the risk of being misinformed. I hope that from now on my reader will rely upon his exposure meter and common sense, and will leave "data" to others.

"Technique" is valuable only in so far as it can be put to practical use. "Know-how" must always be complemented by know-what and know-why. Sometimes, however, knowing "too much" may cause a photographer to risk too little. If you are in doubt whether or not a shot will come off "technically," take it anyway! Only "safe" pictures always come off. However, they are very often very dull. Taking chances, as for example shooting against the light, or directly into the sun, often leads to very exciting photographs. Of course, the resulting halation may be terrific—but then, so is the brilliance of the sun!

HOW TO "SEE IN TERMS OF PICTURES"

I stated before that part of a "good" photographer's success is due to his ability to "see" more, and "better," than his less fortunate colleagues. This faculty for discovering picture possibilities which others overlook is a combination of three different factors: an eye for *interesting* subject matter; a feeling for the "photogenic"; and knowledge, based upon experience, of the subjects that should be avoided because they never make good pictures.

Interesting subject matter. As a rule, something that is alive, or that is unusual, or is a combination of both, is more interesting and makes for more exciting pictures than subjects that are commonplace, static, or dead. The most interesting photographs are always those pictures of people which show their true emotions—the W. Eugene Smith type of photograph. At the other extreme—characterized by the dullest and most pointless pictures—are still lifes and the childish exercises known as "table-top photographs." "Phony" setups, no matter how "artistically conceived," can never result in anything but "phony" photographs.

Photogenic qualities. Every photograph is an "abstraction," in the same sense that words and letters are abstractions. A letter, for example, is a symbol for a sound. A combination of letters is a symbol for a more complicated sound—a word. And a word is a symbol for an object, a quality, an event, etc. Everyone who speaks English knows the meaning of the symbols G-I-R-L. Without such symbols we could not convey to others in written form the meaning of the concept "girl." The same principle applies to photographs. The picture of a girl, for example, is an abstraction in that it lacks color, three-dimensionality, and motion—three of the most important qualities of any living subject. In photography, color is "symbolized" by shades of gray; three-dimensionality is symbolized by perspective; and motion is symbolized by blur. How well a photographer knows his "symbols," and to what extent he utilizes them, are important factors which influence the outcome of his pictures.

The most elementary qualification of a writer is the ability to spell. He has to know his symbols. But few photographers realize that they also work with "symbols"—gray tones, perspective, and blur, to name only the three most important. They take these symbols for granted because they appear "automatically" on the film. But they forget that these symbols, like words, can be "controlled," or changed, or used in many different ways. However, whereas any literate person will spot a mistake in spelling or grammar at once, only a few people are "photographically literate" enough to detect in a photograph a symbol that is used wrongly (I do not mean a "technical mistake," which is always easy to detect). For example: most photographers like their pictures to be sharp. However, the "sharp" photograph of a car in motion differs in no way from the "sharp" photograph of a car that is standing still. In order to indicate movement, one has to use a symbol, since obviously motion can never be rendered directly in a "still." The most common symbol for motion is blur. The more blurred a car appears in a picture, the faster it seems to go. Anyone can "freeze" the motion of a car by taking the picture at a high enough shutter speed. However, such "faulty" use of a photographic symbol results in a picture that creates a "faulty" impression: the impression of a car standing still.

To cite another example: a photographer has to take a fashion shot of a green dress trimmed with red. The brightness value of these two colors is practically the same. An "ordinary" photograph would render the red and green as two identical shades of gray, and contrast would be, there-fore, lost. Since the particular attraction of the dress lies in the vivid contrast between the red and the green, such a picture would obviously create a faulty impression—the dress would appear monochrome and dull. Although such a photograph is *factually correct* (i.e., as far as monochromatically correct translation of color into shades of gray is concerned, see p. 75), it is nevertheless *emotionally wrong*. In order to appear "emotionally correct," the colors green and red have to be adequately separated and "symbolized" by shades of gray indicative of their character. Red is aggressive and warm, green is receding and neutral. Given equality of brilliance, a warm and aggressive color appears lighter than a passive and receding color. To create this impression, the picture of the dress would have to be taken through a light red filter. This would make the red appear as a light shade of gray and the green as a dark shade of gray. Contrast would be created, and the black-and-white "translation" of the dress would seem "emotionally true"—as a result of the correct use of photographic "symbols."

Subjects that have qualities that lend themselves to photographic "symbolization" are called "photogenic." Subjects that do not have such qualities, or have them only to a small degree, are called "unphotogenic." Photogenic subjects possess contrast, roundness, interesting outlines, depth. Unphotogenic subjects are flat, monotonous, contrastless, disorganized, dull in outline and form.

Subjects that do not make for good pictures are basically "unphotogenic." Such subjects, however, are not always obviously so. As a matter of fact, subjects may have much appeal to the eye and still be extremely unphotogenic. This is particularly true of "views" from high vantage points and of wide-open "scaleless" landscapes. The latter are magnificent to behold but will prove disappointing in reproduction unless the feeling of grandeur is "symbolized" through introduction of "scale"—a human figure, a rider on horseback far off in the distance, whose smallness makes the landscape appear large, wide, and "big" by contrast.

All subjects that are too cluttered, that have several "centers of interest," or that have unsuitable background, are basically unphotogenic. Green meadows under cloudless blue skies appeal to most everyone but make the dullest kind of picture. This is also true of photographs of lush vegetation—there is too much "green against green," too little contrast, too little outline and form.

A photographer does not enjoy the same advantage as the painter, who can change and invent in order to improve his painting. However, the photographer can always select and reject. By discriminately choosing his subjects according to their photogenic qualifications he can greatly increase his chances of succeeding.

Thinking in terms of photography is different from thinking in terms of literature. A subject may be extremely interesting, and one may be able to write a fascinating story about it. However, the same subject may be boring as a photograph. For example, let us consider a battle monument. A book could be written about that stage of history to which it belongs, with all its life, color, drama, and significance; but in a picture it probably would appear as many other battle monuments, insignificant and dull.

The reason for this discrepancy between interest and appearance lies in the fact that the camera "sees" objectively, whereas the eye sees through the screen of the imagination. To the camera, a particular battle monument is but a statue surrounded by some old guns. To the eye, it is a symbol of a cause, lost or won, for which men died. The mind wanders—and history comes alive . . . Sherman and Grant and Lee . . . the memory of these names stirs the imagination. But how can such intangibles be expressed in photographs? They usually cannot—which is the reason why this type of picture is often so disappointing. It requires imagination to symbolize an idea: a stark silhouette, black against an emblazoned sky, rays of light breaking through stormy clouds, light streaking the horizon —and the monument comes to "life," the might of battle is signified.

Similar considerations apply throughout photography. Let us suppose you have to photograph a certain man—a man you know. Let us suppose that he is happily married, has children, lives in a comfortable house, and drives a Cadillac. You know him to be a successful businessman, driver of hard bargains, yet he is well liked by his friends for his genial ways. He smokes cigars, plays bridge, and likes to tell jokes. How can such knowledge help you to make a good portrait of him?

If photographed by someone who does not know anything about him, this man very likely would be photographed in a conventional pose with standard lighting. It would be a "standard portrait"—very likely pompous, certainly posed, and impersonal. Since you have some knowledge of this man, you might evaluate this knowledge "in terms of pictures" by reasoning as follows: since he is happily married, has children, and a nice, comfortable home—he must be content and quite pleased with himself. Since he owns his home and drives a Cadillac—he must be prosperous and successful. Since he is known to drive hard bargains—he must be strong and clever. But since his friends speak well of him and he likes to joke—he must be "nice" and have a sense of humor. Knowing these things, the problem then is to incorporate them into the picture. Since he smokes cigars, photograph him with a cigar, and he will feel at ease. Arrange your lights to emphasize the line of the jaw to create a feeling of strength. Talk to him, tell him jokes, to bring forth expressions characteristic of his own humor and his friendliness. Get him to talk to you, watch his gestures, take shot after shot of him, trying to capture those moments when he looks "himself": prosperous, happy, and strong.

Again: The "technical" requirements are simple and few. NOT the number of lights or the quality of the lens determine the outcome of your portrait, but your ability to "see," and to "think in terms of pictures."

COMPOSITION

A painter, for example, can make changes, additions, and deletions to improve composition. He can paint over whole sections and begin again, continuing this until he is satisfied with his work. But a photographer is not given this latitude. Once he releases the shutter, the composition is set. In this sense every photograph is final—unalterable. Before this crucial moment, a photographer has the power to arrange, select, and reject. After that moment, there is little he can do to influence the composition. For this reason, he must "edit" his photographs *before* he makes the exposure. This editing is what is meant when we speak of "composing."

Composing means arranging, and its purpose is to organize the different components of a photograph in such a way that the picture becomes a self-contained unit. To do this, it is necessary to direct and concentrate interest where it belongs, to arrange lines and forms in harmonious patterns, to balance distribution of light and dark in "graphic" equilibrium, and to create organic boundaries—an unobtrusive natural frame which holds the picture together. To do this, the photographer has four choices:

1. *To arrange or direct the subject* until he is satisfied that requirements of good composition are fulfilled. This is the ideal solution, but it presupposes, of course, that the photographer has as much command of the situation as a movie director has of his cast.

2. *To change his viewpoint* until a stationary subject composes properly. This applies particularly to landscape and architectural photographs. Wherever possible, use of a lens with longer than standard focal length will materially improve composition by "pulling the subject together" (the typical "telephoto effect" of "compressed perspective").

3. *To wait for the right moment*, then quickly "snap" his picture. This applies particularly to sports and action photographs in which changes are sudden and unexpected. It also applies to many street scenes and

237

pictures in which it is desirable to have a figure or a group "in just the right place" to provide scale and "human interest."

4. *To improve composition during enlarging* by blowing up only that section of a negative which contains the essence of his picture, and cropping off distracting marginal detail. In this way he can produce "telephoto effects" with a lens of standard focal length (see p. 229). Aside from this, however, composing during enlarging hardly affords more than the possibility of making minor adjustments of a compositional nature, and when taking a picture it must NOT be considered as a remedy for hasty or bad composition.

Contrary to popular belief, there are no definite "rules of composition." All those "rules" about S-curves, L-shapes, triangular composition, pyramidal arrangements, leading lines, the position of the horizon within the rectangle of the picture, and so forth, are at best half-truths which sometimes apply, but for which examples proving the contrary can easily be found among any number of excellent photographs. Only "judges" in photographic juries rate pictures according to such pre-established rigid rules. "Common" people—the people who matter—neither know nor care for such "rules" and judge photographs merely by the way in which they affect them. They judge by the heart instead of the head. But even though they may not be able to appreciate the beauty of an S-curve or a pyramidal arrangement, complete with "leading lines," etc., they make a distinction between phony and sincere pictures. And, ultimately, this is what counts.

As an aid to beginners, here are some aspects to consider when "composing" photographs:

Simplicity is never wrong. The more simply conceived and executed, the stronger the picture will be. Principally, this means that each picture should contain only a single subject. Multiple subjects produce multiple centers of interest and, therefore, divide the attention of the observer. If such is the case, simply take several pictures instead of trying to show "everything" in one.

"Graphic" black and white is often more effective than a long scale of subtle shades of gray. Do not be afraid of using it in your pictures—no matter what you have been told concerning "empty" highlights and shadows. A highlight that is not pure white appears "fogged" and dirty, while a black, detailless shadow can often hold a whole composition together, giving it power and strength.

The background is one of the most important—and most frequently neglected—parts of the picture. Especially if out of focus and filled with shapeless white "spots," a cluttered background ruins any photograph. The best of all backgrounds is the sky.

The horizon—if present at all—divides a picture in two. A low horizon suggests distance, space, and a sense of elevation. A high horizon emphasizes the foreground and the earth, suggesting more materialistic qualities. As long as you are aware of these effects and try to make use of them, you may place the horizon anywhere in the picture—even directly across its center!

Framing the subject with interestingly silhouetted, dark foreground matter leads the eye toward the center of the picture and tends to increase the impression of "depth."

A close-up always creates a stronger impression than a view from farther away. It produces a feeling of intimacy, brings out surface texture ("one can almost feel it . . ."), and presents the very essence of the subject. Keep this in mind when enlarging and trim your picture to the limit. "Cropping" is one of the surest ways to increase the impact of a picture.

Light and shade play a double role: "modulating" light and shade create illusions of three-dimensionality, roundness, and depth; "graphic" light and shade—white and black—set the key of a picture and determine its "graphic" pattern. Light tones and white are aggressive. They suggest joy, youth, ease, and pleasant sensations. Dark shades and black are passive. They suggest somber moods, power, strength, age, and death. Light areas in a picture attract the attention of the observer first. Dark parts allow the eye to rest and provide a picture with strength.

Motion can be symbolized best by blur—the more blurred the image, the more convincing the illusion of speed. As far as subjects in motion are concerned, the sharpest picture is often the least representative. Motion, furthermore, can be suggested by means of a diagonal composition. This applies particularly if the moving subject must for reasons of clarity be rendered sharply. By placing the subject on one of the diagonals of the picture, and by adjusting the main elements of composition so that they run diagonally instead of horizontally-vertically, a "static" arrangement can be transformed into a "dynamic" composition, suggestive of movement and speed.

The proportions of the print should reflect the character of the subject. Many photographers consistently compose their pictures to fit the proportions of the groundglass or finder. This fault is particularly noticeable in cases where the negative is square. Since adherence to such proportions creates monotony and handicaps the effective presentation of many subjects, they should be changed during enlarging. The number of possible proportions of the print is infinite—from extremely narrow horizontal, through square, to extremely narrow vertical. Effective use of these possibilities is an important step in composing.

Cropping during enlarging takes care of small last-minute adjustments. Main forms of the picture should not touch the margins of the print. Either place them well inside its boundaries or cut them partly off. Symmetry is usually boring—try to avoid it, unless there is a specific reason for it. Lines that directly run into a corner seem to split it. Trim the picture so that this does not occur. Small white forms along the edges of a print make the picture look as if mice had gnawed its margins. Trim them off. If this is not possible, darken such areas by "burning in" while enlarging.

Photography can be taught only in part—specifically that part which deals with photo technique. Everything else has to come from within the photographer himself. All that any teacher—or textbook—can do is to guide potentially creative photographers in the right direction by showing them what can be accomplished in photography when it is approached with intelligence and imagination.

From here on it is up to you—where you go, and how you get there. Rules and instructions are for technicians—the creative worker must chart his own course. Discrimination, selection, and the limitations of the medium are his starting points, condensation and stylization are the means by which he turns his material into art. No one cares what tools he uses. Few know the kind of person he is. But millions may participate in his work. This is the essential. If his work is honest and sincere, if it has something to say, if it provides an element of that which helps people to better understand themselves, their neighbors, their surroundings, their world—what difference does it make whether such work was created with brush and paint on canvas, with chisel and mallet in stone, with words and typewriter—or produced with camera and film?

PART NINE

APPENDIX

How to Clean Trays, Tanks, and Hands

Most developers in time leave stains on trays and tanks which, unless removed periodically, flake off, settle on the emulsion, and cause spots in the negatives. The best way to remove such residues is to use the following solution which, however, must not be used on non-acid-proof enamel trays:

Potassium bichromate	3 oz.
Water	32 oz.
Sulfuric acid	5 oz.

Dissolve the potassium bichromate in the water and SLOWLY (!) add the sulfuric acid to the solution. *Caution:* Reversing this procedure would cause a minor explosion!

The best way to remove developer stains from hands and fingernails is as follows: soak the hands in a 20 per cent solution of potassium permanganate. This leaves a brownish stain which disappears when you rinse your hands in a 5 per cent solution of sodium bisulfate. Sometimes milder stains disappear when rubbed with a slice of lemon.

Photographic Chemicals

To compound the nineteen formulas listed in this book—which take care of all the needs of the advanced amateur—only twenty-eight chemicals are needed. They are listed in the survey given below, together with their formulas and more common synonyms. Wherever necessary, instructions for use and storage are added. In the case of poisonous chemicals, the antidotes mentioned are for emergency treatment only. In case of an accident, call a physician at once.

ACETIC ACID (Vinegar acid)—$CH_3.COOH$. Clear, colorless liquid with strong pungent odor. Glacial acetic acid solidifies at about 60° F. Melt by putting bottle in vessel filled with warm water. Gives off inflammable vapors.

CAUTION: Causes burns on contact with skin. Wash off immediately with water. Poisonous. If taken internally, give magnesia or chalk in water; call physician.

Uses: Hardening and acid fixing baths, mostly used in 28 per cent solution. To prepare a 28 per cent working solution from 99½ per cent stock solution of glacial acetic acid, dilute 3 parts of stock solution with 8 parts of water (by volume).

242

AMMONIA WATER (Ammonium Hydroxide)—NH₄OH. Colorless liquid with an intense and suffocating odor. Must be stored in a cool place, in a strong, glass-stoppered bottle. Do not fill the bottle to the top.
Use: Accelerator in developers.

AMMONIUM HYDROXIDE. *See* Ammonia Water.

BORAX (Biborate of Soda, Sodium Biborate, Sodium Borate)—$Na_2B_4O_7.10H_2O$. White crystalline powder, weakly alkaline in solution.
Uses: Low-activity (fine-grain) developers; some acid hardening fixing baths.

ELON. *See* p-Methylamino-phenol Sulfate.

FORMALDEHYDE (Formalin, Formol)—HCHO. Colorless liquid with suffocating odor, intensely irritating to nose and lungs.
CAUTION: Do not inhale vapors. Poisonous. If taken internally, give weak solution of ammonia followed with emetic of mustard.
Uses: Hardening bath, preservative.

GLYCIN. *See* Parahydroxyphenyl Aminoacetic Acid.

GOLD CHLORIDE—$AuCl_3.HCl.4H_2O$. Golden-yellow crystals containing approximately 50 per cent gold. Strongly hygroscopic. Store only in perfectly dry place, in well-stoppered container.
Use: Gold toning (print permanence).

HYDROCHLORIC ACID—HCl. Colorless, or slightly yellowish, fuming liquid.
CAUTION: Acid accidentally brought in contact with the skin must be wiped off immediately but gently, followed by thorough washing with plenty of soap and water. Cover burn with moist magnesia or baking soda. Poisonous. If taken internally, give teaspoonful or more of magnesia, chalk, wall plaster, or small pieces of soap in water or milk. Call a physician!
Uses: Intensifiers, cleaning trays.

HYDROGEN PEROXIDE (Hydrogen Dioxide)—H_2O_2. Colorless liquid, not very stable.
Use: Hypo eliminator.

HYDROQUINONE (Hydrochinon)—$C_6H_4(OH)_2$. White, "silky," needle-like crystals, easily soluble in hot water, difficult to dissolve in cold water. Oxidizes readily, must be kept from excessive contact with air.
Use: Developer.

KODALK is the protected trade name of a balanced alkali produced by the Eastman Kodak Company.
Uses: Developers, fixers. Kodalk Balanced Alkali does not release gas when added to a stop bath or an acid fixer, and minimizes the danger of "blistering." It furthermore retards the formation of sludge in acid hardening fixing baths.

243

p-METHYLAMINO-PHENOL SULFATE (Kodak Elon Developing Agent—Eastman Kodak Co.; Metol—Ansco; Pictol—Mallinckrodt)— $[C_6H_4(OH)NHCH_3]_2H_2SO_4$. White or slightly yellowish powder.
Use: Developer.

METOL. *See* p-Methylamino-phenol Sulfate.

PARAHYDROXYPHENOL AMINOACETIC ACID (Glycin)—$(C_6H_4\cdot OH)(NH.CH_2COOH)$. Shiny white or gray powder.
Use: Developer.

PARAPHENYLENE DIAMINE (BASE)—$NH_2 \cdot C_6H_4 \cdot NH_2$. White or yellowish-white crystals. Slightly toxic, may cause a rash on contact with the skin. Stains hands and clothing.
Use: Ultra fine-grain developer.

POTASSIUM ALUM (Potassium Aluminum Sulfate, Potash Alum)— $K_2Al_2(SO_4)_4.24H_2O$. Large, colorless crystals or white crystalline powder.
Use: Hardening bath.

POTASSIUM BICHROMATE—$K_2Cr_2O_7$. Colorful, reddish-yellow crystals. Poisonous.
Uses: Bleaching solutions, chromium intensifiers, tray cleaners.

POTASSIUM BROMIDE—KBr. White powder or crystalline granules. Slightly hygroscopic, must be protected from dampness.
Use: Developer (restrainer).

POTASSIUM CHROME ALUM (Alum, Chrome, Potassium—Chrome Alum)—$K_2Cr_2(SO_4)_4.24H_2O$. Dark, violet-red crystals, or light violet powder.
Use: Hardener.

POTASSIUM FERRICYANIDE—$K_3Fe(CN)_6$. Ruby-red, shiny crystals, poisonous.
CAUTION: If swallowed, give tablespoonful of hydrogen peroxide, diluted alcohol, or teaspoonful of aromatic spirits of ammonia in water. Call physician!
Use: Reducer (Farmer's).

POTASSIUM PERMANGANATE—$KMnO_4$. Purplish-black, needlelike, metallic-shiny crystals. Stains badly. Stains can be removed with a solution of sodium bisulfite or potassium metabisulfite.
CAUTION: Poison! If swallowed, give emetic of mustard, strong tea or coffee. Call physician!
Uses: Reducer, hypo test, hypo eliminator, bleacher.

POTASSIUM PERSULFATE (Anthion)—$K_2S_2O_8$. Colorless or white crystals. Should be kept in tightly closed container in a cool place.
Use: Reducer, hypo eliminator.

244

SILVER NITRATE—$AgNo_3$. Colorless, flat crystals, producing brownish stains which can be removed from hands by rubbing with tincture of iodine followed by rinsing in a strong solution of hypo. Poisonous.

CAUTION: If swallowed, give large amounts of table salt in water, followed by a tablespoonful of mustard in a glass of warm water. In addition, give dose of Epsom salts followed by milk. Call a physician!

Uses: Emulsion making, intensifying, hypo-eliminator test.

SODIUM BISULFITE—$NaHSO_3$. White crystalline powder.

Use: Clearing bath.

SODIUM CARBONATE (Soda, Washing soda)—$Na_2CO_3XH_2O$. Colorless crystals, or white granules or powder.

Use: Developers (alkali-accelerator).

SODIUM HYDROXIDE (Caustic soda, Soda lye, Sodium Hydrate)—$NaOH$. White sticky lumps or pellets.

CAUTION: Poison! Causes skin burns. Wash off with plenty of water, then apply vinegar. If swallowed, give lemon juice or vinegar (plenty), followed by olive oil. If it gets into the eyes, wash out with a solution of 5 per cent boric acid. Call a physician!

Use: Developer (alkali-accelerator).

SODIUM SULFATE (Glauber's Salt)—Na_2SO_4. White powder.

Use: Developer, stop bath.

SODIUM SULFITE—Na_2SO_3. White powder or crystals. Commonly used in its desiccated (anhydrous) form, which is equivalent to twice the amount in crystals.

Use: Developer (preservative), acid fixer.

SODIUM THIOCYANATE—$NaSCN$. Colorless or white crystals, hygroscopic, must be stored in a dry place in well-stoppered vessel, and must be protected from light.

Use: Fine-grain developer.

SODIUM THIOSULFATE (Hypo)—$Na_2S_2O_35H_2O$. Whitish crystals in large or small size that dissolve easily in hot water or desiccated (anhydrous) powder. Hygroscopic, must be stored in a perfectly dry place.

Uses: Fixing bath, Farmer's reducer.

SULFURIC ACID (Battery acid, Vitriolic acid)—H_2SO_4. Colorless, oily liquid. To dilute, *always* add the acid *slowly* to the water. Reversing the process would cause a violent reaction, splattering acid all over the place. Poisonous and corrosive, never let it touch the skin.

CAUTION: Acid accidentally brought in contact with the skin must be wiped off immediately but gently, followed by thorough washing with plenty of soap and water. Cover burn with moist magnesia or baking soda. If taken internally, give teaspoonful or more of magnesia, chalk, wall plaster, or small pieces of soap in water or milk. Call a physician!

Uses: Acid fixing baths, bleaching solutions.

245

INDEX

247

Speedlights 56, 85, 230
Speed of negative emulsions 41, 46
Spotlights 55, 98
Spotting of prints 139
Spots on prints 166-167
Stains on films 166-167
Standard developer 114
Standard focal length 26
Standard illumination 99
Standard lens 26, 33, 220
Static electricity 35, 147
Stirring rod 112
Stop bath 115, 121, 127, 137, 184
Straightening of prints 138
Super-fast lenses 222
Super-proportional reducer 164
Surfaces of papers 116
Swings of cameras 33, 215

T-stops 29
Tank development of filmpack 129
Tank development of rollfilm 126-128
Tank development of sheet film 129
Technically perfect negative 3, 6
Telephotography 229
Telephoto lenses 26, 32, 33, 221
Temperature of darkroom 108
Temperature of developers 16, 126, 136
Temperature of solutions 174
Test for cameras 216
Test for lenses 217
Test for range finder synchronization 217
Test for washing 187
Theater exposures 94
Thermometer 17, 112
Time-and-temperature method 16, 17, 124

Time of development 16, 126, 137
Timer 17, 112
Trimming of prints 138
Tripod 53
Tripod exposure 12
Tropical developer 115, 182
Twin-lens reflex cameras 9, 22, 215

Ultra fine-grain developer 115
Ultraviolet 41, 67
Underexposed negatives 10, 94, 154
Unsharpness 8, 66, 141, 146

Viewfinders 22
View-type cameras 65, 214
Vignetting 160
Viscose sponge 115
Volt 100

Waist-level finder 22
Washing of negatives 127-128
Washing of prints 137
Water 173
Water damage to negatives 152-153
Watt 100
Weights, conversion tables 178
Weston filmspeed rating 41
Wide-angle lenses 32, 33, 220
"Worm's-eye view" perspective 22

Yellow filters 49-51, 78
Yellow-green safelight 108, 111

Zeiss Dagor wide-angle lens 32
Zeiss Tessar lenses 220